Liberation Day

Liberation Day

Our Nation Empowered
by the Constitution

ERIC MARTIN

The Liberation Day Movement
www.liberationday.com

First Edition: December 2017. Minor Updates: March 31, 2018.

Cover design by Sherwin Soy

Scripture quotations taken from the New American Standard Bible®
(NASB), Copyright © 1960, 1962, 1963, 1968, 1971, 1972, 1973,
1975, 1977, 1995 by The Lockman Foundation
Used by permission. www.Lockman.org

ISBN-13: 978-0-692-04809-2

Dedicated to God.

"Commit your works to the Lord
And your plans will be established."
Proverbs 16:3

CONTENTS

CHAPTER 1

FROM THE HEART

"I just want to read a quote that I find very interesting by Frédéric Bastiat, an economist from the eighteen hundreds, it goes, 'The state is the great fiction through which everyone endeavors to live at the expense of everyone else.' It seems to me that throughout our history the time when we were most prosperous was the time when we did not outsource our desires and wants to the government but rather pulled ourselves up by our own bootstraps and did it ourselves. I'm wondering which candidate will get out of our lives."

Josh Rae spoke those words during the primary season of 2012. They fired me up. I was angry; I was livid at the government and the way it messed up my life and everyone else's lives. Josh spoke those words at an event where the Republican and Democratic candidates for U.S. Congress had to listen to community members and the issues they thought were important. I was one of seven Republican contenders. At the end, we had the opportunity to respond to the audience in about two minutes. Here's a little of what I said, mainly responding to the statement by Josh Rae, "It is so true; we as politicians, we need to get out of your lives. Who cares about us!? We don't matter! You matter!" If only every politician understood those words, or ever even pondered them.

Josh wanted to get his comment in last because he knew the final comment was the most remembered, and he did get it in last, and it worked. When I spoke into the microphone for the first time, at least one person in the audience jerked their head up. I was speaking so loudly because I desired liberty so much for the people of our nation and myself.

I still desire liberty. I desire more freedom—freedom for myself and freedom for others. I wrote this book to help relieve that burden if only a little bit. The goal of this book is to free our nation, but we will need more than a book to free us.

> **"It does not take a majority to prevail ... but rather an irate, tireless minority, keen on setting brushfires of freedom in the minds of men."**
> **—Samuel Adams**

That is what we need. I hope each of you will join me in being the minority that is fighting for freedom. In the Revolutionary War, there were 3% of the people fighting for freedom, 10% actively supporting it, and 20% on the side of freedom.[1] We don't need a bigger minority than what they had.

A lot of this book is detail-oriented and gets into every single entity within the federal government, but right now, I want to forget the details and speak from the heart.

The Constitution breaching federal government disgusts me, and the politicians not following the U.S. Constitution offend me. To swear or affirm that they will uphold the Constitution, with many of them not even seriously reading it, is a disturbing reality of the morality of our leaders today. It's as if people have utterly forgotten or ignored what it means to follow through on their word.

It saddens me when I think about the things that I have to live with today because of our federal government which has stomped, battered, and torn up our Constitution:

- Over 54 million unborn babies have been murdered freely because of a court case that was butchered by the Supreme Court.
- We have had numerous undeclared wars where hundreds of thousands of our men and women were killed or wounded; our opponents in those wars have had hundreds of thousands of more people who have died, not to mention those who were injured, and we're still in undeclared war.
- I have to pay income taxes, in part to pay for hundreds of thousands of pages of unconstitutional laws

and regulations, and trillions of dollars of unconstitutional "transfers" of my money.

- I'm forced to testify against myself by signing my income tax return.
- The Federal Reserve makes our incomes worth very little because they pump inflation through the system that almost exclusively benefits the mega-rich, the military-industrial complex, the banks, other nations, and whoever they choose to bail out.
- Businesses in our nation have to contend with a crushing load of regulations and taxes.
- I can't start a business without considering whether I comply with all of the federal regulations and taxes.
- Farmers have to deal with all of the regulations imposed on them.
- Health insurers and health providers in the United States have to endure a higher number and more restrictive regulations than providers in any other nation in the history of mankind; we pay the price through slower care and higher costs.
- Pharmaceutical companies are in bed with the federal government and force millions and even billions of dollars' worth of testing for drugs that should only be tested according to private sector or state regulations.
- Schools in our nation have to consider what the federal government might say while educating our children; public schools need to comply with an ugly assortment of requirements; and many kids don't want to eat school lunches because Michelle Obama

got involved in making them "healthy": Her 'Healthy, Hunger-Free Kids Act' may have caused over one million kids to stop eating school lunches.[2]

- The citizens of our nation live in fear of constant surveillance because through the Patriot Act, the NSA is carefully watching any or all of us.

- Special interest groups, billionaire bankers, and corporate elites have a virtual stranglehold on Washington and politicians ignore the interests of the people and pass unconstitutional laws written by these entities.

- Issues like gay marriage, gun rights, abortion, drugs, sex, porn, and discrimination by private individuals or firms are being considered at the federal level even though they are clearly meant to stay in the hands of the people and the states: why would we illegalize drugs at the federal level when we don't even illegalize most murders at the federal level?

This list could go on. I hope I've highlighted some key areas that resonate with you. One of the most significant issues I have with all of these unconstitutional intrusions of the federal government is that legislators have a law. It's the supreme law of the land called the U.S. Constitution. How can these legislators expect us to follow the rules that they (or their special interests and career regulators) write when they are not following their law, the U.S. Constitution?

This book is a call to arms. But the arms aren't guns and weapons; the arms are our minds. I'm asking you to consider the words in this book carefully. Are these federal entities constitutional? Are they needed? Are they fair? Are they useful? Are they good?

Liberation Day presents twenty-three executive orders that bring the United States on the path towards the original intent of the Constitution in a single day. It dissolves or significantly downsizes over 250 federal entities, including a handful of entire Departments. We need to use our minds to come together and fight for this plan collectively, or better yet, we should fight for the goal of this plan. The goal of this plan is the restoration of the Constitution in this nation.

If you have any questions about the Constitution or the original meaning that the Founding Fathers' had in mind when they wrote it, please check out "On the U.S. Constitution." It's the appendix near the back of the book. The Constitution is our nation's supreme-law document that informs us that the goals of the executive orders in this book must be achieved to bring a return to legal, constitutional government in our nation. The appendix shows the legal authority a president has to get rid of over 250 federal entities in a single day through twenty-three executive orders.

The executive orders empower the people and their States to live freely and prosper. Our nation is founded on the principle that our state governments and our federal government have no power in and of themselves, but instead, their power flows from the people. By putting power back into the hands of the people, our nation is more powerful. The people are our nation, not the government. The government is merely a product of the people.

Liberation Day also frees the people to obey the government, because it's easier to obey someone who's governing you when the people doing the governing are just. There will be justice when legislators and the rest of the federal government start following their law.

The problems in the list above greatly distress me, and the Liberation Day plan entirely or partially solves most of those issues in a single day. I have many hopes in life, but my greatest hope for our nation is that it starts following the Constitution. Following it means that hundreds of entities would cease to exist, and the respective areas in which they function would be dealt with by the people, and if the people so desire, by their states. Dual regulation by the state and the federal government will cease to exist in hundreds of areas. I might be wrong, but my theory is that I will have a great peace when those problems I listed aren't plaguing my life.

I strive for justice, and Liberation Day will give us a big chunk of it because through it, the Constitution will start being followed. I believe following the Constitution is a part of justice because, in the Bible, Paul writes, "Every person is to be in subjection to the governing authorities.". When it comes to issues of government, the highest legal authority for legislators, lawyers, and executives in this nation to follow is the Constitution of the United States.

That restoration will bring us real freedom. Real freedom means prosperity, but it also means many specific things that, alone, seem small, but together they are enormous. It includes the sovereignty of the states and the people to do as they please regarding guns, unborn babies (though I'm personally 100% pro-life), planes, trains, automobiles, homes, the decision to fight in a war or not, and almost every part of life. The Constitution is not a list of things the government can't do. Those who think they understand the Constitution don't realize that this is perhaps the most misunderstood concept about the Constitution. The truth is, the Constitution is a list of the few things that the federal government can do. It is an exclusive list. In 99.9% of cases this means: if something is not listed as a power of the federal government in the Constitution, the federal government is legally banned from carrying out that power.

You may say, "What about the Bill of Rights? That's in the Constitution, and it contains prohibitions." You would be right. The Bill of Rights is a set of prohibitions on the federal government, but those prohibitions are merely unnecessary reiterations of the prohibitions on the federal government that are already built into the Constitution. Some of the founders wanted the Bill of Rights to be used as a learning tool highlighting the importance of specific freedoms. Others were afraid that, in time, people would forget that the Constitution is a list of powers, not a list of prohibitions. The latter group was correct. Now, we must fix this problem of misunderstanding with our minds. We must understand what the

Constitution truly means and tell our children and the people we can influence about it too.

The Founding Fathers would demand nothing less than for us to follow the original intent of the Constitution. If we have faith in the God of the Bible, He requires nothing less than for us to be perfect, as Jesus said in the Sermon on the Mount, "...be perfect, as your heavenly Father is perfect." I can think of no better, politically feasible thing to do to get our government closer to perfect than to start following the supreme law of the land in our nation. You and I must make this happen: our country depends on it. Without the Constitution, the immoral and unjust things around us will keep happening, and worse things will happen. With the Constitution restored, we will help to create peace and security for ourselves and future generations. For liberty!

Eric Martin

CHAPTER 2

OUR PRESENT CRISIS

"In this present crisis, government is not the solution to our problem, government is the problem."
—President Ronald Reagan

The year is 2017. Our federal government is sitting under $19.97 trillion of debt.[3] That's more debt than the economic output of the entire United States in 2016. The debt surpassed GDP in 2011 for the first time since 1947, just after World War II.[4]

In 15 years, from 2000 to 2015, the federal debt went from $5.7 trillion to $18.2 trillion.[5] That's a compound annual growth rate of 8.06%. If our debt increases at that rate for the next 15 years, we'll be **$64 trillion in debt** in 2032.

That growth of debt is not sustainable, and the markets may not let us get to that level of debt, at least not without massive inflation. That inflation could massively erode the cash in our bank accounts and the bonds in our retirement accounts.

We have a choice. We are at a pivotal point in our nation, perhaps the pivotal point. We can keep on our current path, or we can choose a better path.

The chart below shows the government debt to gross domestic product (or GDP, a nation's economic output in one year) ratio for a few major countries so that you can see where we stand.

Japan	229.20%
Greece	176.90%
Italy	132.70%
Singapore	104.70%
United States	104.17%
Switzerland	34.40%

These are ratios from December 2015.[6] Once we get into that 200 to 300% zone, we'll be in trouble. But right now, we are near the point of no return. The time to reduce our debt is now, or we may have to suffer the consequences of a default on our debt, or a virtual default through hyperinflation.

This 104.17% ratio for the federal debt of the United States does not factor in any state or local debt. Those debts are an additional drag on our ability to pay the federal debt. State and local debt can be thought of as car loans and credit card debt, but there's also the mortgage, which is the federal debt.

If our economy grows even close to the 3.22% that it averaged from 1947-2016, then with 2.5% growth from 2016 until 2032,[7] we'll go from a GDP of $18.56 trillion in 2016 to a GDP of $27.55 trillion in 2032. Imagine having $64 trillion of national debt with a $27.5 trillion economy. That's a debt to GDP ratio of 232.7%. All I've done to calculate that 232.7% is divide the $64 trillion in debt we will have with a similar growth-rate of debt, then divided it by the output we will have in that year when estimating 2.5% yearly growth, and then multiplied by one hundred. Our debt to GDP ratio will have eclipsed Italy, Japan, and Greece's recent ratios.

To look at this another way, let's compare our debt to a typical American household. The current in-come of the federal government, the taxes it collects in a year, is $3.3 trillion. Its debt stands at $19.97 trillion.[8] The median household income in the United States in 2011 was $50,054.[9] For reference, the average household debt that year was $70,000.[10]

If the $50,054 a year household had the same level of debt as the federal government in 2017, it would be a debt of $300,324. Remember, this is like the "mortgage," and it doesn't count the state and local government's "auto" and "credit card" debts.

In 2032, just 15 years from this book's writing, if the government's revenue grows at 2.5% a year, and its debt grows as it did from 2000 to 2015, the federal government will bring in about $4.8 trillion a year, and its debt will have increased to $64 trillion. That's like our median family getting a pay raise and earning about

$72,500 a year, but having a $962,538 mortgage. Now, **imagine earning $72,500 a year, but having a $962,538 mortgage**. At a 30-year 3.92% fixed rate, that's $54,612 per year in mortgage payments. That's where our government is headed by 2032. I don't want that to happen; I don't even think the markets would let that happen. The markets won't let it happen because they won't buy bonds if they doubt they will be paid back, or if they think the bonds will lose real value because of inflation. The markets would require an extremely high interest rate to be willing to buy that bond.

We have to take a stand. We have to say no to just one more penny being added to the federal debt. This book advocates for a radical departure from the way things have been done over the past one hundred years. Our only choice if we want to remain solvent is a radical departure. It's radical in practice, but in theory, it's not radical because it's no change at all. It's simply going back to the meaning of the words of the Constitution when the founders wrote them. It's going back to the meaning of the words when the writers of the amendments wrote them. The time is now to save our nation. But how did we get where we are, and how can we claw our way back out? This book answers those questions.

"...**The truth will set you free.**"—Jesus, John 8:32

How to Read this Book

This book is meant to be read in order; however, any of the chapters and sections in this book can be read alone, and if you ever feel like a section is something you're already familiar with, feel free to skip it: you shouldn't have too much trouble picking up somewhere else.

Eric Martin

CHAPTER 3

WHAT WENT WRONG, WHO'S TO BLAME, AND HOW WE CAN FIX IT

"Government, even in its best state, is but a necessary evil; in its worst state, an intolerable one."—Thomas Paine [11]

We've come to the point where the only entity above the law in our country is the government itself, and the special interests that control it. The federal government thinks it's above the law because it routinely and increaseingly ignores its own law, which it must abide by: The Constitution of the United States of America.

That's all the Constitution is: a simple working document that describes everything which "constitutes" the federal government. It's a working document because anytime it is found to be inadequate to serve our nation, it can be amended. It is the Supreme Law over the rest of the federal government, so the federal government is disobeying the law because it is doing things not contained in the Constitution.

Where Did We Go Wrong?

We've missed the forest for the trees. We've been worrying about whether to raise the debt ceiling, and we need to be focused on lowering the debt ceiling. We're worried about trimming a few trees, and the whole forest is burning down. We need to chop down all the trees around us to save ourselves from being consumed by the fire. This isn't a matter of how much we need to decrease a department's budget (which almost never happens anyway); rather, this is a matter of how many departments we need to completely eradicate.

Total 2015 Federal Spending

Here are the forest and the trees for your reference. Most of these categories of spending are entirely or almost entirely unconstitutional, and therefore illegal.

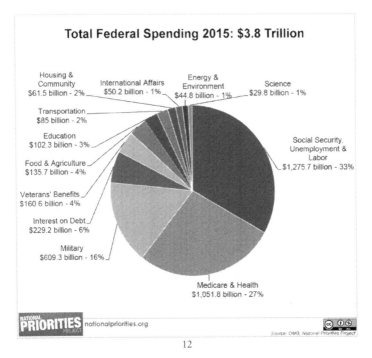

Total Federal Spending 2015: $3.8 Trillion

Housing & Community
$61.5 billion - 2%

International Affairs
$50.2 billion - 1%

Energy & Environment
$44.8 billion - 1%

Science
$29.8 billion - 1%

Transportation
$85 billion - 2%

Education
$102.3 billion - 3%

Food & Agriculture
$135.7 billion - 4%

Veterans' Benefits
$160.6 billion - 4%

Interest on Debt
$229.2 billion - 6%

Military
$609.3 billion - 16%

Social Security, Unemployment & Labor
$1,275.7 billion - 33%

Medicare & Health
$1,051.8 billion - 27%

nationalpriorities.org

Source: OMB, National Priorities Project

12

Who's to Blame?

It seems that The Times of London once posed a similar question, "What's wrong with the world today?" The story goes that G.K. Chesterton responded as follows:

> Dear Sir,
>
> I am.
>
> Yours, G.K. Chesterton.[13]

That sums it up nicely.

I am to blame for the problems of our federal government, and the problems of my state's (Pennsylvania) government, for that matter. I have not been diligent enough in vetting candidates; prior to 2012, I did not vote in every one of the elections; I have not made sure that people running for state office would uphold the state or federal Constitution; I have not done a good enough job of making sure that federal candidates would uphold the Constitution; I haven't run for office much; I have not pressured current officeholders to follow the Constitution; I have not told enough people about the need for a return to the Constitution; and I have caused our nation to be in this terrible state of affairs.

In 2012, I ran for U.S. Congress in the Republican primaries. I got fifth out of seven contenders. It wasn't until I ran for Congress that I realized the significance of voting, even for the lesser positions. Since then, I've voted in every general, primary, and special election, as far as I know.

I don't know if there could be a better education for me about the importance of voting than my run for Congress. I learned that everyone running for office is a flawed human, but we can impact which human gets into office with our vote.

It would not have put him in office, but the person just behind me in the race lost to me by just nine votes. I got a total of 2,159 votes, and he got 2,150 votes. That means that if just five votes that went for me instead went to him, he would have beaten me. That proved to me that every vote counts, and your vote counts.

People would tell me that politics is nasty. All I can say is what I saw: everyone I ran with on the Republican side was quite friendly toward one another, even though people threw a few normal jabs during forums or debates. We did not have too many meet-ups with the two Democrats who were running during events, but they seemed okay at least some of the time.

Running showed me that since we are all flawed, we need to do our best to elect the best person for the job, and also to run more when there's an opportunity when we might be the best person for the job. We need to elect the person who is best able to follow the Constitution, both federal and state if applicable. I still struggle with these things and can do a better job of them. Perhaps we all can.

I'm to blame for the present crisis, but I also see the problem a little more clearly now: because of that, I am working harder to fix it. I want more people to run for office because it may be the best way to understand the flaws of humans in politics and also to understand the enormity of the problem.

Even if you run and don't win, you can change the conversation and hopefully get candidates and the public to think in a new way. I believe I did that in 2012. I ran on a Constitution platform, saying at one venue "the Constitution is the solution." I still believe that it is the solution or at least the best possible first step that I know of, and it will get us about 95% of the way to "perfect" federal government compared to where we are now. I brought up the Constitution so much throughout the campaign that other candidates started talking about it. I think it had quite an impact, and I hope it had an impact on my current congressman, Scott Perry, who eventually got into office out of that field of seven Republicans.

I am the problem, and I am working now to reverse that. I will never be perfect, and the problem is immense, but I must do something because the alternative is that my children and grandchildren, if I am blessed with them, will look at me or think of me one day and say, "Why didn't you do something? Surely you could have done something?"

How does Government Work in the United States?

Of the 195 countries in the world, only about 25 use a federal system of government.[14] Federalism is where there are multiple levels of government with power. The United States has two layers: The state layer with 50 states, and the federal layer with one federal government governing alongside all of the states. A local government within a state, such as a county or a city or a township, doesn't typically have direct power, but rather, it has indirect power. Its indirect power is given to it by the state government of the state where it is located.

At the founding of the United States, power flowed from the people to create the state governments, and later it flowed from the state governments to create the central, federal government. In each case, we have a government created by "We the People." "We the People" wasn't a new concept when it was put into the Preamble of the

Constitution. "We the People" was a concept that ran deep in the minds of Americans because we had recently thrown off the British and we wanted to rule ourselves instead of having British rule.

Our federalist system means that the states hold the keys to all governmental power in our nation, and the people hold the keys to the state governments. The states ceded some of their governmental power over to the federal government with a document that lists specific powers in which the states agreed that the federal government could have a role.

The people who wrote the Constitution would be very confused if they had a look at our government today. It would make no sense to them that we have 50 departments of agriculture, one in each state that governs and regulates agriculture in each state, as well as one Department of Agriculture at the federal level governing and regulating agriculture in every state. We have two sets of regulations for agriculture in every state. That would make no sense to our founding fathers, and it should make no sense to us. The Constitution never ceded any power over agriculture to the federal government, so the states are justified in having departments of agriculture, and the federal government is unjust in having one. The central government usurped power, went against the boundaries created in the Constitution, and has done something illegal. Everything the federal government has done related to agriculture is null and void if the law is being properly interpreted.

It's not that we couldn't have a federal Department of Agriculture, it's just that a simple amendment to the Constitution would first be required in order to make it legal. That's the beauty of the Constitution: it's 100% flexible. There are hundreds of examples of areas where the federal government has usurped power from the states against the Constitution. A government that follows federalism needs to have roles for each level of government that are actually followed, so what we have now would more accurately be called "double government," not federalism. A large portion of this book aims to get rid of double government and restore federalism.

50 Engines of Innovation

When the state governments are free to do as they wish, without the federal government holding them back and strangling them with mandates and extra layers of regulation, the states can shine. Each of the 50 states become a little engine of legislative, executive, and (perhaps) judicial innovation.

Each state can get rid of laws and regulations, or create them as they see fit. When these changes work well, other states can jump on board; when they fail, other states can steer clear.

Right now, the federal government and the states each have their own departments or agencies for education. When the federal government mandates anything, the states' hands are then tied in that area and they can't innovate in that area. The founders of our nation did not intend this. Federal involvement in education and most other areas that they are involved in is unconstitutional. The founders' intent was for the states to be able to innovate freely in every area except for the few enumerated powers that are given over from the states to the federal government through the Constitution.

The legally binding rules for the federal government within the Constitution create a great "barrier to entry" that prohibits the federal government to get involved in the affairs of the states. There is nowhere where the federal government may enter into state affairs except for the areas that the few constitutionally enumerated powers allow. The enumerated powers are like doors through the barrier of entry that allow access into specific rooms (areas of power) within the states. Those few doors have been unlocked by the states through the Constitution, and all other doors remain locked. Only a ratified constitutional amendment could unlock another door.

The doors that the federal government has unconstitutionally pried open need to again be closed, locked, and sealed. The people, the federal government, and the states need to do everything in their power to accomplish this. We will then return to a fully functioning federation of states that are 50 engines of innovation, the likes of which hasn't been seen in this country, or probably even the world, for well over 100 years.

How this Book can Fix Our Government

A government above the law must be stopped, and I believe it can stopped. This book is a plan to be used by the office of the president of the United States to bring our federal government to constitutional governance in just one day. It's not perfect, but it is the starting point which I believe all presidential candidates should start with, tweak if needed, and then carry out. The movement for liberty started at our nation's founding, and it has seen a resurgence since Ron Paul's second presidential campaign, which he announced in 2007. We must continue the fight for liberty, and bring back our constitutional republic. Freedom is good, so let's fight for it.

This book is called *Liberation Day* because we need to be liberated from a government that is no longer following the Constitution of the United States of America; the Constitution is the supreme law of the land. There must be no compromise on every issue contained in the Constitution. There are many, many areas that are constitutional where compromise is totally permitted. For example, "duties, imposts and excises" are certain types of taxes found in the Constitution: Individuals in Congress can, constitutionally speaking, compromise at any time on these taxes because there is no constitutional requirement for them to make an oath that they will raise, lower, eliminate, or create these taxes. There is, however, a requirement that members of Congress swear or affirm to uphold the Constitution. So, on any issue, there can be compromise except for constitutional issues.

Other examples of potential compromise are the rights of the people and the states. These are huge areas where people and entities can act freely in almost every area. Acting freely can be an act of compromising on something.

A person can compromise on his or her values as he or she sees fit. There's not a universally agreed upon the supreme law that people must follow when it comes to values. This is unlike legislators, justices, and presidents, they all have a supreme law which they have agreed to uphold, the Constitution.

The states can compromise as they desire, similar to individuals, as long as they are in line with the United States Constitution and their own state's constitution. Here's an alcohol-related state compromise: Let's say alcohol is heavily regulated in your state. You're a state legislator, and you believe alcohol should be outlawed by the government. You notice that people are bringing in alcohol from other states. People are even moving out of your state because of the strict alcohol regulations that are in place at the state level. Even though you think illegalizing alcohol is the ideal, you may vote to reduce alcohol regulations anyway. So, you want alcohol illegal, but you vote to make it more legal. How could this be? This could be a compromise to your own convictions but done for the wellbeing of your state. As long as this compromise does not go against your state constitution or the US Constitution, it's okay in that it's legal.

But if the federal Constitution says that drugs cannot be made illegal by the federal government within state borders, then there can be no compromise on that issue. This means that federal legislators cannot make drugs illegal within states because that would be a compromise on the Constitution. That would be an unconstitutional law. It is illegal for a congressperson to vote "yes" to a law like that, but unfortunately, we've come to a point where almost everyone is turning a blind eye to these illegal votes. It's not good.

I'm pushing so hard on this topic of compromise because I want you to know that I believe in compromise, and I believe that government cannot function without it. The Constitution would not have been completed without major compromise on the issues of slavery and the voting power of the states. Slave states wanted slavery to be left unchanged, while some northern states thought the immorality of slavery was becoming more evident. Large states wanted more representation in Congress than smaller states. In both cases, there were compromises in the Constitution.

In the slavery example, slavery was originally constitutionally allowed by the states because, in the 1700s, there were states with legal slavery. The Constitution wouldn't have been ratified if slavery was banned because so many states had slavery. It wasn't until 1865 that the Constitution was amended with the Thirteenth Amendment to forbid slavery. Of course, now that the Constitution has abolished slavery, it must remain that way unless the Constitution is amended again to allow slavery. In the 1700s, we needed compromise on slavery, and now we don't because the Constitution has been changed.

Compromise on the Constitution itself, and, now that it has been properly ratified, is tantamount to the end of the rule of law in our land; we are no longer being ruled by the supreme law in our country. Without the rule of law, there can only be one thing remaining, and that thing is tyranny in one form or another. We have tyranny in our nation. We must start abiding by the Constitution to start ridding ourselves of that tyranny.

I can support compromise on many issues. But the Constitution is a very different animal. We, supposedly, live in a constitutional republic. In order for this to be true, our government needs to actually follow the Constitution, which it's not doing. The beauty of a constitutional republic is not only that we get the benefits of elected representation but also that our government is limited by the Constitution.

Would anyone really want an unlimited republic? I hope you know what that means. It means we would have elected officials who could do whatever they felt like with no limits. Even though they're barely abiding by the limits in the Constitution, do you know what we'd have with no constitution? I'm not sure, but perhaps we would have evolved into a dictatorship, or at the very least, special interests would have put a stranglehold on Congress even more than they do now. Congress would bow to every request for competition to be squashed, the power of Congress would be even more entrenched, and perhaps our government would have created an empire out of the entire world, rather than being satisfied with merely near-endless wars and an unjust police state.

I write this book believing that compromises throughout our nation's history have been a large part of what have messed up our nation, but they may have been necessary at the time. I also believe that if we stop compromising on our nation's supreme legal document, the Constitution, many of our government's problems will be solved.

Liberation Day seeks to bring our nation's government back to constitutional governance in just one day. It seeks to make it so that we no longer need any compromise on the Constitution and that we are following it faithfully and based on its original intent when written.

Government and politics are all about compromise; however, we cannot have any compromise on our Constitution because it is the supreme law of the land. By compromising our Constitution, we get an illegal government, and we've had many legislators and presidents at a federal level who have supported illegal measures insofar as they have not upheld the Constitution. It is illegal for federal officials to not uphold the Constitution because every federal legislator, judge, and president is required to swear or affirm to uphold the Constitution as a requirement of their service.

According to Article II of the Constitution, here is what presidents must do:

> Before he enter on the Execution of his Office, he shall take the following Oath or Affirmation:—"I do solemnly swear (or affirm) that I will faithfully execute the Office of President of the United States, and will to the best of my Ability, preserve, protect and defend the Constitution of the United States."

If there's any question about whether states can nullify unconstitutional federal law, it is answered in the last paragraph of Article VI of the U.S. Constitution:

> The Senators and Representatives before mentioned, and the Members of the several State Legislatures, and all executive and judicial Officers, both of the United States and of the several States, shall be bound by Oath or Affirmation, to support this Constitution;

Nullification is the power of a state to ignore and not uphold any unconstitutional federal law. The text above from the Constitution shows us the implication that the Founders wanted state Legislators, Governors, and Judges, as well as all of those people at the federal level, including the President, to be bound to support the Constitution.

This means that nullifying a law that is unconstitutional is perfectly constitutional for any branch of government and even any executive or judicial officer in government. In fact, following the Constitution is a duty and obligation for these people, both in the state and the federal governments.

The founders felt it was so important that the Constitution be followed, and federal tyranny stopped, that they constitutionally commanded people in the state and the federal governments to support the Constitution. This powerful deference to the Constitution by the founders is almost impossible to overemphasize.

The first question that any congressperson, judge, or president should ask when they see any law or action of government is, "Where is this authorized in the Constitution?" If it is not authorized, they are bound to do everything in their power to stop that law or action in its tracks.

When they ask, "Where is this authorized?" we know that our leaders need to follow the original intent of the Constitution, not only because the founders made it clear that they wanted it interpreted that way, but also because original intent is implied in the Constitution. If the founders wanted the words of the Constitution to change in meaning over time depending on who is reading it or when it is read, they would not have written it because it would have no concrete meaning. Also, if the meaning of the Constitution could change on its own without a change of the written words, the founders wouldn't have put a simple system for amending it into the Constitution itself.

I need to more carefully make sure that federal and state officials who I vote for more carefully stick to the Constitution and what it actually intends. As Ron Paul has alluded to, the power of our representatives to do anything in government flows from the people. We need to cut off the power of anyone not following the Constitution.

We need government to no longer be measured for greatness according to what it does, but it needs to be measured for greatness according to what it doesn't do, and for the restraint it maintains. I believe this restraint is what many of the founders wanted as well, and it's the beauty they got to see in the early federal government.

> "When taxes are too high,
> people go hungry.
> When the government is too intrusive,
> people lose their spirit.
>
> Act for the people's benefit.
> Trust them; leave them alone."
> *Tao Te Ching* by Lao-tzu[15]

The Purposes of this Book

This book has three simple purposes: (1) to explain why we need to bring our government back in line with the United States Constitution, (2) to explain how constitutional government will fix many of our nation's current problems, and (3) to detail a specific action plan that our President can use to bring us back to constitutional government in just one day.

A return to the Constitution is something that Democrats, Republicans, and other parties can get behind because it means a return to the rule of law, and it allows the people and the States to live according to their own wills. On average, Democrats should be able to live more according to their ideals, and Republicans more according to their ideals.

Nullification has not Fixed Our Problems Yet

Many people argue that nullification is a solution to the problem of our power-hungry federal government. I agree that nullification, or a state not upholding any federal law which is unconstitutional, is good; however, I am not focusing on this method of returning to the Constitution because it has already been detailed by many people, and it still leaves problematic issues such as those caused by the federal income tax.

The income tax may fund many things, both constitutional and unconstitutional, so how does the state nullify some proportion of the income tax and then ask the federal government to spend it where it sees the spending as proper and constitutional? I think issues like these are nearly impossible to deal with in practice, and I think the federal government would be inclined to collect as much income tax as possible and then spend it wherever it felt like, regardless of what any state has nullified.

There Is Hope in the Executive Branch

I also wrote this book because it presents another possible solution to the federal government's usurpation of powers that were never granted to it: an executive branch that uses its power to "not execute laws," in particular, unconstitutional laws, in order to return us to the Constitution.

I hope most of our federal representatives wake up to the Constitution (since most of them seem to be asleep), but since they continually disregard the Constitution, I feel electing the right president would be a great chance to take back our country for liberty.

I hope this book and its methods can be used in conjunction with nullification and any other strategy or tactic that can bring back our liberty. As far as I can tell, nothing has worked very well to strip the federal government of its power, at least over the past 100 years or so. So, I would like to offer another tool to use, and I would suggest that we use every legal tool available to bring back the Constitution, including using nullification, electing presidents who will nominate a judiciary that interprets the Constitution according to its original intent, voting people into the legislature who are committed to strictly following the Constitution, and demanding a president who is committed to using his or her power to execute or not execute laws, as part of his or her executive power, in order to uphold the Constitution.

The executive orders in this book are an outpouring of executive power. This executive power includes the president's ability to no longer enforce decades, layers, and volumes of laws, minutia, and regulations that have been forced upon us against the will of our people, against the will of our founding document and, consequently, against the supreme law of the land.

Morally Speaking, the Constitution Must be Followed

Most religions and moral systems expect honesty from the people who swear or affirm the Constitution. It's not only Jews or Christians who believe that there is a moral problem when our legislators, judges, and presidents don't uphold the Constitution; it's almost everyone. Our leaders need to follow the Constitution because they have sworn or affirmed to do so, and that makes it the right thing to do.

Article VI is where it says that all legislators, executives, and judges must agree that they are bound to uphold or support the Constitution. Even people in similar positions at the state level must agree to support the federal Constitution. Here's part of Article VI: "The Senators and Representatives before mentioned, and the Members of the several State Legislatures, and all executive and judicial Officers, both of the United States and of the several States, shall be bound by Oath or Affirmation, to support this Constitution; but no religious Test shall ever be required as a Qualification to any Office or public Trust under the United States."

If people don't uphold what they have sworn to uphold, doesn't that make them immoral? Perhaps our federal government is falling apart because its members aren't following through on their moral obligation. Is that what John Adams was talking about in 1798 when he said the following?

"Our Constitution was made only for a moral and religious people. It is wholly inadequate to the government of any other."—John Adams[16]

The Fortress of Liberty

I am so excited by the many movements of liberty sweeping our nation. These movements are helped along by individual people – the books, blogs, and articles they've written; the offices they've won; the podcasts, videos, and speeches they've made; and the organizations they've started. All of these things are building on top of each other, like stones building a great Fortress of Liberty.

In many ways, I feel that Ron Paul has, in recent times, done the most to bring Liberty to the masses. Perhaps I am biased because Ron Paul is the one who most influenced my thinking towards liberty. It's almost as if Ron Paul is a vanguard or rallying cry for the many groups whose ends are Liberty.

I want to give a shout out to a few of those groups who are doing a great job and are helping to lead our nation towards a more prosperous future. There is the Tenth Amendment Center, which has a big thrust for states to nullify any unconstitutional federal law; there's the Tea Party movement, which harkens back to people who dressed up as American Indians and destroyed tea because of their disdain for taxes from a government where they had no representation in parliament; there's the Constitution Party, which is all for the Constitution but also has a focus on God and the Bible; there's the Libertarian Party with a strong disdain for almost all government; there's the Mises Institute, which is about Austrian Economics and ending the Federal Reserve; there's The Future of Freedom Foundation, which educates people about liberty; there's Infowars by Alex Jones, which is exposing corrupt organizations, such as the Bilderberg Group; and of course, there are the organizations that Ron Paul started, including the Campaign for Liberty, the Ron Paul Institute for Peace and Prosperity, and the Ron Paul Liberty Report. I hope that this book is one more strengthening stone laid on top of this nation's strong foundation of liberty.

Is the Constitution Dead?

Early on in my writing of this book, one of my good friends made a great Devil's Advocate argument against it. He said I needed to address the people who would say that the Constitution was written over 200 years ago, and that if we were to interpret it the way the founders would have interpreted it 200 years ago, we wouldn't have a properly functioning government. Or it wouldn't be a realistically sized government.

They would say that the Constitution needs to be interpreted differently because times have changed, the world has changed, and the federal government needs to do a lot more now because the world is a much more complicated place. Industry, in general, has really grown from a very small portion of the economy to a huge portion of it; the service sector has grown to make up a huge section of the economy; when the Constitution was first written, we had a very agrarian society: most people were farmers.

"Times have changed" is a good point against the goal of this book, which is to get us back to the way the founders envisioned our country through the Constitution. However, the remedy to this argument is three-fold. The first two parts of the remedy have to do with the 10th Amendment: anything that we think the government should be doing, we should look to (1) the people (both as individuals and through their organizations) and (2) the states to take care of, rather than the federal government.

For instance, absolutely every state already has an agricultural department of some sort,[17] so there's no need for there to be two layers of law and regulation for agriculture. Isn't it obvious that the people and representatives of the state of Kansas know how to regulate their agriculture better than legislatures and bureaucrats in Washington, a small proportion of which are even from Kansas?

The states and the people are more than capable of taking care of most of these issues. Here's a short list of some of the issues people and states are more than capable of dealing with: education, transportation, health, housing, poverty, and the environment.

The people take care of issues, such as poverty and housing, head on with such organizations as Feeding America, which tackles poverty, and Habitat for Humanity, which tackles housing. In many of these instances, the people could take over any role that the state and federal governments have played, but the key is to allow the states to do whatever they want in these areas: The federal government cannot interfere. There can be no question on this because it's written directly in the Constitution's 10th Amendment: "The powers not dele-gated to the United States by the Constitution, nor prohibited by it to the States, are reserved to the States respectively, or to the people." The word "reserved" means that no other entity, especially not the federal government, can have any of those powers.

The day I understood that the Constitution was not a list of things that the federal government can't do, but rather, a very short list of the only things the federal government can do, my understanding of the govern-- ment changed profoundly. It makes it very simple for any of us to look at any officer in government, or at any law, and determine if what its actions are constitutional. If not, that officer or law needs to be thrown out.

Here's simple explanation of the Constitution:

The Constitution is a very short list of the things the federal government can do, as well as a very short list of the things that state governments can't do.

I don't know if I can find anything in the Constitution that can't fit into one of those two categories. The Constitution excludes almost every power from the federal government and permits almost every power for the state governments. The Constitution section of this book goes into the details of what the federal government can do and what the state governments can't do according to the Constitution.

The reason that we need to allow the states to deal with housing or any other issue is because that's what the Constitution calls for. Also, in general, we virtually never want the federal government limiting the states regarding what they can do. This is because if the federal government is limiting the states, then they are limiting the people, and then, the federal government might start to try to directly impose limitations on the people after being emboldened by successfully limiting the states. Stripping states of power is really just one step away from striping individuals of power.

If a state wants to choose, through their Constitution or otherwise, that they will not in any way be involved with agriculture, housing, et cetera, this is up to them, and it's perfectly acceptable. I just don't want the federal government telling states what they can and can't do, except for the very few cases where the Constitution allows for this kind of interference. The section on the Constitution goes in-depth on the few things that the federal government has the power to do, and the few limits that the Constitution imposes on state governments.

The third and final counter to the argument that states: "We can't go back to the Constitution and its original meaning because the world is much more complicated now that we're in the 21st century" is that the Constitution (3) can be amended. This means that the Constitution can be changed. We can update the Constitution and tweak it so that it fits our 21st-century world. There are a few cases where it makes sense for the federal government to have more power than what the Founders gave to it, and that may be one of the reasons that the founders made the Constitution amendable.

What about Consistency and Efficiency?

Can't the federal government create laws across the entire nation so that all fifty states have the same "rules to follow" and each doesn't have to spend money legislating and regulating various areas? Of course it can, and it does. For example, the Constitution provides for uniform laws of bankruptcy throughout the states. Congress didn't take too long to do this, passing the first bankruptcy law in 1800.[18]

About eight years ago, I had a coworker who wanted gay rights or gay marriage to be the norm across the United States. I explained to him that a federal law would be unconstitutional. He may have been angry at the Constitution. At the time, gay marriage was legal in a few states. I explained to him that that's the beauty of the Constitution—leaving most laws at the state level. If he wanted, he could go to another state to get married. If Congress could legislate on gay marriage, they might do it, and at the time it would have probably meant that gay marriage would be illegal in all fifty states.

I marvel at the genius of states' rights. If you don't like the laws in your state, you can move to another state where things are more in your favor. If something should be done at a federal level, the Constitution can be amended, instead of illegally passing laws or declaring Supreme Court rulings that go against the Constitution.

As far as efficiency goes, you'll see throughout this book that most states, as well as the federal government, have agencies for almost everything, such as education, agriculture, and healthcare. That's not efficient because it means double government and double regulation. The federal government needs to get out of these areas. It's duplication that has not gone away even though the federal government has unconstitutionally stepped on states' rights. There is a federal Department of Agriculture and 50 state departments of agriculture.

If we want the "economies of scale" that a single governmental body could provide for an area, the Constitution must first be amended. We tried that with the prohibition of alcohol in 1920. The amendment didn't go well, so we repealed it with another amendment in 1933. Alcohol has (largely) been in the hands of the states ever since. History shows that less is better when it comes to the federal government.

Perhaps the best argument against the need for consistency is in murder laws. Murder laws are almost exclusively the authority of the state, and yet no one says, "The federal government needs to make murder illegal!" Who is calling for that? Perhaps no one, because the states have all made murder illegal, and they have done so consistently for hundreds of years. Murder is illegal in all 50 states without the federal government needing to say a word on the subject.

The states can govern themselves. We should want to keep murder and almost every other area of governmental interest in the hands of the states because that keeps government closer and more accountable to the people.

The United States is a large nation and a heterogeneous society. Heterogeneous means that we are a mix of very different people. Those differences make the variation in laws from state to state very nice for the various people. If we were all living in Japan, where almost everyone is the same race and has the same culture and language, our federal system of government that empowers states might not make sense. If we were small like Singapore or Monaco, it also might not make sense. But with a large, heterogeneous nation, bringing the power closer to the people makes perfect sense.

Texas is larger than Afghanistan, and Alaska is larger than Iran. Alaska and Hawaii are far away from the rest of the states. If all we had were federal law, it would not be able to govern all of those areas effectively.

What about all the People who will be Fired in one day?

The twenty-three Liberation Day executive orders, if enacted, would take hundreds of thousands of people out of the federal workforce in a single day. This seems staggering and unacceptable. It seems too harsh and too inhumane. But it's not.

There are three reasons that this mass firing is acceptable:

The first reason is that people are resilient: most will be able to find other jobs. People can apply for constitutional, state unemployment insurance until they find a new job.

The second reason this is acceptable is because the people being laid off were doing unconstitutional work. Much of it involved shuffling papers and slowing down the economy through illegal, unnecessary regulations. Every productive, non-government employee shouldn't be made to suffer an inefficient economy because of the government employees' efficiency-draining activities. The work the government employees were doing was unconstitutional and therefore, illegal. But they are not to blame for doing this work. All people working for the federal government do not have to swear or affirm to uphold the

Constitution. Swearing to uphold the Constitution is for the higher-ups: the president, the legislators, and the judges. The higher-ups are at fault, and the average worker is not at fault.

The third reason this mass exodus is acceptable is because without it, our government may implode under its rapidly expanding debt load. If the implosion happens, even more people at the federal level will lose their jobs, along with many other people in the private sector. The huge pain on Liberation Day for those who lose their jobs may pale in comparison to the pain that they and others would have felt if we had done nothing. It's better to pull off a giant, useless band-aid quickly than to drag out the process for years.

One Potential Amendment to the Constitution

A great example of where amendment might be necessary is the executive orders, along with that the ability to have weapons and surveillance equipment in space. The founders had perhaps no idea that we would have military aircraft. They didn't have any self-propelled aircraft in their day, unless you count birds. The Constitution has no provision for an Air Force.

Later in the book, you'll see that there is an executive order that says the Air Force will be disbanded. However, I believe that the people and the states will demand an air force. The plan and hope in this book are to follow the Constitution first and foremost. Therefore, we need to commit to getting rid of the Air Force unless the

Constitution is amended. However, if a presidential candidate commits to getting rid of the Air Force on his or her first day of office through an executive order, contingent on the Constitution not first being amended, he or she can recommend to the people and to Congress that before he or she takes office, they amend the Constitution to allow for an Air Force so that he or she doesn't ever have to sign the executive order.

When the people and the states are faced with the possibility of having no Air Force, I have no doubt that they will quickly ratify an amendment to the Constitution to allow for it. I think they could amend the Constitution within 48 hours in a case like this if needed, through emergency sessions of the federal and state legislatures. In the case of a new president, the legislatures would have almost three months to get an amendment ratified until the president-elect takes office.

When "threatened" with the prospect of a president who has clearly agreed to immediately enforce the Constitution, I believe the people and the states will make the necessary constitutional amendments to keep government at a "modern" level.

The beauty of taking us back to the Constitution is that it forces us to federalize only the most important powers. The amendment process is not easy, which is great because we don't want to make it easy for the federal government to take more power. Unfortunately, allowing easy power-grabs is exactly what we have done in the past.

The goal of this book is not just to bring us back to the Constitution but also to make sure we understand that the Constitution can be amended—it can be changed, and we probably do need to change and tweak our founding document to some extent so that it remains relevant for us in the 21st century.

The Founders foresaw that the Constitution would need to be changed; they knew that it wasn't perfect. But we have to stop making the mistake of thinking that just because the document isn't perfect, we don't need to follow it. We must strive to amend the Constitution to be more perfect while still following it. To the extent that the federal government has stopped following the Constitution, we have a tyrannical federal government.

Is the Constitution Libertarian?

The Constitution is not purely libertarian. However, the Constitution is quite libertarian, particularly regarding the federal government. What I mean by this is that the Constitution essentially says that states can do whatever they want. This means that the states and the people in those states can choose to have state governments that are very libertarian, or they can choose to be quite authoritarian; they can choose to be populist, socialist, conservative, or liberal. The one major constitutional limit on states is that they must have a republican form of government.

The federal government is largely libertarian in that it gives liberty to the states and to the people, so that the states or the people can choose to be whatever they want to be. From here, a totally non-libertarian government is possible in an individual state.

What can the President do?

"The executive Power shall be vested in a President of the United States of America." That's the first sentence in Article II of the Constitution. The president carries out laws. Because any unconstitutional law is actually no law at all (because it's not legal), the president should cease to carry out any law which is unconstitutional. An unconstitutional law is not really a law, because the Constitution is the supreme law of the United States; so, any law that does not abide by the Constitution can be considered null and void. We know that the Constitution is the supreme law of the land because of Section VI of the Constitution:

> This Constitution, and the Laws of the United States which shall be made in Pursuance thereof; and all Treaties made, or which shall be made, under the Authority of the United States, shall be the supreme Law of the Land; and the Judges in every State shall be bound thereby, any Thing in the Constitution or Laws of any State to the Contrary notwithstanding.

This says that the Constitution and the laws made through it are supreme. However, the Constitution is the supreme law over other federal laws because those laws must be made in "Pursuance" of the Constitution. Pursuance means the laws must carry out the Constitution.

The portion of the Constitution above is saying that state judges must abide by constitutional federal laws, but it does not say that state judges need to abide by unconstitutional federal laws. Nullification is a power of the states under the 10th Amendment; because the Constitution doesn't say that states can't nullify laws, therefore, they can. This portion of the Constitution clarifies that only unconstitutional federal laws can be nullified by state courts, but that constitutional federal laws cannot be nullified at the state level.

A quick example of this would be abortion versus federal excise taxes. Abortion within a state's borders is a state's right to ignore, legalize, illegalize, and/or regulate as they see fit, so a state can and should nullify any federal abortion laws, regulations, rulings, or actions, regardless of whether those federal mandates are for or against abortion. Because excise taxes are constitutional, a state cannot nullify federal excise taxes. A state has no right to nullify that tax, and any court, whether state or federal, should strike down that law as Unconstitutional because it goes against a law that is constitutional, thereby violating the above supremacy clause of the Constitution. constitutional federal laws reign supreme over state laws and state actions.

Donald Trump

One of the beauties of Donald Trump's presidency, so far (as of December 2017), is that he's enabling other Presidents to undo what he and others have done. He's creating a precedent of executive power through his numerous executive orders. This is a scary power in the hands of a president who does not uphold the Constitution, but it is a wonderful power in the hands of a president who is committed to the Constitution. Even though a president following the Constitution should be totally accepted by the courts and Congress, executive orders to quickly bring us in line with the Constitution could be questioned if other presidents hadn't issued so many executive orders. Unfortunately, many orders have been outside of constitutional power, which I see as a totally improper and illegal use of executive power.

A Republic

The plan in this book brings us back to a constitutional republic. With it, we can kiss the projected $64 trillion in debt goodbye. The plan almost entirely gets rid of unconstitutional federal programs such as Medicare, Medicaid, and Social Security, as well as undeclared, unconstitutional wars and many other unconstitutional programs. The cut programs are put directly into the hands of the states and the people. With this plan in place, we should have a budget surplus to pay off our debt and then lower taxes.

Hopefully, once we restore the Constitution, we can keep it. I suppose another president could undo the restoration, but as Benjamin Franklin said when asked what type of government we had after the Constitutional Convention was concluded, "**A Republic, if you can keep it.**"[19] Once we have it, we need to keep it, and with God's help, a moral and resolute people can bring it back and keep it.

Eric Martin

CHAPTER 4

ON DEMOCRATS, REPUBLICANS, AND THE POLITICAL SPECTRUM

"Educate and inform the whole mass of the people... They are the only sure reliance for the preservation of our liberty."—Thomas Jefferson[20]

Not long before the 2008 election, I thought that there were two major realms of acceptable political thought. Those were the realms of the Democrats and of the Republicans. I now know that there are other realms of political thought. Here's the political one-dimensional spectrum as I once thought it existed:

I think things started getting more nuanced for me in high school and college, and I realized that there was more to the political spectrum than I had initially thought. It was more complicated; here's a bit about what I thought the political spectrum looked like in my early twenties:

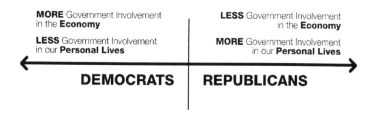

After this, I learned about Ron Paul and the two-dimensional political spectrum. A grasp of this spectrum really shows you know where Democrats, Republicans, and the rest lie. It shows where I see the Constitution. I didn't know about this spectrum for a long time. I didn't realize there were options other than what the Democrats and the Republicans were providing.

I really like one other option in particular: I like the option of freedom, liberty, and getting the government out of our lives, economically, morally, and socially. Hopefully, you've seen something like this before—but if not, please study this. I'm still trying to grapple with the ramifications of this in my own mind. Here's the two-dimensional political spectrum:

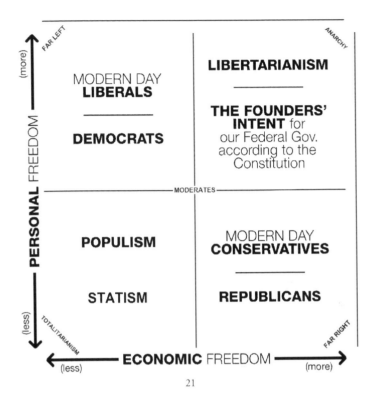

21

As you move up and to the right, you get more and more liberty. This illustrates how much liberty we would have if we were to go all the way up and to the right, where we would have infinite economic and personal liberty. There would be no government, and people call that anarchy.

Anarchy has a negative connotation in our language, but in reality, anarchy could be a good thing, because there's no government, and just pure liberty. However, people argue that pure liberty leads to liberty only for some because if one person has the liberty to kill another, all of the other person's earthly liberties are gone when he or she is killed. This is a good argument for government, and there are counterarguments, but for now, we'll just leave it at that and assume that since most people want government of some sort, there will be some form of government.

If we went down and all the way to the left, we would get the worst form of government: one that controls absolutely everything. This is known as a totalitarian government.

If we went all the way to the right and all the way down, we would get what you might call a strong Republican: someone who wants moral issues to be controlled by the government but who wants economic issues to be totally untouched by government.

We might call someone in the upper left a strong, modern-day liberal: someone who wants the government totally involved in our economic lives, with tons of welfare and regulations for the economy, but no government involvement in our personal lives.

The Constitution creates a federal government within the upper-right on this spectrum. This is the Libertarian quadrant. People and states are virtually anywhere on the spectrum, but Democrats, Republicans, and Libertarians in particular should all rally around the Constitution. If they don't rally around the Constitution, they run the risk of our entire nation falling into a quadrant that they don't believe in. If they vote to uphold the Constitution, then their state will be free to exist virtually anywhere on this political spectrum, unencumbered by the federal government.

CHAPTER 5

THE COMMERCE CLAUSE

"But as Jefferson warned, the natural tendency is for government to grow. Like a poisonous vine, it sprouts through any gap. What is really needed is a repeal of the commerce clause and an amendment to the Bill of Rights that says: 'Congress and the states shall make no law interfering with production and commerce, foreign or domestic.'"—Sheldon Richman [22]

Richman's recommendation would help us and the people in government to understand much of what the government is already legally restricted from doing according to the Constitution. The federal government and the states are already prohibited from any interference in interstate commerce according to the Constitution. Shedding some light on this prohibition is the goal of this chapter.

The Commerce Clause is perhaps the hardest part of the entire Constitution to understand. It took me hours of reading and research to start to grasp its meaning fully.

One of the best explanations I found, and some of what I'll present here, was on The Federalist Blog.[23] There is a great series of original writings or quotes about the Clause at Constitution Mythbuster, some of which I'll list below.[24]

Here's the text of the clause from the Constitution:

[The Congress shall have Power] To regulate Commerce with foreign Nations, and among the several States, and with the Indian Tribes;

Regulating commerce "with foreign Nations" and "with the Indian Tribes" is pretty simple because there's nothing else in the Constitution affecting those powers. The trickiness with this clause is in the portion related to the states, which reads: "[The Congress shall have Power] To regulate Commerce [...] among the several States." This part is tricky because just a little bit later in the Constitution, the power is clarified by two more clauses in Article I, Section 9.

The meaning of the word commerce then essentially means the same as the word trade does now. A little more background on the issue is that "regulating commerce" at that time was thought of as controlling the flow of goods by applying taxes such as duties on those goods, or by applying tonnage duties, which is a fee based on the weight of cargo a ship can carry. By enumerating the power to regulate commerce among the states to the Federal Government, the Constitution was taking that power out of state hands and putting it into federal hands. The fact that the power is out of the hands of the states and in federal hands is made clear in the Supremacy Clause from Article VI:

> This Constitution, and the Laws of the United States which shall be made in Pursuance thereof; and all Treaties made, or which shall be made, under the Authority of the United States, shall be the supreme Law of the Land; and the Judges in every State shall be bound thereby, any Thing in the Constitution or Laws of any State to the Contrary notwithstanding.

The part of Article I, Section 9 that affects "Commerce [...] among the several States," that is written a little before it, is the following:

> No Tax or Duty shall be laid on Articles exported from any State.

> No Preference shall be given by any Regulation of Commerce or Revenue to the Ports of one State over those of another: nor shall Vessels bound to, or from, one State, be obliged to enter, clear, or pay Duties in another.

Two of these three prohibitions flow out of Congress's previously enumerated power to regulate commerce "among the several States." In the first prohibition, the Federal government must ensure that neither the states nor itself lay any tax on any item being exported from one state into another. The last prohibition stops tonnage duties from being assessed by the state governments and the federal government when ships are carrying out trade among the states.

The middle prohibition flows from Congress's power to regulate trade with foreign nations and Indian Tribes: all domestic ports must be treated equally under federal law.

Why have the Framers of the Constitution given Congress the power to regulate interstate trade and then seemingly stripped themselves of it a little later by writing that the same Congress cannot tax any interstate trade, or the ships used for that trade?

The reason is that the states had horrible trade fights raging among themselves at the time under the Articles of Confederation.[25] The Constitution was meant to replace the Articles.

The solution of the Framers in the Constitution was to put regulating interstate commerce into the hands of the federal government in order to put an end to the states' fighting. However, they went further than that. Not only did they keep the states out of fights over trade among themselves, but they also kept the federal government out of taxing interstate trade. The powers given to the federal government over commerce "among the states" were simply the powers to keep the states from taxing or regulating trade, to keep the federal government from taxing trade as well, and to put the regulation of trade into the hands of the federal government. Even so, **the only way the federal government is allowed to**

regulate trade is by keeping the states from regulating or taxing trade.

James Madison, the "father of the Constitution," shows us that the only power Congress has over interstate commerce is to keep the states out of that regulation in an 1829 letter where he talks about the Commerce Clause:

> For a like reason, I made no reference to the "power to regulate commerce among the several States." I always foresaw that difficulties might be started in relation to that power which could not be fully explained without recurring to views of it, which, however just, might give birth to specious though unsound objections. Being in the same terms with the power over foreign commerce, the same extent, if taken literally, would belong to it. *Yet it is very certain that it grew out of the abuse of the power by the importing States in taxing the non-importing, and was intended as a negative and preventive provision against injustice among the States themselves, rather than as a power to be used for the positive purposes of the General Government, in which alone, however, the remedial power could be lodged.*[26]

We can see here that Madison knew that this clause could cause problems, and he explained what its intent and what its power really was. His words show us that the intent of the interstate portion of the Commerce Clause is to stop abuses of the taxation of trade between the states. In other words, the goal of the clause was to stop the trade wars among the states. He tells us that the intent of the clause is not to give the general or federal government any positive powers. The power is a negative power: it is negative for the states and keeps them from regulation (taxing) commerce. I'll show you later how, at the time, "regulating commerce" meant simply taxing commerce, and nothing more.

Madison concludes by telling us that the "remedial power" can only be in the hands of the federal government. In other words, the federal government is regulating trade solely by doing anything necessary and proper to keep the states from regulating (taxing) trade among the states. This is clear in light of Article I, Section 8, which gives the power to regulate commerce among the states to Congress, but then strips both Congress and the states of any taxing power over that category of trade. It's a negative power, not a positive one.

Things like this in the Constitution can really throw me off balance. Why make it so confusing? I'm not sure why, but can we blame the Framers? They had no idea that the Constitution that they were scrambling to create would still be ruling the country over 200 years later. They wanted to finish the Constitution during the hot summer quickly; they had no air conditioning.

If we were in their shoes, we would have written the Constitution just like they did: knowing the full backstory, and knowing the current state of affairs that led them to write what they wrote. We need to try to step into their shoes, and recreate their context, in order to understand the meaning of the Constitution.

The Commerce Clause isn't a one-off confusing portion of the Constitution. There are others. One big example had to do with slavery. The Framers did not want the word "slave" in the Constitution, because it might look bad. The terms "slave" and "slavery" did not exist in the Constitution until the Thirteenth Amendment passed in 1865, which abolished slavery.

The term "slave" was not in the Constitution at first, but slavery was in the Constitution. It's the very first item of Article I, Section 9:

> The Migration or Importation of such Persons as any of the States now existing shall think proper to admit, shall not be prohibited by the Congress prior to the Year one thousand eight hundred and eight, but a Tax or duty may be imposed on such Importation, not exceeding ten dollars for each Person.

Without understanding the context, I thought that this section had to do with immigration, but it is specifically referring to the slave trade. The Founders simply thought of a different way of writing the words so that "slavery" didn't have to be mentioned. We need to understand what the Framers meant when they wrote the Constitution, not only because the meanings of words change but also because the Framers used words that were a euphemism for something else in the case of slavery.[27]

We need to see the original intent of the Framers to understand the power that the Constitution actually hands over from the states to the federal government.

James Madison wrote another letter discussing the Commerce Clause in 1832. Here's an excerpt:

> The power to regulate commerce among the States was well known and so explained by the advocates of the Constitution when before the people for their consideration, to be as a necessary control on the conduct of some of the importing States toward their non-importing neighbors. A recurrence to the angry legislation produced by it among the parties, some of whom had passed commercial laws (duties and imposts on articles of import) more rigid against others than against foreign nations, will well account for the constitutional remedy.

Again, this shows us that the power over commerce among the states, contained in the Constitution, was meant as a control on the states.[28]

James Monroe spoke to the House of Representatives in 1822 about the original meaning of the commerce clause; it seems that people were already starting to forget what it meant. In part:

> **Commerce between independent powers or communities is universally regulated by duties and imposts.** It was so regulated by the States before the adoption of this Constitution, equally in respect to each other and to foreign powers. The goods and vessels employed in the trade are the only subjects of regulation. It can act on none other. **A power, then,**

to impose such duties and imposts in regard to foreign nations and to prevent any on the trade between the States was the only power granted.[29]

Should we take the word of some recent Supreme Court justice or the word of the fifth president of the United States, who was wounded with a musket ball during the Revolutionary War and studied "law under Thomas Jefferson from 1780 to 1783"?[30]

In a very detailed description, the first Attorney General of the United States, Edmund Randolph, explained the interstate commerce clause in 1791, just a few years after the Constitution was ratified:

> The heads of this power with respect to the several States, are little more, than to establish the forms of commercial intercourse between them, & to keep the prohibitions, which the Constitution imposes on that intercourse, undiminished in their operation: that is, to prevent taxes on imports or Exports; preferences to one port over another by any regulation of commerce or revenue; and duties upon the entering or clearing of the vessels of one State in the ports of another.[31]

From the context around this passage, you can see that the "heads of this power" could instead be called the "powers contained in this power." The ability to establish forms of commerce is the ability of Congress to say what constitutes commerce among the states. When Randolph says, "little more," I think he could just have easily had said "nothing more than." I think that's probably what he meant by this colloquialism. In other words, interstate commerce power is nothing more than the ability of Congress to say what commerce is and then to stop the states from taxing that commerce among themselves. The duties of vessels are related to the tonnage duty I mentioned previously. Laying tonnage duties and taxing the trade of goods among the states is not allowed.

If none of this convinces you that the federal government should not be involved in interstate commerce, except to ensure that states cannot impose taxes on goods imported into or exported out of a state, then consider this: There was not one successful passage of a law that regulated industry at the federal level until the Interstate Commerce Act of 1887.[32] From the time the Constitution was first signed in 1787, it took 100 years for a law that regulated commerce in this way to pass. Was that a coincidence? No! It took 100 years for enough people to forget what the Constitution meant to accept this desecration of it. Almost every power given by the Constitution to the federal government was invoked within a year or two of the government's creation; the hundred-year timeframe is because no such power to regulate was ever given. Researching something that was written 100 years ago is not easy. Now, 240 years later, we need to take back that which was lost. We need to dig deep into the annals of history in order to see clearly what our nation is founded upon.

It is founded upon liberty, a liberty so angry at the injuries caused by the British that many people didn't even want the Constitution to be ratified; they thought it gave the federal government too much power. I agree, it did give over too much power, but even if we could bring the government in line with the Constitution, our freedom would be ten or a hundred or a thousand times what it is now. It would be so much greater because we would be living in a country with a federal government that has a few enumerated powers, rather than a few enumerated limits.

One hundred years later and we had the Interstate Commerce Act that regulated the railroads. Two hundred and forty years later and we have so many agencies and departments that use the Commerce Clause to falsely justify themselves that I don't know that anyone has ever before attempted to list them all. I attempt to do that in the pages of this book. Let's take back our Constitution!

Eric Martin

CHAPTER 6

THE LIBERATION DAY PLAN: 23 EXECUTIVE ORDERS TO RESTORE THE CONSTITUTION IN THE UNITED STATES

This is it. This is the plan for any President to bring us back to the Constitution of the United States of America in just one day. All a President needs to do is sign and execute all 23 of the executive orders in this book, and we will have a Liberation Day in our nation. We will be orders of magnitude closer to true, constitutional government.

The 23 orders span several chapters: please check the Executive Order Index at the back of the book to find a specific order.

This plan is for the President, but it is also for Federal and state legislators, executives, and judges, so that they can better understand how our federal government needs to be transformed to become constitutional again. Every person, state or federal, in those offices is bound by oath or affirmation to support the Constitution. In Article VI of the Constitution, it is written, "The Senators and Representatives before mentioned, and the Members of the several State Legislatures, and all executive and judicial Officers, both of the United States and of the several States, shall be bound by Oath or Affirmation, to support this Constitution; but no religious test shall ever be required as a Qualification to any Office or public Trust under the United States."

This plan is also for you and me so that we know to what standards we need to hold the people we vote for. This plan helps us to see what needs to be done and demand it from our government.

Hopefully, it will provide the information needed to convince some of those who were once simply voters to also run for office and then carry out these changes. If those candidates don't win, they can be vocal about these issues during the campaign and help the electorate hold the eventual officeholder accountable for as many of these principles as possible.

In this chapter, I first introduce the plan and talk about our growing debt that makes the plan so necessary. I also go into detail on some of the agencies and why they must be removed from our federal government.

The people of the Liberation Day Movement and I are urging that, if not already implemented, these Executive Orders be signed and executed by the President on the first day of the new President's term, or, if there's not a new President, they should be signed and executed by the current President as soon as possible. We also want all presidential candidates to sign a commitment stating that they will execute these executive orders on their first day in office, as a prerequisite for their candidacy. We will hold them accountable to these commitments. And we will gauge candidacies based on a candidate's commitment to this plan, along with gauging their candidacy according to any other factors that we deem important. The best candidates, as a baseline, will agree to every one of the executive orders contained in this plan, or to similar executive orders that achieve the same goals.

We know that the plan in this book is not perfect, so a candidate who commits to a modified version of this plan will have their plan carefully evaluated for its faithfulness to the sole intent of this plan. The sole intent of this plan is to immediately restore the federal government to the legal, constitutional governance that was originally intended by our founding fathers and the people who ratified each amendment.

The Liberation Day Plan immediately terminates or extremely downsizes over 250 federal departments, agencies, administrations, and other entities. It immediately lays off thousands or even millions of federal employees. People might think, "How can anyone do that!?" or "This is not right!" But those people would be wrong, insofar as the executive orders that the president signs and carries out are constitutional.

Even though this plan seems unrealistic, it is the only detailed plan that I know of that comes close to restoring our Constitution. It may be radical, and for that reason, you may think it is impossible, but I would argue the opposite. The only reason that this plan is possible is that it is so radical. So many plans only go halfway and don't really solve our problems. This plan can solve many of our federal government's problems. One of the biggest problems it will solve is the government's budget deficit and debt.

As of February 2017, our federal government has $19.97 trillion of debt. In 2016, our GDP was $18.56 trillion.[33] Either we will default on the debt, we will pay for it through hyperinflation, or we will pay for it through much, much higher taxes. Or, we can implement the Liberation Day Plan, or something similar, and drastically cut our spending down to constitutional levels and gradually get rid of our debt without any of those negative consequences. All that this plan puts forth is a level of spending that is legal because it is constitutional, which is in contrast to the unconstitutional, illegal federal spending happening right now. The majority of the spending by the federal government is illegal.

I will now give some background and context for the debt projection from the second chapter of the book. Recall that our federal government will have 64 trillion dollars of debt by the year 2032 at the recent rates of debt growth. I will also explain in more detail how I arrived at that projection. And I will try to explain some of the numbers in a way that helps us wrap our heads around them.

Please don't be fooled by people trying to explain away this debt. I believe that most of us are in total denial about the dire consequences that our debt will soon have if left unchecked. People try to simplify the problem and say things like, "This debt is ok: imagine if a household made $100,000 a year, and they owed $110,000 on the house in the form of a mortgage: they could handle that no problem; therefore, the federal government can handle the debt it has incurred without a problem." This is not even remotely true, and I'll explain why.

Not only is this debt a burden on many homeowners in the United States, but any tax burden for homeowners is on top of any mortgage that they are already paying.

If I make $100,000 a year and have $110,000 in debt, I'm actually generating $100,000 in income every year. The federal government essentially makes $0.00 in income every year, and one could argue that because of things such as inefficient programs, they are losing money.

Even if we are very generous and say that the federal government's income is what they take from us in the form of taxes, even though that is in fact "legalized" stealing and not income at all, it presently brings in $3,328,276,580,000 over a year's time.[34]

The $3,328,276,580,000 that the federal government brings in per year is about 18% of the size of our economy in 2016. Therefore, the federal "income" is about 18% of the size of our economy, and that "income" is about 16.7% of our current debt of $19.97 trillion. In other words, our debt is almost 6 times our "income"!

Let's put that into everyday terms. In 2011, the median household income was $50,054.[35] The median household debt in 2011 was $70,000.[36] The average household made $50,054 of income in a year but owed a total of $70,000 to all creditors. This includes people with no debt and people with tons of debt, but I think this average is a pretty good estimate of the typical American.

If the United States were a person, and we assumed that instead of bringing in $3,328,276,580,000 a year they brought in what the average American household brought in, or $50,054, the United States' debt would be $300,324 if it were proportionally equivalent. If the federal government stopped right now and did not incur even one more penny of debt, we might, just might, be able to pay this off. Imagine if you made $50,000 a year and were $300,000 in debt. Would you be able to handle it?

The Liberation Day Plan stops the accumulation of debt right away. The Plan is our best shot at handling the mess we've gotten into, and all it does is have our federal government follow what they (through the Judges, Officers, Legislators, and Presidents) are morally obligated to follow: The Constitution.

I wish the $300,000 of debt for $50,000 of "income" were our only problem, but it's not; the greater problem is where we're headed. We need a constitutional government now more than ever because we're headed toward much greater debt, not to mention the huge unfunded liabilities that we have from Social Security and Medicare.[37]

Our economy will probably grow around 2.5% a year going forward, give or take.[38] However, over the 15-year period from 2000 to 2015, our federal debt has grown from $5,674,178,209,886.86 to $18,150,617,666,484.33.[39] That's a compound annual growth rate (CAGR) of 8.06%. That's the direction we are headed in, and it must be changed.

Almost nobody, but especially nobody in Washington, wants to talk about what this really means. If we continue on our recent growth path of 8.06% per year for our debt, **we will have $64,000,000,000,000 in debt in just 15 years.**

If we assume similar economic growth and a similar level of taxation going forward, we can estimate that the government's revenue will increase by about 2.5% a year. In 15 years, that would put federal revenue around $4,820,000,000,000 a year.

Let's put that debt and revenue into perspective: if the federal government were a household (a loose analogy), it would, in 2032, be making 44.8% more than it was making in 2017, or $72,478.19 a year. Its debt would be 220.5% more, or $962,538.42.

It would be like someone making $72,478.19 a year and having to pay off $962,538.42 in debt. If we do not change course, this is where we are heading! It is absolutely unsustainable. Even someone who knows almost nothing about money can recognize that this is a serious problem.

I need to release this book quickly because this is it. This is perhaps our last chance to save our nation. We have gone from being a Constitutional Republic to an unwieldy empire.

We will not last fifteen years at this rate of debt growth. If we don't change course, we could have inflation like the Weimar Republic in post-World War I Germany. I wish I were wrong, but get ready. Now is our last hope.

I don't know if we have one year or can eek out ten years before this ship can no longer be saved, but this ship must be righted, or we will have to default on our debt, or virtually default on it through hyperinflation.

If we default or go into hyperinflation, we won't be able to borrow any more, especially not at reasonable rates, because no one will want to lend to us. We will be like Greece; only there will be no one to bail us out. At that point, our economy will go into a downward spiral.

Would we come out of the spiral? Yes, I think we would, but at the very least our government programs would need to be slashed by about 20% or more. And the global economic panic that would occur would probably throw the United States and the entire world into another great depression, and stock and bond markets would also probably be ravaged. If we default or go into hyper-inflation, it would be a horrible outcome for anyone who holds bonds, because those bonds would plummet in value or be worthless. Anyone holding cash would be decimated by hyperinflation, because cash would lose so much of its value.

If we default or have hyperinflation, it could trigger a global economic depression the likes of which the world has never seen. The Chinese government could have trillions of dollars in worthless or almost worthless bonds (they have $1.3 trillion worth of our bonds as of 2016[40]). Even more troublesome for us is that many seniors would be hit extremely hard because they tend to invest heavily in U.S. Treasury bonds because they are deemed "safe." Their retirement portfolios could be wiped out.

Every person on earth who held United States bonds would lose some or all of that money, and anyone who had their savings in cash would lose virtually any of their cash value if we end up in hyperinflation, rather than an actual default on our debt.

I can't stress this enough: **We're on track to hit $64 trillion of federal debt by 2032**. Empires fall. Now is our chance to pull ourselves out from under this failed empire and go back to the constitutional republic that the founders intended.

This book is for my children, grandchildren, and great-grandchildren, if I'm ever blessed to have any, and it's for all of the people in our nation for however long we continue to exist. Let's take a stand, let's make it bold, and let's keep our republic! The Constitution will be our guide, along with, I pray, wisdom from God.

Was This Hard to do?

When I started thinking about taking the whole federal government down to a constitutional size, the task seemed daunting and overwhelming. However, when things were broken down into individual agencies and the various components of each department, things became more manageable. The constitutionality of each individual component tends to be pretty simple and clear. I've used this strategy, taking things a piece at a time, in order to start to grasp the entirety of the federal government and then to chop it down to its constitutional size.

You might think our nation's health system would come screeching to a halt if we simply got rid of the Department of Health and Human Services, for example. But it's only when you break things down into the individual components of a department that you see that everything will be fine. Healthcare won't fall apart because some of the components of the department are absurd. Within that department, there is the Child Support Enforcement Office. They make sure that states are enforcing the payment of child support.[41] Why on earth can't states do that themselves? Of course they can. Can you imagine an entire office in the federal government, with ten or maybe a thousand people just sitting there on their telephones? Maybe they're just calling up the Human Services departments of each of the states all day long. They ask, "Are you enforcing child support payments?" They hear, "Yes," hang up, and put a little check on their list. Then they do it again. That's all they do all day.

Child support is a states' rights issue and has nothing to do with the federal government. When I say something is a "states' rights issue," what I mean is that the Constitution forbids the federal government from getting involved in the issue, and therefore, only the states or their people can take any action regarding it.

The federal government has no Murder Punishment Enforcement Office. How could the federal government possibly think that it makes sense to have a child support office like this before it had a similar office for murder? It is absolutely and utterly absurd, and it is perhaps a product of our lack of understanding of the Constitution.

I'll say it again: there is no agency in the federal government tasked solely with making sure that the states enforce murder laws. And there shouldn't be. It would be unconstitutional.

You'll see in the following pages that the Liberation Day Plan gets rid of over 250 "Child Support Enforcement Offices." When a federal agency is unconstitutional, there are typically these truths associated with the agency:

1) It is an agency that does little other than duplicate the work of the state governments and the work of the people,

2) the agency does so in areas where the states and the people have full authority to take care of any issues themselves,

3)   the states and the people would happily use the authority the agency has taken if needed,

4)   and the federal government has no constitutional authority to be taking part in any actions of the agency.

Breaking down the federal government into small, bite-size pieces lets us see how much of it serves no productive purpose whatsoever. Now we just need to bite these pieces out of what has become the carcass of federal government. If we do that, we hopefully can breathe some life back into the carcass.

I don't suspect that anyone in their right mind would want to go through 440 federal entities to figure out whether they're constitutional or not. I did not want to, but I felt it was my duty to the people of this once great nation and to the family which I love so much. I hope that what I've done here can change our federal government so that no one has to do this ever again. If our government ever goes off course again, hopefully, it's only two or three entities that are unconstitutional, not over 250 of them. At least then, a shorter book could be written to get us back to where we need to be.

What Does Our Government Look Like?

For your reference, here is a short list, largely from 2009, of the major federal executive departments of the United States.[42]

Department	Creation Year	2009 Outlays in Billions	Number of Employees
State	1789	$16.39	18,900
Treasury	1789	$19.56	115,897
Justice	1870	$46.20	113,543
Interior	1849	$90.00	71,436
Agriculture	1889	$134.12	109,832
Commerce	1903	$15.77	43,880
Labor	1913	$137.97	17,347
Defense	1947	$651.16	3,000,000
Health and Human Services	1953	$879.20	67,000
Housing and Urban Development	1965	$40.53	10,600
Transportation	1966	$73.20	58,622
Energy	1977	$24.10	109,094
Education	1979	$45.40	4,487
Veterans Affairs	1989	$97.70	235,000
Homeland Security	2003	$40.00	240,000
Total outlays, employees:		**$2,311.30**	**4,215,638**

This is not all of the federal government, but it is a large chunk of it. Can you see how much things have grown in the 20th and 21st centuries? It's almost as if the 20th century came, and all of a sudden, we totally forgot the meaning of the Constitution.

Out of the 15 Departments listed here, only 5 were created in the 18th and the 19th centuries, and 10 have been created in the 20th and 21st centuries. When we look at the ten newest departments, not one of them was created due to a constitutional amendment, which is a testament to how unconstitutional they are. Do you think that all of a sudden, Congress just realized that they had these powers? That is not the case. For the most part, Congress wasn't exercising these powers because they were unconstitutional, illegal powers.

Of the ten newest departments, only four are totally or partly constitutional. Those 4 are the Departments of Defense, Commerce, Veterans Affairs, and Homeland Security. The Departments of Veterans Affairs and Homeland Security can be absorbed into the Department of Defense because their functions are related to the defense of our nation.

Of the five oldest departments, the Departments of the Interior and Agriculture are almost entirely unconstitutional, and any constitutional functions that they carry out can be absorbed by another department or don't require a department.

This would leave us with only five departments. Getting rid of unconstitutional departments will vastly cut our government's expenses. The department with the highest expenditures is the Department of Health and Human Services. Some of the duties of this department go all the way back to 1798, with the creation of the Marine Hospital Service, which helped certain federal beneficiaries.[43]

However, since almost all of what this department does is unconstitutional, let's imagine for a moment that we could get rid of it entirely (which we essentially can). We would be saving $879.2 billion a year. Just getting rid of that one unconstitutional department would bring our spending down to about $3.044 trillion this year, leaving us with a $288 billion surplus to finally start paying off our debt.[44]

You might be concerned that this plan gets rid of Medicare, Medicaid, and Obamacare. It does get rid of federal spending for those programs because that spending is unconstitutional. However, just because those programs will no longer exist at the federal level, it does not follow that those services won't be provided. Those programs focus on medical care for seniors, the poor, and the uninsured, respectively. Private hospitals, churches, and individuals have a long history of caring for the elderly, the poor, and those without insurance, well before the federal government intervened in those areas.

When this federal spending is abolished, if there is any slack that the private sector doesn't take care of, it is the right of state governments to pick up that slack. With people's medical care in the hands of those who are closer to them, in the hands of the people and the states, rather than in the hands of bureaucrats in Washington, D.C., and the special interests controlling them, then on the whole, health care will be cheaper, of higher quality, and more caring of those who can't provide health care for themselves.

When we look at the top spending federal departments, three of the top four with the highest expenses are entirely or almost entirely unconstitutional. These three are the Department of Health and Humans Services that was already mentioned, and the departments of Labor and

Agriculture. Getting rid of just these three unconstitutional departments would save us a lot of money. Spending has grown since 2009, so it should follow that departmental spending has also grown for these three departments. Based on that, we would save over $1.151 trillion per year and free up 194,179 people to do constitutional, legal, and probably much more productive, work.

I hope this gives you a little view of the scope of the problem we are facing. But the problem can be solved by returning many of these categories of federal government intervention directly back to the people and the states, as the Tenth Amendment of the Constitution demands.

Without abiding by the Constitution, we are ignoring the Supreme Law of the Land, and we are therefore living in a lawless society. I would rather live in a society with no government or law at all than live in a society that is lawless with illegal laws. Many of these illegal laws are created by the military-industrial complex, the drug-health-medicine complex, other special interest powers, as well as by elitist millionaires and billionaires through their lobbyists.

How the Executive Order Section Works

I go through each entity (that I have found) of the federal government and state whether it is constitutional or not. I may also give a little background on the department, agency, or other entity.

If the entity is not constitutional, or if it is partially unconstitutional, I have written the executive order which a president should sign on his first day in office, or if already in office, as soon as possible, in order to bring that entity back to the Constitution.

Each executive order is intended to perfectly interpret the Constitution according to the original intent of those who wrote it, but I am not perfect, and so these may be modified for mistakes or misunderstandings.

I hope through this book a few things are achieved. My first hope is that presidential candidates will sign off in agreement that they will execute these or similar orders on day one of their presidency, and then carry them out when they're elected. In conjunction with that, I hope the current President signs these executive orders as soon as it is practical to do so. My second hope is that all legislators now and going forward would agree to uphold the Constitution according to the ideals embodied in these executive orders. My third hope is that all Supreme Court Justices and all other federal judges start interpreting the Constitution according to this plan's ideals. My fourth hope is that every employee and contractor serving the federal government in some capacity would ask themselves if what they are doing is constitutional according to the ideals of this plan, and, if not, I hope that they immediately start refusing to work for the Federal Government in that capacity. If public servants and citizens refuse to enable the federal government to be unconstitutional, we can force the government's hand so that it follows the Constitution. Finally, my hope is that all of the citizens of the United States understand the original intent of the Constitution and that, through that understanding, we have voters and political candidates who are committed to following the Constitution.

Legislative candidates should sign specific statements similar to these orders before their election to help us know more clearly what they mean when they say that they are committed to following the Constitution. Prospective judges should do the same.

To be clear, one or more of these executive orders would not need to be agreed to if the Constitution is amended to make any of these federal entities constitutional.

The Constitutionality of Every Federal Entity

In talking about federal agencies, departments, etc., I will sometimes use the term "entity," because, as you will see, there are so many names of governmental bodies that there's no common term such as agency or department that I can use to describe them.

I hope this to be a list of every entity in the federal government (including quasi-governmental entities). It also includes those entities' constitutionality, occasional explanations of the entities, and executive orders to change or abolish the entities, if necessary. Many of the executive orders are quite similar to each other. There will also be occasional comments and history.

In compiling this list of federal entities, I've found that no one seems to agree on how many agencies there are in the federal government, let alone what they are. I am focusing on Executive Branch agencies according to a Federal Register list. The total for that list is 440 agencies as of 2017.[45]

Wikipedia also has an extremely long list of federal agencies[46] and a list of some quasi-governmental agencies.[47]

Most of these entities are a disgrace to the rights of the people, the rights of the states, the original intent of the Constitution, and the obvious meaning of the Tenth Amendment to the Constitution.

Unfortunately, more items can probably be added to the list, but I think we can get close enough to the entire government with this list as a good start. The goal of this book is to bring us to constitutional government in one day, but please remember that this is a starting point – a baseline litmus test to measure any president against – so it will not be perfect.

We will start with cabinet-level entities and then move to other entities. We will determine if they are constitutional, and if partly or totally not constitutional, an executive order will be presented to deal with the problem. If the entity is totally unconstitutional, the executive order has the President eliminate the entity with the Constitution as the basis for this elimination. If the entity is only partially unconstitutional, the executive order has the President eliminate the unconstitutional portion of the agency with the Constitution as the basis for this elimination.

The cabinet-level listing will be based on the order given in the Cabinet Wikipedia article.[48] I sometimes write a quick overview of an entity, and when I do this, I typically get the information from the description you can get when you click through the agency's link on the Federal Register site.[49]

State Department

This is constitutional. It is focused on foreign affairs and policy. It was created in 1789, the year that George Washington became our first president. I can only imagine that the founders would never have thought that this department would be as big as it is today. The fact that it started the same year as our federal government is a testament to its constitutionality.

Even though fat could be trimmed from this department, it is largely not a constitutional question. You can see in the Constitution from where the Department of State gets its power. Here is some of the constitutional text providing for the State Department, from the Second Article on the powers of the executive: "He shall have Power, by and with the Advice and Consent of the Senate, to make Treaties, provided two thirds of the Senators present concur; and he shall nominate, and by and with the Advice and Consent of the Senate, shall appoint Ambassadors, other public Ministers and Consuls." Notice that these issues are in the hands of the Executive, and have nothing to do with the House of

Representatives, and only get input and confirmation from the Senate.

This department had no Components listed in the Federal Register Index.

Treasury Department

The Treasury itself is constitutional. It is listed in a few places, first in Article I, Section Six: "The Senators and Representatives shall receive a Compensation for their Services, to be ascertained by Law, and paid out of the Treasury of the United States." Later we read, "No Money shall be drawn from the Treasury, but in Consequence of Appropriations made by Law; and a regular Statement and Account of the Receipts and Expenditures of all public Money shall be published from time to time." The Treasury is the accountable place that stores the money of the government of the United States. Much of modern day Treasury has components that have been added to it which are not constitutional. Here it is:

Components of the Treasury Department:

- Alcohol and Tobacco Tax and Trade Bureau - This collects constitutional excise taxes but also administers commercial regulations, and that unconstitutional part must be stopped.
- Bureau of the Fiscal Service - Accounting of what the government takes in and spends is constitutional.

- Community Development Financial Institutions Fund - This is totally unconstitutional. It tries to help "distressed communities," a function that needs to be left up to the people and the states[50]

- Comptroller of the Currency - This agency regulates banks within the U.S. This is utterly unconstitutional and needs to be left up to the states and the people.

- Financial Crimes Enforcement Network - This is an anti-money laundering, anti-terror-funding agency. This is not constitutional and must be left up to the states and the people.

- Fiscal Service - I think this is the same as the Bureau of the Fiscal Service, but if not, this agency should be gone due to the founders not intending to have two separate functions of accountability. I listed it here because I found both it and the Bureau of the Fiscal Service on the Federal Register Index.

- Foreign Assets Control Office - This enforces sanctions and is constitutional in that it may be carrying out treaties, but it should not do anything regarding treaties without two-thirds approval from the Senate.

- Internal Revenue Service - Collecting taxes is constitutional.

- United States Mint - As this makes coins, it is constitutional. The founders only intended for the mint to make coins primarily out of gold or silver.[51] All coins must be greater than or equal to 90% gold, silver, or copper, because that is what the founders saw as money.[52] This needs to immediately be enforced. All other coins must stop being produced.

- The Mint is not responsible for paper money, but in case you were wondering, paper money is unconstitutional. We get a clue that the founders thought of money as precious metals, and only precious metals, in the Constitution: "No State shall [...] coin Money; [or] make any Thing but gold and silver Coin a Tender in Payment of Debts;" So the states aren't allowed to make any federal coins or paper money a "Tender in Payment of Debts" unless they are gold or silver coins, so it must have been gold and silver coins that the founders wanted the federal government to be minting, and not printing paper.

- Customs Service - Dissolved in 2003.

- Engraving and Printing Bureau - Partly const-itutional. Printing military ID cards is fine, but all paper "money" printing, which is this Bureau's main function, must immediately cease because only metal coins are constitutional.

- Financial Research Office - Unconstitutional. Enacted because of the 2010 Dodd-Frank law, it provides financial information and research.

- International Investment Office - Unconstitutional. Now called the Office of Investment Security. They keep foreign people or entities from investing too much in certain U.S. businesses so that foreigners can't control those businesses.

- Monetary Offices - constitutional. They make rules such as not being allowed to melt down coins. That's allowed, but most of the money in circulation is unconstitutional.

- Public Debt Bureau - Constitutional. They issue debt. I doubt we would need this very often if our government was constitutionally limited.

- Thrift Supervision Office - Unconstitutional. It "regulates Federal and State-chartered savings institutions." Federally-chartered savings institutions are unconstitutional, let alone the regulation of them.

The Executive Order related to the Treasury Department:

(Much of the text in the 23 executive orders is repetitive: please feel free to skip through the repetition.)

Executive Order Immediately Dissolving Portions of the United States Department of the Treasury

EXECUTIVE ORDER

- - - - - - -

IMMEDIATELY DISSOLVING PORTIONS OF THE UNITED STATES DEPARTMENT OF THE TREASURY

By the authority vested in me as President by the Constitution and the laws of the United States of America, it is hereby affirmed, declared, and ordered as follows:

Section 1. Policy. It is the policy of the United States to have no involvement within the Department of the Treasury in matters not directly associated with the carrying out a power given to it by the Constitution of the United States.

Sec. 2. Constitutionality and in some instances Ending the Functions of Particular Entities. Portions of the United States Department of the Treasury are unconstitutional. The following entities perform unconstitutional functions: Community Development Financial Institutions Fund, Comptroller of the Currency, Financial Crimes Enforcement Network, Financial Research Office, International Investment Office, and Thrift Supervision Office. No powers regarding the functions of these entities are ever given to the Federal Government or its Legislature in the Constitution. The following entities perform some unconstitutional functions: Alcohol and Tobacco Tax and Trade Bureau - it administers commercial regulations, this is unconstitutional and must immediately cease; Engraving and Printing Bureau - All paper money printing is unconstitutional and must immediately cease; United States Mint - All coins minted going forward must be greater than or equal to 90% gold, silver, or copper, all other coins must stop being produced.

Sec. 3. Presidential Duty and Immediacy. According to the President's duty to uphold the Constitution of the

United States of America, as the President has sworn or affirmed to uphold such Constitution, all sections of this executive order will be immediately understood and carried out by all branches of the United States Federal Government as it pertains to them, without regard to any court order that goes against the Constitution.

Sec. 4. Unenforceable Laws. Any laws, regulations, acts, or other legislation of the Federal Government that unconstitutionally provides for or regulates anything related to the areas served by the previously mentioned entities, and (if applicable) the functions of entities where particular functions have been ceased, will henceforward cease to be executed and will continue to cease to be executed unless and until the Constitution of the United States is amended to give Congress or the Federal Government the power to make laws regarding the areas served by the previously mentioned entities.

Sec. 5. Ending portions of the Department. The following entities within the United States Department of the Treasury will immediately cease to function, and any obligations owed by these entities to servants or from these entities to other entities will be taken over by the Federal Government in accordance with its historical commitment to pay debts, as Congress may prescribe: Community Development Financial Institutions Fund, Comptroller of the Currency, Financial Crimes Enforcement Network, Financial Research Office,

International Investment Office, and Thrift Supervision Office.

Everyone working at the previously mentioned entities must permanently leave their respective entity offices or places of work immediately. Any State Government or other entity may reemploy any Federal worker who has lost a job in this way, to work in a similar or a different capacity.

All property of the previously mentioned entities will now be the property of the governments of the respective State, the District of Columbia, or the United States Territory where the property is situated. If the property is not contained in one of these locations, it will immediately come into the control of the first State government which has a representative at the property physically to claim the property. If two or more States lay claim to property at the same time, they may agree among themselves as to who will own the property, or they will share it among themselves. Any State, the District of Columbia, or any United States Territory that acquires property from the Federal Government in the above two ways may freely pay the Treasury of the United States for such property, if and in the amount that they desire to do so.

Sec. 6. Reaffirmation of the Tenth Amendment of the Constitution. It is reaffirmed that, according to the Tenth Amendment of the Constitution of the United States, and implied by the Constitution before it was ever amended,

all powers of the previously mentioned entities are reserved to the States respectively, or to the People, and, therefore, none of the powers that these previously mentioned entities had will henceforward be exercised by the Federal Government, without there first being a ratified amendment to the Constitution that gives power over some area where these entities served to the Federal Government.

Sec. 7. Responsibilities of the People and their State Governments. Regarding the topic(s) of this Executive Order, the People and their respective State Governments, or the People alone, are urged to take care of anything previously attended to by the Federal Government. If any State desires to take action regarding a topic of this Executive Order, the Congress of the United States is urged to approve such State action so that the state may accomplish these or related things which were previously attended to by the Federal Government, if Congressional approval is Constitutionally required for the State to take such action.

Sec. 8. Pardons and Contracts. (a) A Full and Unconditional Pardon is hereby given to anyone who has been charged or convicted of any Federal crime or offense related to any of the unconstitutional laws that were deemed unenforceable according to this Executive Order.

(b) Regardless of any contracts or agreements that were signed or sworn to towards unconstitutional ends, anyone

who exposes the Federal Government for doing anything unconstitutional, including the items outlined in this Executive Order, will be given a Full and Unconditional Pardon for exposing such unconstitutional Federal actions. Also, regardless of any contracts or agreements that were signed or sworn to towards unconstitutional ends, anyone who has exposed the Federal Government for doing anything unconstitutional, including the items outlined in this Executive Order, is hereby given a Full and Unconditional Pardon for exposing such unconstitutional Federal actions.

Sec. 9. General Provisions. (a) This order is not intended to, and does not, create any right or benefit, substantive or procedural, enforceable at law or in equity by any party against the United States, its departments, agencies, or entities, its officers, employees, or agents, or any other person.

(b) This order is not intended to, and does not, go against the Constitution of the United States. Everything in this order has the intent of restoring the supreme law of the land, which is the Constitution of the United States of America; if any part of this order is deemed as going against the Constitution, any remedy must be at the discretion of each individual charged with that remedy, including judges, officials, secretaries, and people at any and every level of government. Those individuals are each urged to ask if the remedy is Constitutional according to the original intent and spirit of the Constitution when

written by our founding fathers in the seventeen hundreds. If any part of this order is ultimately deemed unconstitutional by any individual or institution, all other parts of this order will remain in full force and effect in perpetuity, or until the Constitution is amended or superseded.

[THE NAME AND SIGNATURE OF THE PRESIDENT OF THE UNITED STATES]

THE WHITE HOUSE,

[Date].

Defense Department

This started as the War Department in 1789, the first year of Washington's Presidency. In its duties running the Army and Navy, it is Constitutional as long as it's carrying out Congressionally declared wars. However, any undeclared wars are unconstitutional and would need to cease immediately.

A president should declare an immediate end to our active military presence in other nations, including an end to drone strikes. The order should bring all troops and offensive equipment back to the United States from foreign military bases.

The president would also be constitutionally required to end the Air Force and remove any forces from space immediately. As mentioned before, I would suggest to

Congress and the states to amend the Constitution so that we can have these modern military divisions, and to do so before a president who has agreed to remove the Air Force comes into power. I believe this amendment would pass, so any air or space forces would remain intact.

Components of the Defense Department:
- Army Department - Constitutional.
- Defense Acquisition Regulations System – Constitutional.
- Engineers Corps - This is largely unconstitutional as it largely deals with generating hydropower and building dams. The only thing that should remain is the construction of needed military structures.
- Navy Department - Constitutional.
- Air Force Department - Currently unconstitutional.
- Defense Contract Audit Agency - Constitutional.
- Defense Criminal Investigative Service - Constitutional.
- Defense Information Systems Agency – Constitutional. It's IT for the Military.
- Defense Intelligence Agency - Constitutional.
- Defense Investigative Service - Constitutional.
- Defense Logistics Agency - Constitutional.
- Defense Mapping Agency - Already ended and functions taken over by National Geospatial-Intelligence Agency.
- Defense Special Weapons Agency - Constitutional.

- National Geospatial-Intelligence Agency – Constitutional.
- National Security Agency/Central Security Service - Started in 1952, the NSA is largely unconstitutional. Military intelligence is fine, but all unwarranted "monitoring" of U.S. citizens (and they do a ton of it) is unconstitutional. The Fourth Amendment applies here, "The right of the people to be secure in their persons, houses, papers, and effects, against unreasonable searches and seizures, shall not be violated, and no Warrants shall issue, but upon probable cause, supported by Oath or affirmation, and particularly describing the place to be searched, and the persons or things to be seized." Every monitoring, however slight, must first have a specific warrant issued through oath or affirmation. The problem is, the warrants would have to show probable cause of Federal criminal activity, and almost all crimes of U.S. citizens within the country would fall under state law, not Federal law. The part of the NSA that can Constitutionally stay in place is its creation of cryptographic systems to help ensure that our enemies can't read our military's communications.
- Uniformed Services University of the Health Sciences - Unconstitutional. Created in 1972, educating people in medicine is not a Constitutional role of government.

The Executive Order related to the Defense Department:

Executive Order Immediately Dissolving Portions of the United States Department of Defense (to be modified to allow for Air and Space forces if an Air and Space Forces amendment is ratified, and I recommend that an amendment such as this is passed and ratified)

EXECUTIVE ORDER

- - - - - - -

IMMEDIATELY DISSOLVING PORTIONS OF THE UNITED STATES DEPARTMENT OF DEFENSE

By the authority vested in me as President by the Constitution and the laws of the United States of America, it is hereby affirmed, declared, and ordered as follows:

Section 1. Policy. It is the policy of the United States to have no involvement within the Department of Defense in matters not directly associated with the carrying out a power given to it by the Constitution of the United States.

Sec. 2. Constitutionality and in some instances Ending the Functions of Particular Entities. Portions of the United States Department of Defense are unconstitutional. The following entities perform unconstitutional functions: Air Force Department and Uniformed Services University of the Health Sciences. No powers regarding the functions of these entities are ever given to the Federal Government or its Legislature in the Constitution. The Engineers Corps - This is partially unconstitutional as it largely deals with generating hydropower and building dams, the only function that should remain is the construction of needed military structures, all other functions of the Corps must immediately cease; National Security Agency/Central Security Service - Military intelligence is Constitutional, but all unwarranted "monitoring" of U.S. citizens is unconstitutional, all surveillance on United States soil, and its territories, must cease immediately.

Sec. 3. Presidential Duty and Immediacy. According to the President's duty to uphold the Constitution of the United States of America, as the President has sworn or affirmed to uphold such Constitution, all sections of this executive order will be immediately understood and carried out by all branches of the United States Federal Government as it pertains to them, without regard to any court order that goes against the Constitution.

Sec. 4. Unenforceable Laws. Any laws, regulations, acts, or other legislation of the Federal Government that unconstitutionally provides for or regulates anything related to the areas served by the previously mentioned entities, and (if applicable) the functions of entities where particular functions have been ceased, will henceforward cease to be executed and will continue to cease to be executed unless and until the Constitution of the United

States is amended to give Congress or the Federal Government the power to make laws regarding the areas served by the previously mentioned entities.

Sec. 5. Ending portions of the Department. The following entities within the United States Department of Defense will immediately cease to function, and any obligations owed by these entities to servants or from these entities to other entities will be taken over by the Federal Government in accordance with its historical commitment to pay debts, as Congress may prescribe: Air Force Department and Uniformed Services University of the Health Sciences.

Everyone working at the previously mentioned entities must permanently leave their respective entity offices or places of work immediately. Any State Government or other entity may reemploy any Federal worker who has lost a job in this way, to work in a similar or a different capacity.

All property of the previously mentioned entities will now be the property of the governments of the respective State, the District of Columbia, or the United States Territory where the property is situated. If the property is not contained in one of these locations, it will immediately come into the control of the first State government which has a representative at the property physically to claim the property. If two or more States lay claim to property at the same time, they may agree among themselves as to who will own the property, or they will share it among themselves. Any State, the District of Columbia, or any United States Territory that acquires property from the Federal Government in the above two ways may freely pay the Treasury of the United States for such property, if and in the amount that they desire to do so.

Sec. 6. Reaffirmation of the Tenth Amendment of the Constitution. It is reaffirmed that, according to the Tenth Amendment of the Constitution of the United States, and implied by the Constitution before it was ever amended, all powers of the previously mentioned entities are reserved to the States respectively, or to the People, and, therefore, none of the powers that these previously mentioned entities had will henceforward be exercised by the Federal Government, without there first being a ratified amendment to the Constitution that gives power over some area where these entities served to the Federal Government.

Sec. 7. Responsibilities of the People and their State Governments. Regarding the topic(s) of this Executive Order, the People and their respective State Governments, or the People alone, are urged to take care of anything previously attended to by the Federal Government. If any State desires to take action regarding a topic of this Executive Order, the Congress of the United States is urged to approve such State action so that the state may accomplish these or related things which were previously attended to by the Federal Government, if Congressional approval is Constitutionally required for the State to take such action.

Sec. 8. Pardons and Contracts. (a) A Full and Unconditional Pardon is hereby given to anyone who has been charged or convicted of any Federal crime or offense related to any of the unconstitutional laws that were deemed unenforceable according to this Executive Order.

(b) Regardless of any contracts or agreements that were signed or sworn to towards unconstitutional ends, anyone who exposes the Federal Government for doing anything unconstitutional, including the items outlined in this Executive Order, will be given a Full and Unconditional Pardon for exposing such unconstitutional Federal actions. Also, regardless of any contracts or agreements that were signed or sworn to towards unconstitutional ends, anyone who has exposed the Federal Government for doing anything unconstitutional, including the items outlined in this Executive Order, is hereby given a Full and Unconditional Pardon for exposing such unconstitutional Federal actions.

Sec. 9. General Provisions. (a) This order is not intended to, and does not, create any right or benefit, substantive or procedural, enforceable at law or in equity by any party against the United States, its departments, agencies, or entities, its officers, employees, or agents, or any other person.

(b) This order is not intended to, and does not, go against the Constitution of the United States. Everything in this order has the intent of restoring the supreme law of the land, which is the Constitution of the United States of America; if any part of this order is deemed as going against the Constitution, any remedy must be at the discretion of each individual charged with that remedy, including judges, officials, secretaries, and people at any and every level of government. Those individuals are each urged to ask if the remedy is Constitutional according to the original intent and spirit of the Constitution when written by our founding fathers in the seventeen hundreds. If any part of this order is ultimately deemed unconstitutional by any individual or institution, all other parts of this order will remain in full force and effect in perpetuity, or until the Constitution is amended or superseded.

[THE NAME AND SIGNATURE OF THE PRESIDENT OF THE UNITED STATES]

THE WHITE HOUSE,

[Date].

Justice Department

This department is constitutional because it embodies the judicial power established by the Constitution. However, many of its subagencies are unconstitutional because they are concerned with carrying out unconstitutional laws. This department started off as a part-time job for one person in 1789. As of 2012, it employs 113,543 people.[53] Because of the illegal and unconstitutional nature of most of this department, I estimate that we could downsize it to just a few hundred people.

Components of the Justice Department:

- Alcohol, Tobacco, Firearms, and Explosives Bureau - The only time any of this could have been constitutional would have been the alcohol portion when the Constitution was amended to ban alcohol throughout the United States, but that amendment was repealed by the 21st Amendment in 1933, so all of this agency should be immediately dissolved. Fun fact: Walgreens grew substantially during prohibition because they legally fulfilled alcohol prescriptions from doctors who were using prescription whiskey to treat "ailments." Walgreens grew from 20 stores in 1919 to 397 stores in 1930.[54] An interesting fact about guns: each year in the U.S., one child under ten dies each year from each million (or more) guns, and one child dies from every 11,000 residential pools. There are more guns than pools in the United States, and yet more children die from the pools.[55] Anyone who thinks that guns should be banned for the safety of children should first be enraged that all swimming pools haven't been filled in, and make that their first priority.

- Antitrust Division - Unconstitutional.
- Drug Enforcement Administration – Unconstitutional.
- Executive Office for Immigration Review – Unconstitutional. Immigration is a State's Rights issue. In our nation's early history, states had immigration laws.[56] It wasn't until 1882 that the first major Federal immigration law was passed, without any constitutional amendment giving that power to the Federal Government.[57] Naturalization is in the hands of the Federal Government because it's listed in the Constitution. Naturalization is rules for and the granting of citizenship into the United States. Immigration is not listed in the Constitution, and so it rests with the states and the people according to the 10th Amendment.
- Foreign Claims Settlement Commission - This department may be Constitutional in that it can carry out Treaties, which are Constitutional. But the Federal funding of claims to U.S. nationals from the U.S. taxpayer is not Constitutional and must be stopped. This should be left up to the people and the states.
- Justice Programs Office - This is for crime prevention. As almost all crime is at the state level and the Federal Government has no jurisdiction over it, this should be dissolved as unconstitutional.
- Parole Commission - This is Constitutional because it can be part of the "punishment" provided for in the Constitution, but there are very few people violating

Constitutional Federal laws who would be in prison and needing parole. Some of the few crimes that the Federal Government can make illegal are: "Treason," "counterfeiting the Securities and current Coin of the United States," "Piracies and Felonies committed on the high Seas, and Offences against the Law of Nations." Federal parole for all unconstitutional offenses would not make any sense, as those people disobeyed an invalid Federal law.

- Federal Bureau of Investigation - Almost totally unconstitutional. The only crimes that the Federal Government has jurisdiction over that might pertain to this are crimes on the high seas, counterfeiting, evading Constitutional Federal taxes, and anything specifically mentioned in the Constitution. Things like murder, computer crime, and drug crimes are all state-level issues, and the states are more than capable of taking care of them. This agency should be reduced to almost nothing compared to what it is now.

- Federal Prison Industries - Trying to train and make money from prisoners. This is Constitutional as part of their punishment, but there will be almost no Federal prisoners since there are very few Constitutional Federal crimes.

- Immigration and Naturalization Service - This agency has been broken up and its duties dispersed throughout government.

- Juvenile Justice and Delinquency Prevention Office - Unconstitutional.

- National Institute of Corrections - Constitutional, but should be almost non-existent since there are so few Constitutional Federal crimes.
- National Institute of Justice - Unconstitutional. Supports criminal justice research.
- Prisons Bureau - Constitutional, but should be almost non-existent since there are so few Constitutional Federal crimes.
- United States Marshals Service - Constitutional, but should be almost non-existent since there are so few Constitutional Federal crimes.

The Executive Order related to the Justice Department:

Executive Order Immediately Dissolving Portions of the United States Department of Justice

EXECUTIVE ORDER

- - - - - - -

IMMEDIATELY DISSOLVING PORTIONS OF THE UNITED STATES DEPARTMENT OF JUSTICE

By the authority vested in me as President by the Constitution and the laws of the United States of America, it is hereby affirmed, declared, and ordered as follows:

Section 1. Policy. It is the policy of the United States to have no involvement within the Department of Justice in matters not directly associated with the carrying out a power given to it by the Constitution of the United States.

Sec. 2. Constitutionality and in some instances Ending the Functions of Particular Entities. Portions of the United States Department of Justice are unconstitutional. The following entities perform unconstitutional functions: Alcohol, Tobacco, Firearms, and Explosives Bureau; Antitrust Division; Drug Enforcement Administration; Executive Office for Immigration Review; Justice Programs Office; Juvenile Justice and Delinquency Prevention Office; and National Institute of Justice. No powers regarding the functions of these entities are ever given to the Federal Government or its Legislature in the Constitution. Foreign Claims Settlement Commission - The Federal funding of claims to U.S. nationals from the U.S. taxpayer is not Constitutional and must be stopped immediately; Federal Bureau of Investigation - The only crimes that the Federal Government has jurisdiction over that might pertain to this Bureau are crimes on the high seas, counterfeiting, evading Constitutional Federal taxes, and anything specifically mentioned in the Constitution, all other functions must cease immediately.

Sec. 3. Presidential Duty and Immediacy. According to the President's duty to uphold the Constitution of the

United States of America, as the President has sworn or affirmed to uphold such Constitution, all sections of this executive order will be immediately understood and carried out by all branches of the United States Federal Government as it pertains to them, without regard to any court order that goes against the Constitution.

Sec. 4. Unenforceable Laws. Any laws, regulations, acts, or other legislation of the Federal Government that unconstitutionally provides for or regulates anything related to the areas served by the previously mentioned entities, and (if applicable) the functions of entities where particular functions have been ceased, will henceforward cease to be executed and will continue to cease to be executed unless and until the Constitution of the United States is amended to give Congress or the Federal Government the power to make laws regarding the areas served by the previously mentioned entities.

Sec. 5. Ending portions of the Department. The following entities within the United States Department of Justice will immediately cease to function, and any obligations owed by these entities to servants or from these entities to other entities will be taken over by the Federal Government in accordance with its historical commitment to pay debts, as Congress may prescribe: Alcohol, Tobacco, Firearms, and Explosives Bureau; Antitrust Division; Drug Enforcement Administration; Executive Office for Immigration Review; Justice

Programs Office; Juvenile Justice and Delinquency Prevention Office; and National Institute of Justice.

Everyone working at the previously mentioned entities must permanently leave their respective entity offices or places of work immediately. Any State Government or other entity may reemploy any Federal worker who has lost a job in this way, to work in a similar or a different capacity.

All property of the previously mentioned entities will now be the property of the governments of the respective State, the District of Columbia, or the United States Territory where the property is situated. If the property is not contained in one of these locations, it will immediately come into the control of the first State government which has a representative at the property physically to claim the property. If two or more States lay claim to property at the same time, they may agree among themselves as to who will own the property, or they will share it among themselves. Any State, the District of Columbia, or any United States Territory that acquires property from the Federal Government in the above two ways may freely pay the Treasury of the United States for such property, if and in the amount that they desire to do so.

Sec. 6. Reaffirmation of the Tenth Amendment of the Constitution. It is reaffirmed that, according to the Tenth Amendment of the Constitution of the United States, and

implied by the Constitution before it was ever amended, all powers of the previously mentioned entities are reserved to the States respectively, or to the People, and, therefore, none of the powers that these previously mentioned entities had will henceforward be exercised by the Federal Government, without there first being a ratified amendment to the Constitution that gives power over some area where these entities served to the Federal Government.

Sec. 7. Responsibilities of the People and their State Governments. Regarding the topic(s) of this Executive Order, the People and their respective State Governments, or the People alone, are urged to take care of anything previously attended to by the Federal Government. If any State desires to take action regarding a topic of this Executive Order, the Congress of the United States is urged to approve such State action so that the state may accomplish these or related things which were previously attended to by the Federal Government, if Congressional approval is Constitutionally required for the State to take such action.

Sec. 8. Pardons and Contracts. (a) A Full and Unconditional Pardon is hereby given to anyone who has been charged or convicted of any Federal crime or offense related to any of the unconstitutional laws that were deemed unenforceable according to this Executive Order.

(b) Regardless of any contracts or agreements that were signed or sworn to towards unconstitutional ends, anyone who exposes the Federal Government for doing anything unconstitutional, including the items outlined in this Executive Order, will be given a Full and Unconditional Pardon for exposing such unconstitutional Federal actions. Also, regardless of any contracts or agreements that were signed or sworn to towards unconstitutional ends, anyone who has exposed the Federal Government for doing anything unconstitutional, including the items outlined in this Executive Order, is hereby given a Full and Unconditional Pardon for exposing such unconstitutional Federal actions.

Sec. 9. General Provisions. (a) This order is not intended to, and does not, create any right or benefit, substantive or procedural, enforceable at law or in equity by any party against the United States, its departments, agencies, or entities, its officers, employees, or agents, or any other person.

(b) This order is not intended to, and does not, go against the Constitution of the United States. Everything in this order has the intent of restoring the supreme law of the land, which is the Constitution of the United States of America; if any part of this order is deemed as going against the Constitution, any remedy must be at the discretion of each individual charged with that remedy, including judges, officials, secretaries, and people at any and every level of government. Those individuals are each

urged to ask if the remedy is Constitutional according to the original intent and spirit of the Constitution when written by our founding fathers in the seventeen hundreds. If any part of this order is ultimately deemed unconstitutional by any individual or institution, all other parts of this order will remain in full force and effect in perpetuity, or until the Constitution is amended or superseded.

[THE NAME AND SIGNATURE OF THE PRESIDENT OF THE UNITED STATES]

THE WHITE HOUSE,

[Date].

Interior Department

This department was started in 1849, and it took over some duties that were Constitutional, but it has since grown to many unconstitutional duties as well. The very name Interior implies issues that are domestic to each state, and so most of these entities should not exist and should be left up to the states and to the people.

Components of the Interior Department:
- Fish and Wildlife Service - Started in 1871 without any Constitutional amendment. Almost every power that the Constitution gives was enacted by the Federal Government quite quickly, typically within one year

of when it was created. How, almost a hundred years later, can we think that this is ok without an amendment? Of course it is not ok, as there's nothing about Fish or Wildlife mentioned in the Constitution.[58] In case you're worried that the states and the people can't handle this, please don't be. Every single state already has something like a wildlife and/or fish agency of its own already.[59]

- Geological Survey - This started in 1879 and is responsible for surveying the land. This is unconstitutional and is to be left up to the states, territories, and the people. You might argue that the Louisiana Purchase couldn't be properly assessed before purchase without first surveying the land, and you would be right. Surveying lands for potential purchase should be a power added to the Constitution before the power to survey is used.[60]

- Indian Affairs Bureau - This started in 1824 and is largely unconstitutional. While Indians are mentioned in the Constitution, all it really says is that they're not to be taxed, they don't count towards vote totals, and commerce with them may be regulated. So, regulating commerce with Indians is Constitutional, but nothing else is.[61]

- Land Management Bureau - This started in 1946 and is Constitutional.[62] Congress can manage the land upon which sits "Forts, Magazines, Arsenals, dock-Yards, and other needful Buildings." But any other land is unconstitutional and must immediately be ceded back to the states. The states can then determine a fair amount to pay the Federal Government for the land. In particular, all Federal parkland within the states must be ceded back to the states.

- National Indian Gaming Commission - Started in 1988 to regulate Native American gaming activities such as casinos, this is clearly unconstitutional.[63]

- National Park Service - Started in 1916 with no new Constitutional amendment, this is totally unconstitutional. It must immediately be ended. All land must be ceded to the states.[64]

- Ocean Energy Management Bureau - Created in 2011, this is for dealing with things like oil in the ocean. There's nothing in the Constitution about this, so we must get rid of it.[65]

- Reclamation Bureau - Started in 1902, this is unconstitutional. It deals with water resources primarily in the western states, which is an issue to be left to the states and the people according to the 10th Amendment.[66]

- Safety and Environmental Enforcement Bureau - Started in 2011 as the successor to the 1982 Minerals Management Service, this agency largely deals with oil spills.[67] It is unconstitutional and must be ended. This sort of issue might be a good place to have Congressional regulation, but the Constitution must be amended first. In the meantime, it seems that nature largely takes care of oil spills on its own through microbes that digest the oil spill.[68]

- Surface Mining Reclamation and Enforcement Office - Started around 1977, to the extent that this agency is collecting an excise tax on coal, it is Constitutional. But all of its mining regulations and any other actions beyond this are unconstitutional and must be stopped immediately.[69]

- Indian Arts and Crafts Board - Unconstitutional.

- Hearings and Appeals Office, Interior Department - Constitutional.

- Indian Trust Transition Office - Not running anymore.

- Minerals Management Service - Now called the Ocean Energy Management Bureau.

- Mines Bureau - Not running anymore, except some functions transferred to the Secretary of Energy.

- National Biological Service - Unconstitutional. It studies the support of plants and animals.

- National Civilian Community Corps – Unconstitutional community service program.

- Natural Resources Revenue Office - Unconstitutional. Most of these resources shouldn't be owned by the Federal Government Constitutionally.

- Ocean Energy Management, Regulation, and Enforcement Bureau - Unconstitutional.

- Special Trustee for American Indians Office – Unconstitutional.

The Executive Order related to the Interior Department:

Executive Order Immediately Dissolving Portions of the United States Department of the Interior

EXECUTIVE ORDER

- - - - - - -

IMMEDIATELY DISSOLVING PORTIONS OF THE UNITED STATES DEPARTMENT OF THE INTERIOR

By the authority vested in me as President by the Constitution and the laws of the United States of America, it is hereby affirmed, declared, and ordered as follows:

Section 1. Policy. It is the policy of the United States to have no involvement within the Department of the Interior in matters not directly associated with the carrying out a power given to it by the Constitution of the United States.

Sec. 2. Constitutionality and in some instances Ending the Functions of Particular Entities. Portions of the United States Department of the Interior are unconstitutional. The following entities perform unconstitutional functions: Fish and Wildlife Service, Geological Survey, National Indian Gaming Commission, National Park Service, Ocean Energy Management Bureau, Reclamation Bureau, Safety and Environmental Enforcement Bureau, Indian Arts and

Crafts Board, National Biological Service, National Civilian Community Corps, Natural Resources Revenue Office, Ocean Energy Management, Regulation, and Enforcement Bureau, and Special Trustee for American Indians Office. No powers regarding the functions of these entities are ever given to the Federal Government or its Legislature in the Constitution. Land Management Bureau - According to the Constitution, it may manage the land upon which sits "Forts, Magazines, Arsenals, dock-Yards, and other needful Buildings", any other land within the fifty United States that is managed by this Bureau is unconstitutionally owned (if owned by the Federal Government) and must immediately be ceded back to the states and their people, and those lands must immediately cease to be managed by this Bureau, the states can then determine a fair amount to pay the Federal Government for the land, if any, all Federal park land within the states must be ceded back to the states and their people; Surface Mining Reclamation and Enforcement Office - This may collect excise tax on coal, but all of its mining regulations and any other actions beyond this are unconstitutional and must be stopped immediately.

Sec. 3. Presidential Duty and Immediacy. According to the President's duty to uphold the Constitution of the United States of America, as the President has sworn or affirmed to uphold such Constitution, all sections of this executive order will be immediately understood and carried out by all branches of the United States Federal

Government as it pertains to them, without regard to any court order that goes against the Constitution.

Sec. 4. Unenforceable Laws. Any laws, regulations, acts, or other legislation of the Federal Government that unconstitutionally provides for or regulates anything related to the areas served by the previously mentioned entities, and (if applicable) the functions of entities where particular functions have been ceased, will henceforward cease to be executed and will continue to cease to be executed unless and until the Constitution of the United States is amended to give Congress or the Federal Government the power to make laws regarding the areas served by the previously mentioned entities.

Sec. 5. Ending portions of the Department. The following entities within the United States Department of the Interior will immediately cease to function, and any obligations owed by these entities to servants or from these entities to other entities will be taken over by the Federal Government in accordance with its historical commitment to pay debts, as Congress may prescribe: Fish and Wildlife Service, Geological Survey, National Indian Gaming Commission, National Park Service, Ocean Energy Management Bureau, Reclamation Bureau, Safety and Environmental Enforcement Bureau, Indian Arts and Crafts Board, National Biological Service, National Civilian Community Corps, Natural Resources Revenue Office, Ocean Energy Management, Regulation, and Enforcement Bureau, and Special Trustee for American Indians Office.

Everyone working at the previously mentioned entities must permanently leave their respective entity offices or places of work immediately. Any State Government or other entity may reemploy any Federal worker who has lost a job in this way, to work in a similar or a different capacity.

All property of the previously mentioned entities will now be the property of the governments of the respective State, the District of Columbia, or the United States Territory where the property is situated. If the property is not contained in one of these locations, it will immediately come into the control of the first State government which has a representative at the property physically to claim the property. If two or more States lay claim to property at the same time, they may agree among themselves as to who will own the property, or they will share it among themselves. Any State, the District of Columbia, or any United States Territory that acquires property from the Federal Government in the above two ways may freely pay the Treasury of the United States for such property, if and in the amount that they desire to do so.

Sec. 6. Reaffirmation of the Tenth Amendment of the Constitution. It is reaffirmed that, according to the Tenth Amendment of the Constitution of the United States, and

implied by the Constitution before it was ever amended, all powers of the previously mentioned entities are reserved to the States respectively, or to the People, and, therefore, none of the powers that these previously mentioned entities had will henceforward be exercised by the Federal Government, without there first being a ratified amendment to the Constitution that gives power over some area where these entities served to the Federal Government.

Sec. 7. Responsibilities of the People and their State Governments. Regarding the topic(s) of this Executive Order, the People and their respective State Governments, or the People alone, are urged to take care of anything previously attended to by the Federal Government. If any State desires to take action regarding a topic of this Executive Order, the Congress of the United States is urged to approve such State action so that the state may accomplish these or related things which were previously attended to by the Federal Government, if Congressional approval is Constitutionally required for the State to take such action.

Sec. 8. Pardons and Contracts. (a) A Full and Unconditional Pardon is hereby given to anyone who has been charged or convicted of any Federal crime or offense related to any of the unconstitutional laws that were deemed unenforceable according to this Executive Order.

(b) Regardless of any contracts or agreements that were signed or sworn to towards unconstitutional ends, anyone who exposes the Federal Government for doing anything unconstitutional, including the items outlined in this Executive Order, will be given a Full and Unconditional Pardon for exposing such unconstitutional Federal actions. Also, regardless of any contracts or agreements that were signed or sworn to towards unconstitutional ends, anyone who has exposed the Federal Government for doing anything unconstitutional, including the items outlined in this Executive Order, is hereby given a Full and Unconditional Pardon for exposing such unconstitutional Federal actions.

Sec. 9. General Provisions. (a) This order is not intended to, and does not, create any right or benefit, substantive or procedural, enforceable at law or in equity by any party against the United States, its departments, agencies, or entities, its officers, employees, or agents, or any other person.

(b) This order is not intended to, and does not, go against the Constitution of the United States. Everything in this order has the intent of restoring the supreme law of the land, which is the Constitution of the United States of America; if any part of this order is deemed as going against the Constitution, any remedy must be at the discretion of each individual charged with that remedy, including judges, officials, secretaries, and people at any and every level of government. Those individuals are each

urged to ask if the remedy is Constitutional according to the original intent and spirit of the Constitution when written by our founding fathers in the seventeen hundreds. If any part of this order is ultimately deemed unconstitutional by any individual or institution, all other parts of this order will remain in full force and effect in perpetuity, or until the Constitution is amended or superseded.

[THE NAME AND SIGNATURE OF THE PRESIDENT OF THE UNITED STATES]

THE WHITE HOUSE,

[Date].

Agriculture Department

This is one of those uglies that is totally and utterly unconstitutional. There's nothing about agriculture or farming in the Constitution. This is to be left up to the states and the people, and must immediately be eliminated. Absolutely every state has their own version of a department of agriculture.[70] The founders never intended two layers of laws, regulation, and government for agriculture at the state and federal level. What bizarre redundancy that would have been, and now is.

There is really only one major place where the Constitution wanted redundant government, and that was with the military because defense is so important.

Perhaps defense was so important to the founders because they saw it as one of the few legitimate purposes of government and probably the primary purpose of the Federal Government.

You can see clearly in the Constitution that the founders cared about defense: The states can have militias, and the federal government can have an army and a navy. Both levels of government can defend the country.

The Agriculture Department was started in 1862 without any amendment to the Constitution, this department should not exist.[71]

Components of the Agriculture Department:
- Agricultural Marketing Service - This marketing service is totally unconstitutional and should be left up to the states and the people.[72]
- Agricultural Research Service - Created in 1953, this research agency is unconstitutional.[73]
- Animal and Plant Health Inspection Service - Created in 1972, this health inspection agency needs to be left to the people and the states.[74]
- Farm Service Agency - Creating any farm programs need to be left to the states.[75]
- Food and Nutrition Service - Started in 1969, it now addresses "hunger".[76] This is totally unconstitutional and needs to be left to the states and the people. Whenever I say that a whole agency should be eliminated, please don't think that the purposes of that agency are bad. The purposes of many agencies like this are good. I think we should do something

about the hungry in this nation. However, I think that the free market, including non-profit organizations such as soup kitchens and food banks, is the best way to achieve less hunger, and without Federal funds. There are a few reasons for this. Those funds come from the people, so the government needs to take by force in order to feed others. I would rather people do it voluntarily. The Federal Government tends to spend more and achieves less than private enterprises or other levels of government, because it is the most removed from the people, so it gives us the smallest bang for our buck. Finally, it is illegal for the Federal Government to get involved. If any government entity should be getting involved, it is state and/or local government, because that's the only legal way for government to be involved according to the 10th Amendment. In essentially every case where I call for the elimination of an agency, the purposes of that agency would be better achieved through the people or the states.

- Food Safety and Inspection Service - This agency regulates food and is totally unconstitutional.[77]
- Forest Service - Started in 1905, all Federal forests and grasslands need to be ceded to the states. There's nothing about forests or grasslands in the Constitution. The states can decide what a fair amount to pay the Federal Government for these lands is. Those funds could make a dent in the National Debt.[78]
- Grain Inspection, Packers and Stockyards Administration - Formed in 1994, it's about marketing and

competition for meat, cereal, and oil, and is totally unconstitutional.[79]

- National Agricultural Statistics Service - This is unconstitutional.
- Procurement and Property Management, Office of - Unconstitutional.
- Rural Housing Service - Unconstitutional, this needs to be done by the states or the people.
- Rural Utilities Service - Unconstitutional, this needs to be done by the states or the people.
- Advocacy and Outreach Office- Unconstitutional, it improves access and knowledge of Department of Agriculture services.
- Commodity Credit Corporation - Unconstitutional, it stabilizes farm income and prices.
- Cooperative State Research, Education, and Extension Service - Unconstitutional, does and promotes research.
- Foreign Agricultural Service - Unconstitutional.
- Inspector General Office, Agriculture Department - Unconstitutional.
- National Agricultural Library - Unconstitutional.
- National Agricultural Statistics Service – Unconstitutional.
- National Institute of Food and Agriculture - Unconstitutional.
- Office of the Chief Financial Officer, Agriculture Department - Unconstitutional.

- Economic Analysis Staff - Unconstitutional, already gone.
- Economic Research Service - Unconstitutional.
- Energy Policy and New Uses Office – Unconstitutional.
- Federal Crop Insurance Corporation - Unconstitutional.
- Food and Consumer Service - Unconstitutional.
- Natural Resources Conservation Service – Unconstitutional.
- Operations Office - Unconstitutional.
- Risk Management Agency - Unconstitutional.
- Rural Business-Cooperative Service – Unconstitutional.
- Rural Housing and Community Development Service - Unconstitutional.
- Rural Telephone Bank - Unconstitutional, already mostly dissolved.
- Transportation Office - Unconstitutional.

The Executive Order related to the Agriculture Department:

Executive Order Immediately Dissolving the United States Department of Agriculture

EXECUTIVE ORDER

- - - - - - -

IMMEDIATELY DISSOLVING THE UNITED STATES DEPARTMENT OF AGRICULTURE

By the authority vested in me as President by the Constitution and the laws of the United States of America, it is hereby affirmed, declared, and ordered as follows:

Section 1. Policy. It is the policy of the United States to have no involvement in matters regarding agriculture not directly associated with carrying out a power given to it by the Constitution of the United States.

Sec. 2. Constitutionality. The United States Department of Agriculture is unconstitutional. The term "agriculture" is not contained in the Constitution of the United States of America and no power regarding agriculture is ever given to the Federal Government or its Legislature in the Constitution. The following entities from the Department of Agriculture are entirely unconstitutional and must immediately cease functioning: Agricultural Marketing Service, Agricultural Research Service, Animal and Plant Health Inspection Service, Farm Service Agency; Food and Nutrition Service; Food Safety and Inspection Service; Forest Service; Grain Inspection, Packers and Stockyards Administration; National Agricultural Statistics Service; Office of Procurement and Property Management; Rural Housing Service; Rural Utilities Service; Advocacy and Outreach Office;

Commodity Credit Corporation; Cooperative State Research, Education, and Extension Service; Foreign Agricultural Service; Inspector General Office, Agriculture Department; National Agricultural Library; National Agricultural Statistics Service; National Institute of Food and Agriculture; Office of the Chief Financial Officer; Agriculture Department; Economic Research Service; Energy Policy and New Uses Office; Federal Crop Insurance Corporation; Food and Consumer Service; Natural Resources Conservation Service; Operations Office; Risk Management Agency; Rural Business-Cooperative Service; Rural Housing and Community Development Service; Rural Telephone Bank; and Transportation Office.

Sec. 3. Presidential Duty and Immediacy. According to the President's duty to uphold the Constitution of the United States of America, as the President has sworn or affirmed to uphold such Constitution, all sections of this executive order will be immediately understood and carried out by all branches of the United States Federal Government as it pertains to them, without regard to any court order that goes against the Constitution.

Sec. 4. Unenforceable Laws. Any laws, regulations, acts, or other legislation of the Federal Government that unconstitutionally provide for or regulate agriculture will henceforward cease to be executed and will continue to cease to be executed unless and until the Constitution of the United States is amended to give Congress or the

Federal Government the power to make laws regarding agriculture.

Sec. 5. Ending the Department. The United States Department of Agriculture will immediately cease to function, and any obligations owed by the United States Department of Agriculture to its servants or from the United States Department of Agriculture to other entities will be taken over by the Federal Government in accordance with its historical commitment to pay debts, as Congress may prescribe.

The Secretary of Agriculture will remain in his or her position for ninety days to make sure that all unconstitutional agriculture functions throughout the Federal Government are eradicated and to make sure that agriculture is firmly in the hands of the people and their respective States. The Secretary of Agriculture will give a report to the President on how agriculture matters have been eradicated from the Federal Government, and will permanently leave his or her office when ninety days have passed.

Everyone working at the United States Department of Agriculture must permanently leave their respective Department offices or places of work immediately. Any State Government or other entity may reemploy any Federal worker who has lost a job in this way, to work in a similar or a different capacity.

Any property which was owned by the United States Department of Agriculture will now be the property of the governments of the respective State, the District of Columbia, or the United States Territory where the property is situated. If the property is not contained in one of these locations, it will immediately come into the control of the first State government which has a representative at the property physically to claim the property. If two or more States lay claim to property at the same time, they may agree among themselves as to who will own the property, or they will share it among themselves. Any State, the District of Columbia, or any United States Territory that acquires property from the Federal Government in the above two ways may freely pay the Treasury of the United States for such property, if and in the amount that they desire to do so.

Sec. 6. Reaffirmation of the Tenth Amendment of the Constitution. It is reaffirmed that, according to the Tenth Amendment of the Constitution of the United States, and implied by the Constitution before it was ever amended, all agriculture powers are reserved to the States respectively, or to the People, and, therefore, nothing regarding agriculture will henceforward be done by the Federal Government, without there first being a ratified amendment to the Constitution that gives power over agriculture to the Federal Government.

Sec. 7. Responsibilities of the People and their State Governments. Regarding the topic(s) of this Executive

Order, the People and their respective State Governments, or the People alone, are urged to take care of anything previously attended to by the Federal Government. If any State desires to take action regarding a topic of this Executive Order, the Congress of the United States is urged to approve such State action so that the state may accomplish these or related things which were previously attended to by the Federal Government, if Congressional approval is Constitutionally required for the State to take such action.

Sec. 8. Pardons and Contracts. (a) A Full and Unconditional Pardon is hereby given to anyone who has been charged or convicted of any Federal crime or offense related to any of the unconstitutional laws that were deemed unenforceable according to this Executive Order.

(b) Regardless of any contracts or agreements that were signed or sworn to towards unconstitutional ends, anyone who exposes the Federal Government for doing anything unconstitutional, including the items outlined in this Executive Order, will be given a Full and Unconditional Pardon for exposing such unconstitutional Federal actions. Also, regardless of any contracts or agreements that were signed or sworn to towards unconstitutional ends, anyone who has exposed the Federal Government for doing anything unconstitutional, including the items outlined in this Executive Order, is hereby given a Full and Unconditional Pardon for exposing such unconstitutional Federal actions.

Sec. 9. General Provisions. (a) This order is not intended to, and does not, create any right or benefit, substantive or procedural, enforceable at law or in equity by any party against the United States, its departments, agencies, or entities, its officers, employees, or agents, or any other person.

(b) This order is not intended to, and does not, go against the Constitution of the United States. Everything in this order has the intent of restoring the supreme law of the land, which is the Constitution of the United States of America; if any part of this order is deemed as going against the Constitution, any remedy must be at the discretion of each individual charged with that remedy, including judges, officials, secretaries, and people at any and every level of government. Those individuals are each urged to ask if the remedy is Constitutional according to the original intent and spirit of the Constitution when written by our founding fathers in the seventeen hundreds. If any part of this order is ultimately deemed unconstitutional by any individual or institution, all other parts of this order will remain in full force and effect in perpetuity, or until the Constitution is amended or superseded.

[THE NAME AND SIGNATURE OF THE PRESIDENT OF THE UNITED STATES]

THE WHITE HOUSE,

[Date].

Commerce Department

I explained the regulation of commerce earlier in the book. Other than dealing with international commerce, the only thing the federal government is constitutionally allowed to do in regard to commerce is to make sure that the states aren't restricting trade among the other states. Commerce within and among states may not be restricted or regulated by the central government. The department's mission is to "promote job creation and improved living standards for all Americans by creating an infrastructure that promotes economic growth, technological competitiveness, and sustainable development."[80] This has little to do with the constitutional powers that the Commerce Department has.

Components of the Commerce Department:
- Census Bureau - The census once every ten years is allowed, but the unnecessary questions beyond how many people are in a household and whether someone is an Indian or not are unconstitutional.
- Economic Development Administration - This group "invests" in things. Definitely unconstitutional.[81]
- Foreign-Trade Zones Board - Created from a law passed in 1934, these seem to allow foreign trade near ports so that goods can be repackaged without owing any U.S. duties or other taxes, but they also allow

things to be manufactured there, and there are fewer taxes owed when things are exported out of the United States. The government actually oversees these zones. This overseeing is not provided for in the Constitution and needs to be taken over by the states.[82]

- Industry and Security Bureau - Started in 2001, this partly focuses on stopping the export of certain encryption technology. Foreign commerce can be regulated by Congress, so to the extent that this agency is regulating foreign commerce, it's constitutional.[83]

- International Trade Administration - Its goals are: "1. Provide practical information to help Americans select markets and products. 2. Ensure that Americans have access to international markets as required by the U.S. trade agreements. 3. Safeguard Americans from unfair competition from dumped and subsidized imports." Only goal 2 is Constitutional. Information and ensuring competition are not.[84]

- National Institute of Standards and Technology - Congress can "fix the standard of weights and measures," but anything beyond this is unconstitutional.

- National Oceanic and Atmospheric Administration - Created in 1970, it deals with stuff like weather. It is unconstitutional and must be dissolved unless the Constitution is amended. Its functions can instantly be given to the states where its buildings reside or are nearest to, and the states can reimburse the Federal Government for this property as they see fit. The states can decide how to deal with any civil servants (as they will with all closed agencies).[85]

- National Telecommunications and Information Administration - There's nothing constitutional about this agency, started in 1978.[86]
- Patent and Trademark Office - Patents are constitutional in that they secure, for a limited time, exclusive right to discoveries. But trademarks are not Constitutional and should be left to the people and the states. Congress tried creating trademarks in 1870, but the Supreme Court struck it down. They later tried again with unconstitutional success.[87]
- Economic Analysis Bureau - Unconstitutional.
- Economics and Statistics Administration – Unconstitutional.
- Export Administration Bureau - Enforcing treaties and export rules is allowed.
- Minority Business Development Agency – Unconstitutional.
- National Shipping Authority - Unconstitutional, it directs "emergency merchant marine" shipping.[88]
- National Technical Information Service – Unconstitutional.
- Travel and Tourism Administration – Unconstitutional.

The Executive Order related to the Commerce Department:

Executive Order Immediately Dissolving Portions of the United States Department of Commerce
EXECUTIVE ORDER

- - - - - - -

IMMEDIATELY DISSOLVING PORTIONS OF THE UNITED STATES DEPARTMENT OF COMMERCE

By the authority vested in me as President by the Constitution and the laws of the United States of America, it is hereby affirmed, declared, and ordered as follows:

Section 1. Policy. It is the policy of the United States to have no involvement within the Department of Commerce in matters not directly associated with the carrying out a power given to it by the Constitution of the United States.

Sec. 2. Constitutionality and in some instances Ending the Functions of Particular Entities. Portions of the United States Department of Commerce are unconstitutional. The following entities perform unconstitutional functions: Economic Development Administration, National Oceanic and Atmospheric Administration, National Telecommunications and Information Administration, Economic Analysis Bureau, Economics and Statistics Administration, Minority Business Development Agency, National Shipping

Authority, National Technical Information Service, and Travel and Tourism Administration. No powers regarding the functions of these entities are ever given to the Federal Government or its Legislature in the Constitution. Census Bureau - The census once every ten years is allowed, but the unnecessary questions beyond how many people are in a household and whether someone is an Indian or not are unconstitutional and must cease to be asked immediately; Foreign-Trade Zones Board - The Federal Government must immediately cease to oversee these Zones and give that responsibility to the states and their people; International Trade Administration - It must immediately cease to, "Provide practical information to help Americans select markets and products." and "Safeguard Americans from unfair competition from dumped and subsidized imports."; National Institute of Standards and Technology - Congress can "fix the standard of weights and measures" but anything beyond this is unconstitutional and must immediately cease; and Patent and Trademark Office - Trademarks are not Constitutional, and must immediately cease being dealt with by the Federal Government, this office will henceforward be called the Patent Office.

Sec. 3. Presidential Duty and Immediacy. According to the President's duty to uphold the Constitution of the United States of America, as the President has sworn or affirmed to uphold such Constitution, all sections of this executive order will be immediately understood and carried out by all branches of the United States Federal Government as it pertains to them, without regard to any court order that goes against the Constitution.

Sec. 4. Unenforceable Laws. Any laws, regulations, acts, or other legislation of the Federal Government that unconstitutionally provides for or regulates anything related to the areas served by the previously mentioned entities, and (if applicable) the functions of entities where particular functions have been ceased, will henceforward cease to be executed and will continue to cease to be executed unless and until the Constitution of the United States is amended to give Congress or the Federal Government the power to make laws regarding the areas served by the previously mentioned entities.

Sec. 5. Ending portions of the Department. The following entities within the United States Department of Commerce will immediately cease to function, and any obligations owed by these entities to servants or from these entities to other entities will be taken over by the Federal Government in accordance with its historical commitment to pay debts, as Congress may prescribe: Economic Development Administration, National Oceanic and Atmospheric Administration, National Telecommunications and Information Administration, Economic Analysis Bureau, Economics and Statistics Administration, Minority Business Development Agency, National Shipping Authority, National Technical

Information Service, and Travel and Tourism Administration.

Everyone working at the previously mentioned entities must permanently leave their respective entity offices or places of work immediately. Any State Government or other entity may reemploy any Federal worker who has lost a job in this way, to work in a similar or a different capacity.

All property of the previously mentioned entities will now be the property of the governments of the respective State, the District of Columbia, or the United States Territory where the property is situated. If the property is not contained in one of these locations, it will immediately come into the control of the first State government which has a representative at the property physically to claim the property. If two or more States lay claim to property at the same time, they may agree among themselves as to who will own the property, or they will share it among themselves. Any State, the District of Columbia, or any United States Territory that acquires property from the Federal Government in the above two ways may freely pay the Treasury of the United States for such property, if and in the amount that they desire to do so.

Sec. 6. Reaffirmation of the Tenth Amendment of the Constitution. It is reaffirmed that, according to the Tenth Amendment of the Constitution of the United States, and implied by the Constitution before it was ever amended,

all powers of the previously mentioned entities are reserved to the States respectively, or to the People, and, therefore, none of the powers that these previously mentioned entities had will henceforward be exercised by the Federal Government, without there first being a ratified amendment to the Constitution that gives power over some area where these entities served to the Federal Government.

Sec. 7. Responsibilities of the People and their State Governments. Regarding the topic(s) of this Executive Order, the People and their respective State Governments, or the People alone, are urged to take care of anything previously attended to by the Federal Government. If any State desires to take action regarding a topic of this Executive Order, the Congress of the United States is urged to approve such State action so that the state may accomplish these or related things which were previously attended to by the Federal Government, if Congressional approval is Constitutionally required for the State to take such action.

Sec. 8. Pardons and Contracts. (a) A Full and Unconditional Pardon is hereby given to anyone who has been charged or convicted of any Federal crime or offense related to any of the unconstitutional laws that were deemed unenforceable according to this Executive Order.

(b) Regardless of any contracts or agreements that were signed or sworn to towards unconstitutional ends, anyone

who exposes the Federal Government for doing anything unconstitutional, including the items outlined in this Executive Order, will be given a Full and Unconditional Pardon for exposing such unconstitutional Federal actions. Also, regardless of any contracts or agreements that were signed or sworn to towards unconstitutional ends, anyone who has exposed the Federal Government for doing anything unconstitutional, including the items outlined in this Executive Order, is hereby given a Full and Unconditional Pardon for exposing such unconstitutional Federal actions.

Sec. 9. General Provisions. (a) This order is not intended to, and does not, create any right or benefit, substantive or procedural, enforceable at law or in equity by any party against the United States, its departments, agencies, or entities, its officers, employees, or agents, or any other person.

(b) This order is not intended to, and does not, go against the Constitution of the United States. Everything in this order has the intent of restoring the supreme law of the land, which is the Constitution of the United States of America; if any part of this order is deemed as going against the Constitution, any remedy must be at the discretion of each individual charged with that remedy, including judges, officials, secretaries, and people at any and every level of government. Those individuals are each urged to ask if the remedy is Constitutional according to the original intent and spirit of the Constitution when

written by our founding fathers in the seventeen hundreds. If any part of this order is ultimately deemed unconstitutional by any individual or institution, all other parts of this order will remain in full force and effect in perpetuity, or until the Constitution is amended or superseded.

[THE NAME AND SIGNATURE OF THE PRESIDENT OF THE UNITED STATES]

THE WHITE HOUSE,

[Date].

Labor Department

This started in 1913, the same year as the Federal Reserve and the income tax (what a bad year). It has absolutely no constitutional basis, nor does it have any amendment ratified near when it was created to give its existence any legality.[89]

This department and every subagency listed under it must be dissolved. Labor is totally and utterly meant to be taken care of by the states and the people, not the federal government. There's nothing about labor in the Constitution.

The states have taken it upon themselves to take care of many of these issues. All fifty states have their own equivalent of a department of labor.[90]

We don't need two layers of regulations, rules, and laws. It disturbs me that the federal government has trampled on the rights of the people and the states in this area. When this department is dissolved, the states can take over anything the federal government was doing (if anything) as they deem necessary.

The minimum wage is a perfect example of why the federal government needs to stay out of labor regulations. Could Congress, comprised of people from all fifty states, possibly know the proper minimum wage for an individual state better than a legislature comprised entirely of people from that particular state? Unless we are giving Congress some God-like status above state legislatures, the answer is almost definitely "No."

Congress's Joint Economic Committee published a research review in 1995 that showed that minimum wage laws do the following - these are a selection of effects nearly verbatim from the report. They show that it would be better for the Federal Government and state governments to get rid of minimum wage laws. The minimum wage:

- reduces employment
- hurts the unskilled
- hurts low wage workers
- hurts low wage workers particularly during cyclical downturns
- increases job turnover
- reduces average earnings of young workers

- reduces employment in low-wage industries, such as retailing
- hurts small businesses generally
- causes employers to cut back on training
- leads employers to cut back on fringe benefits
- encourages employers to install labor-saving devices.
- increases the number of people on welfare
- hurts the poor generally
- increases inflationary pressure
- encourages employers to hire illegal aliens
- has reduced employment in foreign countries [91]

Components of the Labor Department:
- Employee Benefits Security Administration - This is unconstitutional. Requiring and regulating the benefits of private employees throughout the nation is abhorrent. It started in 1970 under President Nixon.[92]
- Employment and Training Administration – Unconstitutional.
- Labor-Management Standards Office – Unconstitutional.
- Mine Safety and Health Administration – Unconstitutional.
- Occupational Safety and Health Administration - Unconstitutional. What a beautiful thing it will be for OSHA to be gone. If there's any need for safety, that's for the people and the states to decide.
- Wage and Hour Division - Unconstitutional. Getting rid of this will get rid of the Federal Minimum wage,

overtime requirements, child labor laws, and much more. These things are required to be in the hands of the states and the people.

- Workers Compensation Programs Office – Unconstitutional. Won't it be nice for workers comp to lose all Federal regulations?

- Disability Employment Policy Office – Unconstitutional.

- Employees Compensation Appeals Board - This constitutional because it deals with worker's compensation for Federal employees and can be moved to the Executive Office of the President.

- Employment Standards Administration - Dissolved in 2009, its functions stayed alive through the agencies that were under it.

- Federal Contract Compliance Programs Office – Constitutional. Hardly needed because there should be so much fewer Federal contractors. It can be moved to the Executive Office of the President.

- Labor Statistics Bureau - Unconstitutional.

- Pension and Welfare Benefits Administration - Partly Constitutional. Any regulation or control of state-level or private sector pension or welfare benefits is unconstitutional and needs to be left to the states and the people. Administering benefits for Federal employees is Constitutional and should be moved to the Executive Office of the President.

- Veterans Employment and Training Service - Constitutional as pay for veterans. Should immediately be moved to the Department of Veterans Affairs.

The Executive Order related to the Labor Department:

Executive Order Immediately Dissolving the United States Department of Labor and Moving Portions of it to Other Parts of the Government

EXECUTIVE ORDER

- - - - - - -

IMMEDIATELY DISSOLVING THE UNITED STATES DEPARTMENT OF LABOR AND MOVING PORTIONS OF IT TO OTHER PARTS OF THE GOVERNMENT

By the authority vested in me as President by the Constitution and the laws of the United States of America, it is hereby affirmed, declared, and ordered as follows:

Section 1. Policy. It is the policy of the United States to have no involvement within the Department of Labor in matters not directly associated with the carrying out a power given to it by the Constitution of the United States.

Sec. 2. Constitutionality. Portions of the United States Department of Labor are unconstitutional. The following entities from the Department of Labor are entirely unconstitutional and must immediately cease functioning: Employee Benefits Security Administration, Employment and Training Administration, Labor-Management Standards Office, Mine Safety and Health Administration, Occupational Safety and Health Administration, Wage and Hour Division, Workers Compensation Programs Office, Disability Employment Policy Office, and Labor Statistics Bureau. No powers regarding the functions of these entities are ever given to the Federal Government or its Legislature in the Constitution. Employees Compensation Appeals Board - This Constitutional Board must immediately be moved under the Executive Office of the President; Federal Contract Compliance Programs Office - This Constitutional Office must immediately be moved under the Executive Office of the President; Pension and Welfare Benefits Administration - Any regulation or control of state-level or private sector pension or welfare benefits is unconstitutional and must immediately cease and be left to the states and their people, administering benefits for Federal employees is Constitutional and must immediately be moved under the Executive Office of the President; and Veterans Employment and Training Service - This is Constitutional and must immediately be moved under the Department of Veterans Affairs.

Sec. 3. Presidential Duty and Immediacy. According to the President's duty to uphold the Constitution of the United States of America, as the President has sworn or affirmed to uphold such Constitution, all sections of this executive order will be immediately understood and carried out by all branches of the United States Federal Government as it pertains to them, without regard to any court order that goes against the Constitution.

Sec. 4. Unenforceable Laws. Any laws, regulations, acts, or other legislation of the Federal Government that unconstitutionally provides for or regulates anything related to the areas served by the previously mentioned entities, and (if applicable) the functions of entities where particular functions have been ceased, will henceforward cease to be executed and will continue to cease to be executed unless and until the Constitution of the United States is amended to give Congress or the Federal Government the power to make laws regarding the areas served by the previously mentioned entities.

Sec. 5. Ending the Department. The United States Department of Labor will immediately cease to function, except for the portions of it that have moved under other parts of the Federal Government and are henceforward no longer considered part of the Department of Labor, and any obligations owed by the United States Department of Labor to its servants or from the United States Department of Labor to other entities will be taken over by the Federal Government in accordance with its historical commitment to pay debts, as Congress may prescribe.

The Secretary of Labor will remain in his or her position for ninety days to make sure that all unconstitutional labor functions throughout the Federal Government are eradicated and to make sure that labor is firmly in the hands of the people and their respective States. The Secretary of Labor will give a report to the President on how labor matters have been eradicated from the Federal Government, and will permanently leave his or her office when ninety days have passed.

Everyone working at the United States Department of Labor must permanently leave their respective Department offices or places of work immediately. Any State Government or other entity may reemploy any Federal worker who has lost a job in this way, to work in a similar or a different capacity.

Any property that was not taken over by Constitutional Departments, which was owned by the United States Department of Labor, will now be the property of the governments of the respective State, the District of Columbia, or the United States Territory where the property is situated. If the property is not contained in one of these locations, it will immediately come into the control of the first State government which has a representative at the property physically to claim the property. If two or more States lay claim to property at the same time, they may agree among themselves as to who will own the property, or they will share it among themselves. Any State, the District of Columbia, or any United States Territory that acquires property from the Federal Government in the above two ways may freely pay the Treasury of the United States for such property, if and in the amount that they desire to do so.

Sec. 6. Reaffirmation of the Tenth Amendment of the Constitution. It is reaffirmed that, according to the Tenth Amendment of the Constitution of the United States, and implied by the Constitution before it was ever amended, all powers of the previously mentioned entities are reserved to the States respectively, or to the People, and, therefore, none of the powers that these previously mentioned entities had will henceforward be exercised by the Federal Government, without there first being a ratified amendment to the Constitution that gives power over some area where these entities served to the Federal Government.

Sec. 7. Responsibilities of the People and their State Governments. Regarding the topic(s) of this Executive Order, the People and their respective State Governments, or the People alone, are urged to take care of anything previously attended to by the Federal Government. If any State desires to take action regarding a topic of this Executive Order, the Congress of the United States is urged to approve such State action so that the state may accomplish these or related things which were previously attended to by the Federal Government, if Congressional approval is Constitutionally required for the State to take such action.

Sec. 8. Pardons and Contracts. (a) A Full and Unconditional Pardon is hereby given to anyone who has been charged or convicted of any Federal crime or offense related to any of the unconstitutional laws that were deemed unenforceable according to this Executive Order.

(b) Regardless of any contracts or agreements that were signed or sworn to towards unconstitutional ends, anyone who exposes the Federal Government for doing anything unconstitutional, including the items outlined in this Executive Order, will be given a Full and Unconditional Pardon for exposing such unconstitutional Federal actions. Also, regardless of any contracts or agreements that were signed or sworn to towards unconstitutional ends, anyone who has exposed the Federal Government for doing anything unconstitutional, including the items outlined in this Executive Order, is hereby given a Full and Unconditional Pardon for exposing such unconstitutional Federal actions.

Sec. 9. General Provisions. (a) This order is not intended to, and does not, create any right or benefit, substantive or procedural, enforceable at law or in equity by any party against the United States, its departments, agencies, or entities, its officers, employees, or agents, or any other person.

(b) This order is not intended to, and does not, go against the Constitution of the United States. Everything in this order has the intent of restoring the supreme law of the land, which is the Constitution of the United States of America; if any part of this order is deemed as going against the Constitution, any remedy must be at the discretion of each individual charged with that remedy, including judges, officials, secretaries, and people at any and every level of government. Those individuals are each urged to ask if the remedy is Constitutional according to the original intent and spirit of the Constitution when written by our founding fathers in the seventeen hundreds. If any part of this order is ultimately deemed unconstitutional by any individual or institution, all other parts of this order will remain in full force and effect in perpetuity, or until the Constitution is amended or superseded.

[THE NAME AND SIGNATURE OF THE PRESIDENT OF THE UNITED STATES]

THE WHITE HOUSE,

[Date].

Health and Human Services Department

This was started in 1953 as the Department of Health, Education, and Welfare with no constitutional amendment then or since to authorize its activities.[93]

This department is almost entirely unconstitutional, and all of its subagencies need to be instantly abolished while providing for those services owed as payment to current or former federal employees or military. Constitutionally speaking, every function that this agency performs is to be reserved for the states or the people, except for payments to military and federal employees. The words "health" and "healthcare" are non-existent in the Constitution, and services like the ones supposedly carried out by this department are non-existent in the Constitution as well.

The states can handle any of these things if needed. Should there be any doubt on this fact, please check the reference list in the endnote that shows that each one of the fifty states has its own equivalent of a department of health.[94]

I also know from firsthand practical experience that anything related to health (unless someone is in the service of the military, where it should probably be left to private people and organizations hired by the government) should be kept out of the hands of the federal government. From 2007 to 2010, I worked part-time at Martin Foot and Ankle, the podiatric practice where my dad, Rick, and my uncle, Craig, were doctors. Seeing the level of federal intrusion into healthcare was appalling.

There were all sorts of weird rules, many of which are probably improperly understood by the medical industry and not even understood by those who wrote them. We had to get patients' pictures, check their government-issued IDs, and try not to call anyone by his or her last name in front of another patient. There were so many more issues, many of which I didn't have to deal with. For example, there are currently around 7,800 CPT (Current Procedural Terminology) codes that doctors (and perhaps their assistants) have to juggle. It's a nightmare.

One thing that really bugged me had to do with durable medical equipment (DME). DME could be a medical boot that stabilizes your foot and ankle after an injury, for example. We had a system where anytime people got this boot, they had to sign a statement that the DME was "satisfactory and not substandard," or something much longer to that effect. I thought this was ridiculous and looked it up. From what I recall, the law or rule was that for Medicare Guidelines, we needed to have a resolution procedure in place in case any of the DME we sold was defective or substandard.

It seems like we had people sign off that the DME was not substandard to fulfill this procedural requirement, even though we were actually supposed to have a documented procedure for issues that cropped up after the DME was taken home. When reading the actual law or rule, some of it literally did not make sense, almost like the words were scrambled.

How does the Federal Government hope for any respect when it does not even make sense? We didn't understand the law, the law-writers didn't understand it, and there was no way to understand it. But here's the kicker, these were guidelines given for people getting DME under Medicare, but many insurance companies say that doctors must follow "Medicare Guidelines" in order to be reimbursed. In other words, our healthcare industry is almost entirely following Medicare guidelines for every patient, even though most people don't yet fall under Medicare. These regulations are at an enormous cost to the healthcare consumer.

The Obamacare "law" currently stands at 974 pages, and that's just one law related to health care.[95] It is impossible to properly follow a law like this, and the founders never intended for the federal government to pass this type of law.

Our healthcare problems got kicked into high gear with the passing of Medicare for all U.S. seniors. This was spearheaded by President Lyndon Johnson and came into effect in 1965.[96]

While this book can't prove that this action led to the rapidly rising cost of healthcare, I have no doubt that Medicare was a large part of it. A disproportionate amount of healthcare expenses arises at the end of most people's lives, and that's when the government has guaranteed to foot the bill for most people. Therefore, the government, either on purpose or inadvertently, decided to drive health care inflation in the most impactful possible age band.

Medicare for the masses started in 1965. Check out this chart showing health care costs from 1935 to 2010. You can see that 1965 is when medical expenses broke away and became much higher than the average rate of inflation. It's hard to argue that this isn't causation.

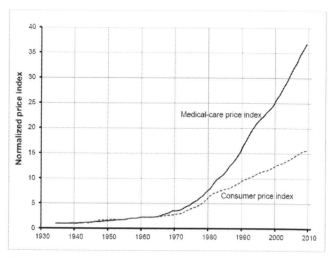

Figure 1

Credit goes to the Mises Institute for this chart.[97]

Components of the Health and Human Services Department:

- Agency for Healthcare Research and Quality – Unconstitutional.
- Agency for Toxic Substances and Disease Registry - Unconstitutional.
- Centers for Disease Control and Prevention – Unconstitutional.
- Centers for Medicare & Medicaid Services - These can simply be taken over by state governments, to the

extent that the states would like to. Medicare is primarily for the elderly and Medicaid is for the poor. If a state decides to not provide any of these welfare programs, someone can move to another state. No more Federal payroll deductions for this boondoggle. Yay! However, in 1965 Medicare was the expansion of a military benefits program. Military benefits are an obligation we have made to our military as payment. Because of this we owe them and will pay them, as an exception to entirely getting rid of Medicare. Although not Constitutionally required, I would recommend to Congress to allow veterans to be in charge of their healthcare and any insurance purchases. I like the idea of the government finding an uncapped private insurance that the Federal government will pay the cash-equivalent for, and the veteran can choose to buy it, or another insurance, or just pocket the cash. We could keep a skeleton crew in the meantime within Medicare to administer the military benefits.

- Children and Families Administration – Unconstitutional.
- Community Living Administration - Unconstitutional.
- Food and Drug Administration - Drugs can still be issued patents under the Constitution, but any drug safety or other testing needs to be done by private companies, individuals, and/or the states.
- Health Resources and Services Administration - Unconstitutional. This tries to see that healthcare is

given to the uninsured and those in hard to reach places. Its precursor agencies started in 1973 with, you guessed it, no corresponding Constitutional amendment.

- Indian Health Service - Unconstitutional.
- National Institutes of Health - If health research is needed, the states and/or private groups or individuals are more than capable. Privatization is almost universally more efficient. Regardless, this is totally unconstitutional and illegal.
- Substance Abuse and Mental Health Services Administration - Unconstitutional.
- Aging Administration - Unconstitutional.
- Child Support Enforcement Office - This requires states to enforce child support on absent parents. Utterly unconstitutional and needs to be left up to the states and the people. Can you believe that our money is being wasted on an entire office dedicated to this?
- Family Assistance Office - Unconstitutional. Tries to force welfare for stuff like childcare for the poor upon the states.
- Health Care Finance Administration – Unconstitutional.
- Inspector General Office, Health and Human Services Department - Unconstitutional.
- National Library of Medicine - Unconstitutional.
- Program Support Center - Unconstitutional.
- Public Health Service - Unconstitutional, except for the United States Public Health Service Comm-

issioned Corps which should be moved under the armed forces.

- Refugee Resettlement Office - Unconstitutional.

The Executive Order related to the Health and Human Services Department:

Executive Order Immediately Dissolving the United States Department of Health and Human Service

EXECUTIVE ORDER

- - - - - - -

IMMEDIATELY DISSOLVING THE UNITED STATES DEPARTMENT OF HEALTH AND HUMAN SERVICES

By the authority vested in me as President by the Constitution and the laws of the United States of America, it is hereby affirmed, declared, and ordered as follows:

Section 1. Policy. It is the policy of the United States to have no involvement in matters regarding health or human services when not directly associated with carrying out a power given to it by the Constitution of the United States. The following entities from the Department of Health and Human Services are entirely unconstitutional and must immediately cease functioning: Agency for

Healthcare Research and Quality; Agency for Toxic Substances and Disease Registry; Centers for Disease Control and Prevention; Children and Families Administration; Community Living Administration; Food and Drug Administration; Health Resources and Services Administration; Indian Health Service; National Institutes of Health; Substance Abuse and Mental Health Services Administration; Aging Administration; Child Support Enforcement Office; Family Assistance Office; Health Care Finance Administration; Inspector General Office, Health and Human Services Department; National Library of Medicine; Program Support Center; and Refugee Resettlement Office. Public Health Service - This is unconstitutional and must immediately cease to exist, except for the United States Public Health Service Commissioned Corps which shall immediately be moved under the Department of Defense and shall henceforward not be a part of the Department of Health and Human Services; Centers for Medicare & Medicaid Services - This is unconstitutional and must immediately cease to exist, except for military benefits provided by these Centers: they are an obligation we have made to our military as payment, we will pay them, and anyone in the Centers for Medicare & Medicaid Services who is administering benefits for military personnel will keep working, doing the same thing, under the Department of Defense and shall henceforward not be a part of the Department of Health and Human Services, the Centers are encouraged to cut any unneeded personnel due to these changes.

Sec. 2. Constitutionality and Transfer of some functions of the Department to other parts of the Federal Government. The United States Department of Health and Human Services is unconstitutional. The terms "health" and "human" are not contained in the Constitution of the United States of America and no power regarding health or human services is ever given to the Federal Government or its Legislature in the Constitution.

Sec. 3. Presidential Duty and Immediacy. According to the President's duty to uphold the Constitution of the United States of America, as the President has sworn or affirmed to uphold such Constitution, all sections of this executive order will be immediately understood and carried out by all branches of the United States Federal Government as it pertains to them, without regard to any court order that goes against the Constitution.

Sec. 4. Unenforceable Laws. Any laws, regulations, acts, or other legislation of the Federal Government that unconstitutionally provide for or regulate health or human services will henceforward cease to be executed and will continue to cease to be executed unless and until the Constitution of the United States is amended to give Congress or the Federal Government the power to make laws regarding health or human services.

Sec. 5. Ending the Department. The United States Department of Health and Human Services will immediately cease to function, and any obligations owed by the United States Department of Health and Human Services to its servants or from the United States Department of Health and Human Services to other entities will be taken over by the Federal Government in accordance with its historical commitment to pay debts, as Congress may prescribe.

The Secretary of Health and Human Services will remain in his or her position for ninety days to make sure that all unconstitutional health and human services functions throughout the Federal Government are eradicated and to make sure that health and human services are firmly in the hands of the people and their respective States. The Secretary of Health and Human Services will give a report to the President on how health and human services matters have been eradicated from the Federal Government, and will permanently leave his or her office when ninety days have passed.

Everyone working at the United States Department of Health and Human Services must permanently leave their respective Department offices or places of work immediately. Any State Government or other entity may reemploy any Federal worker who has lost a job in this way, to work in a similar or a different capacity.

Any property that was not taken by Constitutional Departments, which was owned by the United States Department of Health and Human Services, will now be the property of the governments of the respective State, the District of Columbia, or the United States Territory where the property is situated. If the property is not contained in one of these locations, it will immediately come into the control of the first State government which has a representative at the property physically to claim the property. If two or more States lay claim to property at the same time, they may agree among themselves as to who will own the property, or they will share it among themselves. Any State, the District of Columbia, or any United States Territory that acquires property from the Federal Government in the above two ways may freely pay the Treasury of the United States for such property, if and in the amount that they desire to do so.

Sec. 6. Reaffirmation of the Tenth Amendment of the Constitution. It is reaffirmed that, according to the Tenth Amendment of the Constitution of the United States, and implied by the Constitution before it was ever amended, all health and human services powers are reserved to the States respectively, or to the People, and, therefore, nothing regarding health or human services will henceforward be done by the Federal Government, without there first being a ratified amendment to the Constitution that gives power over health or human services to the Federal Government.

Sec. 7. Responsibilities of the People and their State Governments. Regarding the topic(s) of this Executive Order, the People and their respective State Governments, or the People alone, are urged to take care of anything previously attended to by the Federal Government. If any State desires to take action regarding a topic of this Executive Order, the Congress of the United States is urged to approve such State action so that the state may accomplish these or related things which were previously attended to by the Federal Government, if Congressional approval is Constitutionally required for the State to take such action.

Sec. 8. Pardons and Contracts. (a) A Full and Unconditional Pardon is hereby given to anyone who has been charged or convicted of any Federal crime or offense related to any of the unconstitutional laws that were deemed unenforceable according to this Executive Order.

(b) Regardless of any contracts or agreements that were signed or sworn to towards unconstitutional ends, anyone who exposes the Federal Government for doing anything unconstitutional, including the items outlined in this Executive Order, will be given a Full and Unconditional Pardon for exposing such unconstitutional Federal actions. Also, regardless of any contracts or agreements that were signed or sworn to towards unconstitutional ends, anyone who has exposed the Federal Government for doing anything unconstitutional, including the items outlined in this Executive Order, is hereby given a Full

and Unconditional Pardon for exposing such unconstitutional Federal actions.

Sec. 9. General Provisions. (a) This order is not intended to, and does not, create any right or benefit, substantive or procedural, enforceable at law or in equity by any party against the United States, its departments, agencies, or entities, its officers, employees, or agents, or any other person.

(b) This order is not intended to, and does not, go against the Constitution of the United States. Everything in this order has the intent of restoring the supreme law of the land, which is the Constitution of the United States of America; if any part of this order is deemed as going against the Constitution, any remedy must be at the discretion of each individual charged with that remedy, including judges, officials, secretaries, and people at any and every level of government. Those individuals are each urged to ask if the remedy is Constitutional according to the original intent and spirit of the Constitution when written by our founding fathers in the seventeen hundreds. If any part of this order is ultimately deemed unconstitutional by any individual or institution, all other parts of this order will remain in full force and effect in perpetuity, or until the Constitution is amended or superseded.

[THE NAME AND SIGNATURE OF THE PRESIDENT OF THE UNITED STATES]

THE WHITE HOUSE,

[Date].

Housing and Urban Development Department

Another beauty by President Lyndon Johnson, this unconstitutional department was created in 1965.[98] A quick search shows that all five of the most populous states have government services regarding housing and/or house financing. The states are more than capable of providing any of these services if they feel it is necessary.

People have owned or rented homes for thousands of years, and suddenly, in 1965, the Federal Government decides that they need to step up their involvement. They couldn't be more wrong (which is true of many constitutional matters).

There is nothing in the Constitution allowing the Federal Government to provide for or regulate housing or home financing. That is the right of the states and the people. The Housing and Urban Development Department must be immediately dissolved, and any veterans' benefit functions it serves must immediately be put under the Department of Veterans Affairs.

Components of the Housing and Urban Development Department:
- Board of Directors of the Hope for Homeowners Program - Unconstitutional.

- Federal Housing Enterprise Oversight Office - Unconstitutional. This agency oversees the Federal National Mortgage Association (Fannie Mae) and the Federal Home Loan Mortgage Corporation (Freddie Mac).
- Government National Mortgage Association - Mostly unconstitutional. Also known as Ginnie Mae, this entity provides government-guaranteed mortgages. There are VA (Veterans Affairs) guaranteed loans provided through this. Since that benefit can be considered pay for the military, which is constitutional, that portion of this entity can be moved under the Department of Veterans Affairs. Everything else needs to be dissolved.

The Executive Order related to the Housing and Urban Development Department:

Executive Order Immediately Dissolving the United States Department of Housing and Urban Development

EXECUTIVE ORDER

- - - - - - -

IMMEDIATELY DISSOLVING THE UNITED STATES DEPARTMENT OF HOUSING AND URBAN DEVELOPMENT

By the authority vested in me as President by the Constitution and the laws of the United States of America, it is hereby affirmed, declared, and ordered as follows:

Section 1. Policy. It is the policy of the United States to have no involvement in matters regarding housing or urban development when not directly associated with carrying out a power given to it by the Constitution of the United States.

Sec. 2. Constitutionality and one Function to be Moved. The United States Department of Housing and Urban Development is unconstitutional. The terms "housing," "urban," and "development" are not contained in the Constitution of the United States of America and no power regarding housing or urban development is ever given to the Federal Government or its Legislature in the Constitution. The following entities from the Department of Housing and Urban Development are entirely unconstitutional and must immediately cease functioning: Board of Directors of the Hope for Homeowners Program, and Federal Housing Enterprise Oversight Office. Government National Mortgage Association - All parts of this Association are unconstitutional and must be dissolved except for VA (Veterans Affairs) guaranteed loans provided through this Association because they are benefit pay for military personnel and their families, those guarantees and benefits from this Association must immediately be assumed by and moved under the Department of Veterans Affairs, henceforward the portion of the Association that moved to the Department of Veterans Affairs is not a part of the Department of Housing and Urban Development.

Sec. 3. Presidential Duty and Immediacy. According to the President's duty to uphold the Constitution of the United States of America, as the President has sworn or affirmed to uphold such Constitution, all sections of this executive order will be immediately understood and carried out by all branches of the United States Federal Government as it pertains to them, without regard to any court order that goes against the Constitution.

Sec. 4. Unenforceable Laws. Any laws, regulations, acts, or other legislation of the Federal Government that unconstitutionally provide for or regulate housing or urban development will henceforward cease to be executed and will continue to cease to be executed unless and until the Constitution of the United States is amended to give Congress or the Federal Government the power to make laws regarding housing or urban development.

Sec. 5. Ending the Department. The United States Department of Housing and Urban Development will immediately cease to function, and any obligations owed by the United States Department of Housing and Urban Development to its servants or from the United States Department of Housing and Urban Development to other entities will be taken over by the Federal

Government in accordance with its historical commitment to pay debts, as Congress may prescribe.

The Secretary of Housing and Urban Development will remain in his or her position for ninety days to make sure that all unconstitutional housing and urban development functions throughout the Federal Government are eradicated and to make sure that housing and urban development is firmly in the hands of the people and their respective States. The Secretary of Housing and Urban Development will give a report to the President on how housing and urban development matters have been eradicated from the Federal Government, and will permanently leave his or her office when ninety days have passed.

Everyone working at the United States Department of Housing and Urban Development must permanently leave their respective Department offices or places of work immediately. Any State Government or other entity may reemploy any Federal worker who has lost a job in this way, to work in a similar or a different capacity.

Any property that was not taken by Constitutional Departments, which was owned by the United States Department of Housing and Urban Development, will now be the property of the governments of the respective State, the District of Columbia, or the United States Territory where the property is situated. If the property is not contained in one of these locations, it will immediately come into the control of the first State government which has a representative at the property physically to claim the property. If two or more States lay claim to property at the same time, they may agree among themselves as to who will own the property, or they will share it among themselves. Any State, the District of Columbia, or any United States Territory that acquires property from the Federal Government in the above two ways may freely pay the Treasury of the United States for such property, if and in the amount that they desire to do so.

Sec. 6. Reaffirmation of the Tenth Amendment of the Constitution. It is reaffirmed that, according to the Tenth Amendment of the Constitution of the United States, and implied by the Constitution before it was ever amended, all housing and urban development powers are reserved to the States respectively, or to the People, and, therefore, nothing regarding housing and urban development will henceforward be done by the Federal Government, without there first being a ratified amendment to the Constitution that gives power over housing and urban development to the Federal Government.

Sec. 7. Responsibilities of the People and their State Governments. Regarding the topic(s) of this Executive Order, the People and their respective State Governments, or the People alone, are urged to take care of anything previously attended to by the Federal Government. If any State desires to take action regarding a topic of this Executive Order, the Congress of the United States is urged to approve such State action so that the state may accomplish these or related things which were previously attended to by the Federal Government, if Congressional approval is Constitutionally required for the State to take such action.

Sec. 8. Pardons and Contracts. (a) A Full and Unconditional Pardon is hereby given to anyone who has been charged or convicted of any Federal crime or offense related to any of the unconstitutional laws that were deemed unenforceable according to this Executive Order.

(b) Regardless of any contracts or agreements that were signed or sworn to towards unconstitutional ends, anyone who exposes the Federal Government for doing anything unconstitutional, including the items outlined in this Executive Order, will be given a Full and Unconditional Pardon for exposing such unconstitutional Federal actions. Also, regardless of any contracts or agreements that were signed or sworn to towards unconstitutional ends, anyone who has exposed the Federal Government for doing anything unconstitutional, including the items outlined in this Executive Order, is hereby given a Full and Unconditional Pardon for exposing such unconstitutional Federal actions.

Sec. 9. General Provisions. (a) This order is not intended to, and does not, create any right or benefit, substantive or procedural, enforceable at law or in equity by any party against the United States, its departments, agencies, or entities, its officers, employees, or agents, or any other person.

(b) This order is not intended to, and does not, go against the Constitution of the United States. Everything in this order has the intent of restoring the supreme law of the land, which is the Constitution of the United States of America; if any part of this order is deemed as going against the Constitution, any remedy must be at the discretion of each individual charged with that remedy, including judges, officials, secretaries, and people at any and every level of government. Those individuals are each urged to ask if the remedy is Constitutional according to the original intent and spirit of the Constitution when written by our founding fathers in the seventeen hundreds. If any part of this order is ultimately deemed unconstitutional by any individual or institution, all other parts of this order will remain in full force and effect in perpetuity, or until the Constitution is amended or superseded.

[THE NAME AND SIGNATURE OF THE PRESIDENT OF THE UNITED STATES]

THE WHITE HOUSE,

[Date].

Transportation Department

Why can't we trust the states and the people to finance and build their own roads, bridges, airports, and seaports? They can, and that's what the founders intended when they wrote the Constitution. We know that commerce among the states does not include building roads or other public works like that. Here's one reason why, as mentioned before:

The preeminent constitutional expert President James Madison wrote the following in 1817 when vetoing a bill trying to fund roads and other means of transportation. He essentially said that "regulating commerce" did not mean building roads when the Constitution was written. He wrote:

> "The power to regulate commerce among the several States" cannot include a power to construct roads and canals, and to improve the navigation of water courses in order to facilitate, promote, and secure such a commerce without a latitude of construction departing from the ordinary import of the terms strengthened by the known inconveniences which doubtless led to the grant of this remedial power to Congress.[99]

The Transportation Department and all its subentities must be immediately dissolved, except for part of the Maritime Administration and the Saint Lawrence Seaway Development Corporation, as described below. In case there's any question on whether the states and the people can handle the transportation issue, each of the 50 states already has its own equivalent of a department of transportation.[100]

Components of the Transportation Department:

- Federal Aviation Administration - This is unconstitutional. It might be scary to think that Air Traffic control will be lost, but I think there will be a fairly seamless transition when this and other duties of the FAA are taken over by the people, airlines, airports and/or the states. This is an example of the importance of the people, corporations, and states knowing ahead of time that a President will carry out these executive orders, and when he will carry them out.
- Federal Highway Administration - This is unconstitutional. Highways are a state's right. Think of how much fairer it is for the states and people to allocate money to this than the Federal Government. Right now, people taxed across the nation have to pay for up to 95% of the cost of some interstate highways, and the states only pay 5%.[101] That means that a politically powerful state in the Federal Congress could get much better roads that another state. I see this all of the time. It seems like Maryland's interstate highways are much nicer that Pennsylvania's (my home state), and the state of Maryland is probably only paying 10% of that cost, whereas the nation at large is footing 90% of the bill. I don't want to pay Maryland's road building bill, and it makes no sense for me to do so.

- Federal Motor Carrier Safety Administration – Unconstitutional.
- Federal Railroad Administration - Unconstitutional.
- Federal Transit Administration - This is unconstitutional. It is meant to assist local public transportation efforts and should be left up to the private sector and the states.
- Maritime Administration - This agency is primarily responsible for the U.S. Merchant Marine. To the extent that the Merchant Marine is an extension of the Navy, it is Constitutional, but any activities involving commercial shipping, when done by the Federal Government, are unconstitutional.
- National Highway Traffic Safety Administration - Unconstitutional.
- Pipeline and Hazardous Materials Safety Administration - Unconstitutional.
- Saint Lawrence Seaway Development Corporation - This agency helps the flow of trade along the Great Lakes. This is unconstitutional and should be left up to the states and the people, except to the extent that this creates regulations for international trade. That legal portion should be moved under the Department of Commerce.
- Commercial Space Transportation Office – Unconstitutional. It regulates the private space industry.
- Office of Motor Carrier Safety - Unconstitutional.
- Research and Innovative Technology Administration - Unconstitutional.

- Research and Special Programs Administration - Unconstitutional. But has already been abolished.
- Transportation Statistics Bureau - Unconstitutional.

The Executive Order related to the Transportation Department:

Executive Order Immediately Dissolving the United States Department of Transportation

EXECUTIVE ORDER

- - - - - - -

IMMEDIATELY DISSOLVING THE UNITED STATES DEPARTMENT OF TRANSPORTATION

By the authority vested in me as President by the Constitution and the laws of the United States of America, it is hereby affirmed, declared, and ordered as follows:

Section 1. Policy. It is the policy of the United States to have no involvement in matters regarding transportation when not directly associated with carrying out a power given to it by the Constitution of the United States.

Sec. 2. Constitutionality. The United States Department of Transportation is unconstitutional. The term "transportation" is not contained in the Constitution of the United States of America except in an amendment that was repealed, and in the repeal amendment, and no power regarding transportation is given to the Federal Government or its Legislature in the Constitution. The following entities from the Department of Transportation are entirely unconstitutional and must immediately cease functioning: Federal Aviation Administration, Federal Highway Administration, Federal Motor Carrier Safety Administration, Federal Railroad Administration, Federal Transit Administration, National Highway Traffic Safety Administration, Pipeline and Hazardous Materials Safety Administration, Commercial Space Transportation Office, Office of Motor Carrier Safety, Research and Innovative Technology Administration, and Transportation Statistics Bureau. Maritime Administration - This agency is primarily responsible for the U.S. Merchant Marine, to the extent that the Merchant Marine is an extension of the Navy it is Constitutional, but any activities involving commercial shipping, when done by the Federal Government, are unconstitutional and must cease immediately, any Constitutional portions are now a part of the Navy and henceforward are not part of the Department of Transportation; Saint Lawrence Seaway Development Corporation - It is unconstitutional for this agency to help the flow of trade along the Great Lakes, this function must cease immediately, and must be left up to the states and the people, except to the extent that this creates regulations for international trade, that legal portion should be moved under the Department of Commerce and henceforward is not part of the Department of Transportation.

Sec. 3. Presidential Duty and Immediacy. According to the President's duty to uphold the Constitution of the United States of America, as the President has sworn or affirmed to uphold such Constitution, all sections of this executive order will be immediately understood and carried out by all branches of the United States Federal Government as it pertains to them, without regard to any court order that goes against the Constitution.

Sec. 4. Unenforceable Laws. Any laws, regulations, acts, or other legislation of the Federal Government that unconstitutionally provide for or regulate transportation will henceforward cease to be executed and will continue to cease to be executed unless and until the Constitution of the United States is amended to give Congress or the Federal Government the power to make laws regarding general transportation.

Sec. 5. Ending the Department. The United States Department of Transportation will immediately cease to function, and any obligations owed by the United States Department of Transportation to its servants or from the United States Department of Transportation to other entities will be taken over by the Federal Government in accordance with its historical commitment to pay debts, as Congress may prescribe.

The Secretary of Transportation will remain in his or her position for ninety days to make sure that all unconstitutional transportation functions throughout the Federal Government are eradicated and to make sure that transportation is firmly in the hands of the people and their respective States. The Secretary of Transportation will give a report to the President on how general transportation matters have been eradicated from the Federal Government, and will permanently leave his or her office when ninety days have passed.

Everyone working at the United States Department of Transportation must permanently leave their respective Department offices or places of work immediately. Any State Government or other entity may reemploy any Federal worker who has lost a job in this way, to work in a similar or a different capacity.

Any property that was not taken by Constitutional Departments, which was owned by the United States Department of Transportation, will now be the property of the governments of the respective State, the District of Columbia, or the United States Territory where the property is situated. If the property is not contained in one of these locations, it will immediately come into the control of the first State government which has a representative at the property physically to claim the property. If two or more States lay claim to property at the same time, they may agree among themselves as to who will own the property, or they will share it among themselves. Any State, the District of Columbia, or any United States Territory that acquires property from the Federal Government in the above two ways may freely pay the Treasury of the United States for such property, if and in the amount that they desire to do so.

Sec. 6. Reaffirmation of the Tenth Amendment of the Constitution. It is reaffirmed that, according to the Tenth Amendment of the Constitution of the United States, and implied by the Constitution before it was ever amended, all general transportation powers are reserved to the States respectively, or to the People, and, therefore, nothing regarding general transportation will henceforward be done by the Federal Government, without there first being a ratified amendment to the Constitution that gives power over general transportation to the Federal Government.

Sec. 7. Responsibilities of the People and their State Governments. Regarding the topic(s) of this Executive Order, the People and their respective State Governments, or the People alone, are urged to take care of anything previously attended to by the Federal Government. If any State desires to take action regarding a topic of this Executive Order, the Congress of the United States is urged to approve such State action so that the state may accomplish these or related things which were previously attended to by the Federal Government, if Congressional approval is Constitutionally required for the State to take such action.

Sec. 8. Pardons and Contracts. (a) A Full and Unconditional Pardon is hereby given to anyone who has been charged or convicted of any Federal crime or offense related to any of the unconstitutional laws that were deemed unenforceable according to this Executive Order.

(b) Regardless of any contracts or agreements that were signed or sworn to towards unconstitutional ends, anyone who exposes the Federal Government for doing anything unconstitutional, including the items outlined in this Executive Order, will be given a Full and Unconditional Pardon for exposing such unconstitutional Federal actions. Also, regardless of any contracts or agreements that were signed or sworn to towards unconstitutional ends, anyone who has exposed the Federal Government for doing anything unconstitutional, including the items outlined in this Executive Order, is hereby given a Full and Unconditional Pardon for exposing such unconstitutional Federal actions.

Sec. 9. General Provisions. (a) This order is not intended to, and does not, create any right or benefit, substantive or procedural, enforceable at law or in equity by any party against the United States, its departments, agencies, or entities, its officers, employees, or agents, or any other person.

(b) This order is not intended to, and does not, go against the Constitution of the United States. Everything in this order has the intent of restoring the supreme law of the land, which is the Constitution of the United States of America; if any part of this order is deemed as going against the Constitution, any remedy must be at the discretion of each individual charged with that remedy, including judges, officials, secretaries, and people at any and every level of government. Those individuals are each urged to ask if the remedy is Constitutional according to the original intent and spirit of the Constitution when written by our founding fathers in the seventeen hundreds. If any part of this order is ultimately deemed unconstitutional by any individual or institution, all other parts of this order will remain in full force and effect in perpetuity, or until the Constitution is amended or superseded.

[THE NAME AND SIGNATURE OF THE PRESIDENT OF THE UNITED STATES]

THE WHITE HOUSE,

[Date].

Energy Department

Energy is totally the right of the people and the states and not the responsibility of the Federal Government.

Unfortunately, defense has been mixed into this department as some of its responsibility is for creating nuclear weapons. To the extent that these weapons are for the Navy or the Army, this function is Constitutional and should immediately be moved into the Defense Department.

To the extent that the Federal Energy Regulatory Commission is creating regulations for international commerce, it is Constitutional and should be moved into the Commerce Department.

After these moves occur, this department should be entirely dissolved because it is unconstitutional.

Components of the Energy Department:

- Energy Efficiency and Renewable Energy Office - It's about researching clean, renewable energy. This is unconstitutional. It was formed in 1981 with no Constitutional amendment to allow for it.[102]

- Energy Information Administration – Unconstitutional.

- Federal Energy Regulatory Commission - This deals with electricity and natural gas regulations. International commerce that is regulated can continue to exist, but this should be put under the Commerce Department. Any regulations not part of an international commercial transaction is unconstitutional and must be declared illegal.

- Southwestern Power Administration - These guys sell Federally-run hydroelectric dam power. Selling the energy and the Federal running of dams are both unconstitutional.

- Western Area Power Administration - Another federal power seller, this needs to be instantly taken over by the states in which it resides, because it's unconstitutional.

- National Nuclear Security Administration - This is Constitutional when providing weapons for the Navy or Army.
- Alaska Power Administration - Unconstitutional. It's directly part of the Department of Energy, now.
- Bonneville Power Administration - Unconstitutional. It's in the Pacific Northwest.
- Energy Research Office - Unconstitutional.
- Environment Office, Energy Department – Unconstitutional.
- Hearings and Appeals Office, Energy Department - Unconstitutional.
- Minority Economic Impact Office – Unconstitutional.
- Nuclear Energy Office - Unconstitutional.
- Southeastern Power Administration – Unconstitutional.

The Executive Order related to the Energy Department:

Executive Order Immediately Dissolving the United States Department of Energy (to be modified to allow for Air and Space weapons if an Air and Space Forces amendment is ratified)

EXECUTIVE ORDER

- - - - - - -

IMMEDIATELY DISSOLVING THE UNITED STATES DEPARTMENT OF ENERGY

By the authority vested in me as President by the Constitution and the laws of the United States of America, it is hereby affirmed, declared, and ordered as follows:

Section 1. Policy. It is the policy of the United States to have no involvement in matters regarding energy when not directly associated with carrying out a power given to it by the Constitution of the United States.

Sec. 2. Constitutionality. The United States Department of Energy is unconstitutional. The term "energy" is not contained in the Constitution of the United States of America and no power regarding energy is ever given to the Federal Government or its Legislature in the Constitution. The following entities from the Department of Energy are entirely unconstitutional and must immediately cease functioning: Energy Efficiency and Renewable Energy Office; Energy Information Administration; Southwestern Power Administration; Western Area Power Administration; Alaska Power Administration; Bonneville Power Administration; Energy Research Office; Environment Office, Energy Department; Hearings and Appeals Office, Energy Department; Minority Economic Impact Office; Nuclear

Energy Office; and Southeastern Power Administration. Federal Energy Regulatory Commission - International commerce that is regulated by this Commission can continue, but will immediately be put under the Commerce Department, any regulations not regarding an international commercial transaction are unconstitutional and must cease immediately, the Constitutional portion of this Commission is henceforward not part of the Department of Energy; National Nuclear Security Administration - This is Constitutional when providing weapons for the Navy or Army, all other functions of this Administration must immediately cease, the Constitutional portion of this Administration will immediately become part of the Department of Defense and henceforward is not a part of the Department of Energy.

Sec. 3. Presidential Duty and Immediacy. According to the President's duty to uphold the Constitution of the United States of America, as the President has sworn or affirmed to uphold such Constitution, all sections of this executive order will be immediately understood and carried out by all branches of the United States Federal Government as it pertains to them, without regard to any court order that goes against the Constitution.

Sec. 4. Unenforceable Laws. Any laws, regulations, acts, or other legislation of the Federal Government that unconstitutionally provide for or regulate energy will henceforward cease to be executed and will continue to cease to be executed unless and until the Constitution of the United States is amended to give Congress or the Federal Government the power to make laws regarding energy.

Sec. 5. Ending the Department. The United States Department of Energy will immediately cease to function, and any obligations owed by the United States Department of Energy to its servants or from the United States Department of Energy to other entities will be taken over by the Federal Government in accordance with its historical commitment to pay debts, as Congress may prescribe.

The Secretary of Energy will remain in his or her position for ninety days to make sure that all unconstitutional energy functions throughout the Federal Government are eradicated and to make sure that energy is firmly in the hands of the people and their respective States. The Secretary of Energy will give a report to the President on how energy matters have been eradicated from the Federal Government, and will permanently leave his or her office when ninety days have passed.

Everyone working at the United States Department of Energy must permanently leave their respective Department offices or places of work immediately. Any State Government or other entity may reemploy any Federal worker who has lost a job in this way, to work in a similar or a different capacity.

Any property that was not taken by Constitutional Departments, which was owned by the United States Department of Energy, will now be the property of the governments of the respective State, the District of Columbia, or the United States Territory where the property is situated. If the property is not contained in one of these locations, it will immediately come into the control of the first State government which has a representative at the property physically to claim the property. If two or more States lay claim to property at the same time, they may agree among themselves as to who will own the property, or they will share it among themselves. Any State, the District of Columbia, or any United States Territory that acquires property from the Federal Government in the above two ways may freely pay the Treasury of the United States for such property, if and in the amount that they desire to do so.

Sec. 6. Reaffirmation of the Tenth Amendment of the Constitution. It is reaffirmed that, according to the Tenth Amendment of the Constitution of the United States, and implied by the Constitution before it was ever amended, all energy powers are reserved to the States respectively, or to the People, and, therefore, nothing regarding general energy powers will henceforward be done by the Federal Government, without there first being a ratified amendment to the Constitution that gives power over general energy to the Federal Government.

Sec. 7. Responsibilities of the People and their State Governments. Regarding the topic(s) of this Executive Order, the People and their respective State Governments, or the People alone, are urged to take care of anything previously attended to by the Federal Government. If any State desires to take action regarding a topic of this Executive Order, the Congress of the United States is urged to approve such State action so that the state may accomplish these or related things which were previously attended to by the Federal Government, if Congressional approval is Constitutionally required for the State to take such action.

Sec. 8. Pardons and Contracts. (a) A Full and Unconditional Pardon is hereby given to anyone who has been charged or convicted of any Federal crime or offense related to any of the unconstitutional laws that were deemed unenforceable according to this Executive Order.

(b) Regardless of any contracts or agreements that were signed or sworn to towards unconstitutional ends, anyone who exposes the Federal Government for doing anything unconstitutional, including the items outlined in this Executive Order, will be given a Full and Unconditional Pardon for exposing such unconstitutional Federal actions. Also, regardless of any contracts or agreements that were signed or sworn to towards unconstitutional ends, anyone who has exposed the Federal Government for doing anything unconstitutional, including the items outlined in this Executive Order, is hereby given a Full

and Unconditional Pardon for exposing such unconstitutional Federal actions.

Sec. 9. General Provisions. (a) This order is not intended to, and does not, create any right or benefit, substantive or procedural, enforceable at law or in equity by any party against the United States, its departments, agencies, or entities, its officers, employees, or agents, or any other person.

(b) This order is not intended to, and does not, go against the Constitution of the United States. Everything in this order has the intent of restoring the supreme law of the land, which is the Constitution of the United States of America; if any part of this order is deemed as going against the Constitution, any remedy must be at the discretion of each individual charged with that remedy, including judges, officials, secretaries, and people at any and every level of government. Those individuals are each urged to ask if the remedy is Constitutional according to the original intent and spirit of the Constitution when written by our founding fathers in the seventeen hundreds. If any part of this order is ultimately deemed unconstitutional by any individual or institution, all other parts of this order will remain in full force and effect in perpetuity, or until the Constitution is amended or superseded.

[THE NAME AND SIGNATURE OF THE PRESIDENT OF THE UNITED STATES]

THE WHITE HOUSE,

[Date].

Education Department

This department is my personal pet peeve. Education is the last place, perhaps in the entire universe, where we should want government involvement. This is because when government educates our children, it is likely teaching the children the benefits of government, with no countervailing argument on the problems of government.

Whenever the government mandates that only one side of an argument be taught, things get skewed toward that side of the argument. Therefore, government-run education is the best way to ensure a growing, overbearing government.

I only need to mention four words to make most American teachers cringe, "No Child Left Behind." Education is totally and utterly to be left up to the states and the people according to the Constitution. This department needs to be dissolved immediately.

The words Educate, Education, Teach, Teaching, Teacher, School, and Schools do not even exist in the Constitution, and Federal actions on these issues are unconstitutional. Education became its own department in 1977 under Jimmy Carter.

Stopping Federal involvement in education would be entirely seamless because the states and the people can take care of any education-related things. All 50 states have their own equivalent of a department of edu-cation.[103]

No Child Left Behind is a great example of the Federal Government messing things up. It was signed into law in 2002 by President George W. Bush.[104] Under this act, children are under immense pressure to do well in standardized exams because school funding depends on their performance. I remember hearing complaints that mentally disabled children were held to perform to the same standard as everyone else.

This law was such a horrible disaster that it was replaced by the Every Student Succeeds Act, signed by President Barack Obama in 2015. The new act puts more power over education in the hands of the states but does not remove the federal government's power entirely, as it should.[105]

The closer education is to the people, the better it is. I hope that states (regardless of intrusion attempts by the federal government) enact school voucher systems, where parents can take the money intended for use in a particular district and use it for any school where they would like to send their children. This makes education more like a market, with more competition. Competition typically leads to better services at a lower cost, but this is an issue for the states to decide, not this book.

In order to show that "closer" education is better education, let's go over the fact that private education is better than public education. Private education tends to be closer to those it serves because it is run locally, whereas public education tends to have State and Federal rulers who are in some city far away. It's nice, and parents get to choose where they send their kids to private school regardless of where they live, unlike most public schools.

Directly from the Council for American Private Education's website, here are some facts I selected on the benefits of private schooling. In America:

- Private school students perform better than their public school counterparts on standardized achievement tests.
- Sixty-seven percent of private high school graduates attend four-year colleges compared to 40 percent of public high school graduates.
- Private school students from low socio-economic backgrounds are more than three times more likely than comparable public school students to attain a bachelor's degree by their mid-20s, which means that private schools contribute to breaking the cycle of poverty for their students.
- Private schools are racially, ethnically, and economically diverse. Twenty-seven percent of private school students are students of color; 27 percent are from families with annual incomes under $75,000 (another 18 percent of families did not report income).[106]

What about the cost of education? In the United States, for the 2011-2012 school year, the average tuition at private schools was $10,740 per child.[107] In 2011, the spending per student for public schools was

$10,608.28.[108]

The tuition and cost for these two methods of education are virtually the same, yet private education tends to be much better. Private education exists on a much smaller scale than public education in this country, so there could be great economies of scale to create more savings if every school were private, because many of those private schools could grow much larger.

Many private schools are run by churches, so the church could subsidize some of the expenses to drive tuition down. Because of this, costs per student could be higher than what is stated here, but that's the beauty of the government getting out of education entirely. The free market tends to make education higher quality and more affordable and encourages benefactors to take on some of the costs.

This department had no Components listed in the Federal Register Index.

The Executive Order related to the Education Department:

Executive Order Immediately Dissolving the United States Department of Education

EXECUTIVE ORDER

- - - - - - -

Eric Martin

IMMEDIATELY DISSOLVING THE UNITED STATES DEPARTMENT OF EDUCATION

By the authority vested in me as President by the Constitution and the laws of the United States of America, it is hereby affirmed, declared, and ordered as follows:

Section 1. Policy. It is the policy of the United States to have no involvement in the education of its people or its citizens when that education is not directly associated with carrying out a power given to it by the Constitution of the United States.

Sec. 2. Constitutionality. The United States Department of Education is unconstitutional. The United States Department of Education is unconstitutional. The term "education" is not contained in the Constitution of the United States of America and no power regarding general education is ever given to the Federal Government or its Legislature in the Constitution.

Sec. 3. Presidential Duty and Immediacy. According to the President's duty to uphold the Constitution of the United States of America, as the President has sworn or affirmed to uphold such Constitution, all sections of this executive order will be immediately understood and carried out by all branches of the United States Federal Government as it pertains to them, without regard to any court order that goes against the Constitution.

Sec. 4. Unenforceable Laws. Any laws, regulations, acts, or other legislation of the Federal Government that unconstitutionally provide for or regulate education will henceforward cease to be executed and will continue to cease to be executed unless and until the Constitution of the United States is amended to give Congress or the Federal Government the power to make laws regarding general education.

Sec. 5. Ending the Department. The United States Department of Education will immediately cease to function, and any obligations owed by the United States Department of Education to its servants or from the United States Department of Education to other entities will be taken over by the Federal Government in accordance with its historical commitment to pay debts, as Congress may prescribe.

The Secretary of Education will remain in his or her position for ninety days to make sure that all unconstitutional educational functions throughout the Federal Government are eradicated and to make sure that education is firmly in the hands of the people and their respective States. The Secretary of Education will give a report to the President on how general education matters have been eradicated from the Federal Government, and will permanently leave his or her office when ninety days have passed.

Anyone else working at the United States Department of Education, who is educating in relation to Constitutional activities, such as those related to War, will move to a Constitutional department that can absorb them, such as, in this case, the Department of Defense; the Constitutional Departments will take any property that is Constitutional in nature for their purposes, as they see fit.

Everyone else working at the United States Department of Education, who is not educating in relation to Constitutional activities, must permanently leave their respective Department offices or places of work immediately. Any State Government or other entity may reemploy any Federal worker who has lost a job in this way, to work in a similar or a different capacity.

Any property that was not taken by Constitutional Departments, which was owned by the United States Department of Education, will now be the property of the governments of the respective State, the District of Columbia, or the United States Territory where the property is situated. If the property is not contained in one of these locations, it will immediately come into the control of the first State government which has a representative at the property physically to claim the property. If two or more States lay claim to property at the same time, they may agree among themselves as to who will own the property, or they will share it among themselves. Any State, the District of Columbia, or any United States Territory that acquires property from the

Federal Government in the above two ways may freely pay the Treasury of the United States for such property, if and in the amount that they desire to do so.

Sec. 6. Reaffirmation of the Tenth Amendment of the Constitution. It is reaffirmed that, according to the Tenth Amendment of the Constitution of the United States, and implied by the Constitution before it was ever amended, all general education powers are reserved to the States respectively, or to the People, and, therefore, nothing regarding general education will henceforward be done by the Federal Government, without there first being a ratified amendment to the Constitution that gives power over general education to the Federal Government.

Sec. 7. Responsibilities of the People and their State Governments. Regarding the topic(s) of this Executive Order, the People and their respective State Governments, or the People alone, are urged to take care of anything previously attended to by the Federal Government. If any State desires to take action regarding a topic of this Executive Order, the Congress of the United States is urged to approve such State action so that the state may accomplish these or related things which were previously attended to by the Federal Government, if Congressional approval is Constitutionally required for the State to take such action.

Sec. 8. Pardons and Contracts. (a) A Full and Unconditional Pardon is hereby given to anyone who has been charged or convicted of any Federal crime or offense related to any of the unconstitutional laws that were deemed unenforceable according to this Executive Order.

(b) Regardless of any contracts or agreements that were signed or sworn to towards unconstitutional ends, anyone who exposes the Federal Government for doing anything unconstitutional, including the items outlined in this Executive Order, will be given a Full and Unconditional Pardon for exposing such unconstitutional Federal actions. Also, regardless of any contracts or agreements that were signed or sworn to towards unconstitutional ends, anyone who has exposed the Federal Government for doing anything unconstitutional, including the items outlined in this Executive Order, is hereby given a Full and Unconditional Pardon for exposing such unconstitutional Federal actions.

Sec. 9. General Provisions. (a) This order is not intended to, and does not, create any right or benefit, substantive or procedural, enforceable at law or in equity by any party against the United States, its departments, agencies, or entities, its officers, employees, or agents, or any other person.

(b) This order is not intended to, and does not, go against the Constitution of the United States. Everything in this order has the intent of restoring the supreme law of the land, which is the Constitution of the United States of America; if any part of this order is deemed as going against the Constitution, any remedy must be at the discretion of each individual charged with that remedy, including judges, officials, secretaries, and people at any and every level of government. Those individuals are each urged to ask if the remedy is Constitutional according to the original intent and spirit of the Constitution when written by our founding fathers in the seventeen hundreds. If any part of this order is ultimately deemed unconstitutional by any individual or institution, all other parts of this order will remain in full force and effect in perpetuity, or until the Constitution is amended or superseded.

[THE NAME AND SIGNATURE OF THE PRESIDENT OF THE UNITED STATES]

THE WHITE HOUSE,

[Date].

Veterans Affairs Department

When administered by laws directly by Congress, this department is constitutional because it pays military personnel what they are owed in the form of benefits. So, this Department can exist, but personally, I think virtually all of the functions of this Department should be privatized, and choice should be given to veterans on where they would like to receive care. However, this is a matter for Congress to decide.

Homeland Security Department

This department was created in 2002 by President George W. Bush in response to the terrorist attacks on September 11th, 2001. It is unnecessary as its Constitutional functions should be under the Department of Defense.

Components of the Homeland Security Department:

- Coast Guard - This should be transferred to be part of the Navy to make it Constitutional.
- Federal Emergency Management Agency - This agency was started through executive order by president Jimmy Carter in 1979.[109] It is totally unconstitutional as the word emergency doesn't exist in the Constitution. This is something that needs to be left up to the states and the people.
- Transportation Security Administration - These are the "guards" at airports who often seem to be doing nothing. It is totally unconstitutional, and I believe private individuals, private airports, and private airlines would do a much better job of providing security for aviation than the Federal Government. This agency must be dissolved immediately.
- U.S. Citizenship and Immigration Services - This is somewhat Constitutional, as rules for citizenship are clearly delegated to the Congress in the Constitution as the "Rule of Naturalization"; however, immigration is not a power given to Congress and must be left to the states and the people. The name of this agency

should be changed to "U.S. Citizenship Services," and it should be moved under the State Department.

- U.S. Customs and Border Protection - This is similar to the U.S. Citizenship and Immigration Services entity in that the Customs part is Constitutional. It should be called "U.S. Customs" and be moved under the Commerce Department. The "Border Protection" part should be dissolved as this is unconstitutional and is a right of the states and the people.

- U.S. Immigration and Customs Enforcement - The Customs part is Constitutional, but the Immigration part is not. This should be moved to the Department of Commerce and anything unconstitutional dissolved.

- Federal Law Enforcement Training Center - Mostly unconstitutional, like running law enforcement training centers in other countries. The only thing that can remain is training federal agents to enforce the few Constitutional Federal laws. Should be transferred to the Department of Justice.

- National Communications System - Constitutional. Should be transferred to the departments of defense and interior, depending on the function.

- Secret Service - Somewhat Constitutional. Move it to the Executive Office of the President. Its activities in preventing and investigating "financial institution fraud, identity theft, and computer fraud and computer-based attacks on our Nation's financial, banking, and telecommunications infrastructure" are unconstitutional.[110]

The Executive Order related to the Homeland Security Department:

Executive Order Immediately Dissolving the United States Department of Homeland Security

EXECUTIVE ORDER

- - - - - - -

IMMEDIATELY DISSOLVING THE UNITED STATES DEPARTMENT OF HOMELAND SECURITY

By the authority vested in me as President by the Constitution and the laws of the United States of America, it is hereby affirmed, declared, and ordered as follows:

Section 1. Policy. It is the policy of the United States to have no involvement in matters regarding homeland security when not directly associated with carrying out a power given to it by the Constitution of the United States.

Sec. 2. Constitutionality. The United States Department of Homeland Security is unconstitutional. The term "homeland" is not contained in the Constitution of the United States of America, the term "security" only appears once in the Constitution, and it is regarding the right to bear arms. The following entities from the Department of Homeland Security are entirely unconstitutional and must immediately cease functioning: Federal Emergency Management Agency, and Transportation Security Administration. Coast Guard - Must immediately become part of the Navy, it will henceforward no longer be a part of the Department of Homeland Security; U.S. Citizenship and Immigration Services - Rules for citizenship are clearly delegated to the Congress in the Constitution as the "Rule of Naturalization", but immigration is not a power given to Congress and this function must immediately cease, the name of this agency must be immediately changed to "U.S. Citizenship Services", it will immediately be moved under the Department of State, and it will henceforward no longer be a part of the Department of Homeland Security; U.S. Customs and Border Protection - The "Border Protection" function is unconstitutional and must cease immediately, the name must immediately be changed to "U.S. Customs", what remains must immediately be moved under the Department of Commerce, and it will henceforward no longer be a part of the Department of Homeland Security; U.S. Immigration and Customs Enforcement - The Immigration function is unconstitutional and must cease immediately, the Customs function is Constitutional and must immediately be moved under the Department of Commerce, anything else unconstitutional must cease immediately, and it will henceforward no longer be a part of the Department of Homeland Security; Federal Law

Enforcement Training Center - Running law enforcement training centers in other countries is unconstitutional and must cease immediately, all other functions are unconstitutional and must cease immediately, except for training federal agents to enforce the few Constitutional Federal laws, this Constitutional function may continue, and the Center will henceforward no longer be a part of the Department of Homeland Security but will immediately be under the Department of Justice; National Communications System - This Constitutional system must immediately be divided up and transferred to the Departments of Defense and the Interior, according to the function of each part of the system, and it will henceforward no longer be a part of the Department of Homeland Security; Secret Service - This Service must immediately be moved to the Executive Office of the President, its activities in preventing and investigating "financial institution fraud, identity theft, and computer fraud and computer-based attacks on our Nation's financial, banking, and telecommunications infrastructure" are unconstitutional and must cease immediately, and it will henceforward no longer be a part of the Department of Homeland Security.

Sec. 3. Presidential Duty and Immediacy. According to the President's duty to uphold the Constitution of the United States of America, as the President has sworn or affirmed to uphold such Constitution, all sections of this executive order will be immediately understood and carried out by all branches of the United States Federal

Government as it pertains to them, without regard to any court order that goes against the Constitution.

Sec. 4. Unenforceable Laws. Any laws, regulations, acts, or other legislation of the Federal Government that unconstitutionally provide for or regulate emergencies or transportation security will henceforward cease to be executed and will continue to cease to be executed unless and until the Constitution of the United States is amended to give Congress or the Federal Government the power to make laws regarding emergencies or transportation security.

Sec. 5. Ending the Department. The United States Department of Homeland Security will immediately cease to function, and any obligations owed by the United States Department of Homeland Security to its servants or from the United States Department of Homeland Security to other entities will be taken over by the Federal Government in accordance with its historical commitment to pay debts, as Congress may prescribe.

The Secretary of Homeland Security will remain in his or her position for ninety days to make sure that all unconstitutional emergency management and transportation security functions throughout the Federal Government are eradicated and to make sure that emergency management and transportation security is firmly in the hands of the people and their respective States. The Secretary of Homeland Security will give a report to the President on how emergency management and transportation security matters have been eradicated from the Federal Government, and will permanently leave his or her office when ninety days have passed.

Everyone working at the United States Department of Homeland Security must permanently leave their respective Department offices or places of work immediately. Any State Government or other entity may reemploy any Federal worker who has lost a job in this way, to work in a similar or a different capacity.

Any property that was not taken by Constitutional Departments, which was owned by the United States Department of Homeland Security, will now be the property of the governments of the respective State, the District of Columbia, or the United States Territory where the property is situated. If the property is not contained in one of these locations, it will immediately come into the control of the first State government which has a representative at the property physically to claim the property. If two or more States lay claim to property at the same time, they may agree among themselves as to who will own the property, or they will share it among themselves. Any State, the District of Columbia, or any United States Territory that acquires property from the Federal Government in the above two ways may freely pay the Treasury of the United States for such property, if and in the amount that they desire to do so.

Sec. 6. Reaffirmation of the Tenth Amendment of the Constitution. It is reaffirmed that, according to the Tenth Amendment of the Constitution of the United States, and implied by the Constitution before it was ever amended, all emergency management and transportation security powers are reserved to the States respectively, or to the People, and, therefore, nothing regarding emergency management or transportation security will henceforward be done by the Federal Government, without there first being a ratified amendment to the Constitution that gives power over emergency management or transportation security to the Federal Government.

Sec. 7. Responsibilities of the People and their State Governments. Regarding the topic(s) of this Executive Order, the People and their respective State Governments, or the People alone, are urged to take care of anything previously attended to by the Federal Government. If any State desires to take action regarding a topic of this Executive Order, the Congress of the United States is urged to approve such State action so that the state may accomplish these or related things which were previously attended to by the Federal Government, if Congressional approval is Constitutionally required for the State to take such action.

Sec. 8. Pardons and Contracts. (a) A Full and Unconditional Pardon is hereby given to anyone who has been charged or convicted of any Federal crime or offense related to any of the unconstitutional laws that were deemed unenforceable according to this Executive Order.

(b) Regardless of any contracts or agreements that were signed or sworn to towards unconstitutional ends, anyone who exposes the Federal Government for doing anything unconstitutional, including the items outlined in this Executive Order, will be given a Full and Unconditional Pardon for exposing such unconstitutional Federal actions. Also, regardless of any contracts or agreements that were signed or sworn to towards unconstitutional ends, anyone who has exposed the Federal Government for doing anything unconstitutional, including the items outlined in this Executive Order, is hereby given a Full and Unconditional Pardon for exposing such unconstitutional Federal actions.

Sec. 9. General Provisions. (a) This order is not intended to, and does not, create any right or benefit, substantive or procedural, enforceable at law or in equity by any party against the United States, its departments, agencies, or entities, its officers, employees, or agents, or any other person.

(b) This order is not intended to, and does not, go against the Constitution of the United States. Everything in this order has the intent of restoring the supreme law of the land, which is the Constitution of the United States of America; if any part of this order is deemed as going against the Constitution, any remedy must be at the discretion of each individual charged with that remedy, including judges, officials, secretaries, and people at any and every level of government. Those individuals are each urged to ask if the remedy is Constitutional according to the original intent and spirit of the Constitution when written by our founding fathers in the seventeen hundreds. If any part of this order is ultimately deemed unconstitutional by any individual or institution, all other parts of this order will remain in full force and effect in perpetuity, or until the Constitution is amended or superseded.

[THE NAME AND SIGNATURE OF THE PRESIDENT OF THE UNITED STATES]

THE WHITE HOUSE,

[Date].

This Concludes Each Cabinet Department of the Federal Government.

Isn't it shocking how far away we've gotten from the Constitution? Many, if not all, of our founders would be appalled. The fallout is a devastating defeat for our Congress, our People, our Justices, our States, and our Presidents. But the Liberation Day Plan is a victory that wipes out this massive set of problems. How could we allow such obvious, ongoing abuses to the governmental limits which our legislators, judges, and presidents swore or affirmed to uphold through our United States Constitution?

It's hard to comprehend how it happened, but I have hope that together, we can fix this. It may seem daunting, but when we look at each Federal entity, one at a time, it becomes pretty clear which ones are unconstitutional, and which ones are Constitutional.

As I said before, this book is meant to be one more stone on the foundation of Liberty that our nation has built. The work that was built by our founders may have crumbled to its very foundation. The time is now to get us back to a much smaller central government, and the time is now to allow the citizens and their states to do what they want to do without the incessant intrusion of the federal government. If we don't do it now, we may be too far gone to overcome the interests in Washington that have become entrenched.

Other Agencies and Entities

There are, unfortunately, many other agencies and entities in the federal government. This section will attempt to categorize them as constitutional, unconstitutional, or partly constitutional. If needed, there will be an executive order to get rid of the agency or bring it down to constitutional size. Some of the categorization may happen within the executive order since there are so many entities.

There are a few cabinet-level positions that have entities connected to them that I'd like to talk about first, since they are cabinet-level but not part of the cabinet.

White House Chief of Staff

This person works under the President. It's a good time to bring up the legitimacy of the entity that is the Presidency. It is legitimate under the Constitution, and the President has the power to execute the law - this is clearly written in the Constitution. The Chief of Staff is the closest cabinet-level position that embodies that power, and this person tends to be the "gatekeeper" to the President.[111]

Office of the United States Trade Representative

The President, with Senate approval, has the power to establish treaties with other countries that can tax trade. That the office was created in 1962 makes it suspect, but I believe this office is an extension of the treaty power. Its offices in other countries are not Constitutional since they are not primarily serving ambassadors, which is the only official (and their underlings) which can have U.S. offices outside of the United States. All the trade officers in foreign countries need to immediately close their office or come under the authority of an ambassador. The order:

Executive Order Immediately Closing All Offices of Trade Officers or Moving Them Under the Authority of an Ambassador

EXECUTIVE ORDER

- - - - - - -

IMMEDIATELY CLOSING ALL OFFICES OF TRADE OFFICERS OR MOVING THEM UNDER THE AUTHORITY OF AN AMBASSADOR

By the authority vested in me as President by the Constitution and the laws of the United States of America, it is hereby affirmed, declared, and ordered as follows:

Section 1. Policy. It is the policy of the United States to have no trade officers in foreign countries not directly under the authority of an ambassador.

Sec. 2. Constitutionality. The Constitution only provides for ambassadors, not trade officers.

Sec. 3. Presidential Duty and Immediacy. According to the President's duty to uphold the Constitution of the United States of America, as the President has sworn or affirmed to uphold such Constitution, all sections of this executive order will be immediately understood and carried out by all branches of the United States Federal Government as it pertains to them, without regard to any court order that goes against the Constitution.

Sec. 4. Unenforceable Laws. Any laws, regulations, acts, or other legislation of the Federal Government that unconstitutionally provides for or regulates anything related to the areas served by the previously mentioned entities, and (if applicable) the functions of entities where particular functions have been ceased, will henceforward cease to be executed and will continue to cease to be executed unless and until the Constitution of the United States is amended to give Congress or the Federal Government the power to make laws regarding the areas served by the previously mentioned entities.

Sec. 5. Ending of a Role. All trade officers must immediately come under the supervision of an Ambassador; if they cannot do this, they must immediately leave their post and return themselves and all property of the United States back to the United States. Any property that cannot safely be returned shall be the property of the first state of the United States to claim it.

Sec. 6. Reaffirmation of the Tenth Amendment of the Constitution. It is reaffirmed that, according to the Tenth Amendment of the Constitution of the United States, and implied by the Constitution before it was ever amended, all powers of the previously mentioned entities are reserved to the States respectively, or to the People, and, therefore, none of the powers that these previously mentioned entities had will henceforward be exercised by the Federal Government, without there first being a ratified amendment to the Constitution that gives power over some area where these entities served to the Federal Government.

Sec. 7. Responsibilities of the People and their State Governments. Regarding the topic(s) of this Executive Order, the People and their respective State Governments, or the People alone, are urged to take care of anything previously attended to by the Federal Government. If any State desires to take action regarding a topic of this Executive Order, the Congress of the United States is urged to approve such State action so that the state may accomplish these or related things which were previously attended to by the Federal Government, if Congressional approval is Constitutionally required for the State to take such action.

Sec. 8. Pardons and Contracts. (a) A Full and Unconditional Pardon is hereby given to anyone who has been charged or convicted of any Federal crime or offense related to any of the unconstitutional laws that were deemed unenforceable according to this Executive Order.

(b) Regardless of any contracts or agreements that were signed or sworn to towards unconstitutional ends, anyone who exposes the Federal Government for doing anything unconstitutional, including the items outlined in this

Executive Order, will be given a Full and Unconditional Pardon for exposing such unconstitutional Federal actions. Also, regardless of any contracts or agreements that were signed or sworn to towards unconstitutional ends, anyone who has exposed the Federal Government for doing anything unconstitutional, including the items outlined in this Executive Order, is hereby given a Full and Unconditional Pardon for exposing such unconstitutional Federal actions.

Sec. 9. General Provisions. (a) This order is not intended to, and does not, create any right or benefit, substantive or procedural, enforceable at law or in equity by any party against the United States, its departments, agencies, or entities, its officers, employees, or agents, or any other person.

(b) This order is not intended to, and does not, go against the Constitution of the United States. Everything in this order has the intent of restoring the supreme law of the land, which is the Constitution of the United States of America; if any part of this order is deemed as going against the Constitution, any remedy must be at the discretion of each individual charged with that remedy, including judges, officials, secretaries, and people at any and every level of government. Those individuals are each urged to ask if the remedy is Constitutional according to the original intent and spirit of the Constitution when written by our founding fathers in the seventeen hundreds. If any part of this order is ultimately deemed unconstitutional by any individual or institution, all other parts of this order will remain in full force and effect in perpetuity, or until the Constitution is amended or superseded.

[THE NAME AND SIGNATURE OF THE PRESIDENT OF THE UNITED STATES]

THE WHITE HOUSE,

[Date].

Office of the Director of National Intelligence

Headed by the Director of National Intelligence, this entity can be considered Constitutional as long as it is carrying out and supporting other Constitutional powers, such as the war power, and the powers to have a navy and an army.

Ambassador to the United Nations

Here's an ugly one. The Federal Government has no Constitutional authority to join an organization that can make binding laws upon the United States. Only the Congress can write laws for the United States. We can send an ambassador to the United Nations simply as an observer, but we cannot be a member and must withdraw from the United Nations, as anything it or its Security Council passes can have no bearing on us. The order:

Executive Order Immediately Leaving the United Nations and a Declaration by the United States that It Gives No Authority for Any Law or Resolution that has Passed or ever will Pass in the United Nations

EXECUTIVE ORDER

- - - - - - -

IMMEDIATELY LEAVING THE UNITED NATIONS AND A DECLARATION BY THE UNITED STATES THAT IT GIVES NO AUTHORITY FOR ANY LAW OR RESOLUTION THAT HAS PASSED OR EVER WILL PASS IN THE UNITED NATIONS

By the authority vested in me as President by the Constitution and the laws of the United States of America, it is hereby affirmed, declared, and ordered as follows:

Section 1. Policy. It is the policy of the United States to not be involved in the United Nations in any way, or heed any of its laws or resolutions, except to send an observer to the body as an Ambassador to various nations.

Sec. 2. Constitutionality. The Constitution does not allow Congress to give its legislative powers to any other body; the United Nations can have no legislative power over the United States.

Sec. 3. Presidential Duty and Immediacy. According to the President's duty to uphold the Constitution of the United States of America, as the President has sworn or affirmed to uphold such Constitution, all sections of this executive order will be immediately understood and carried out by all branches of the United States Federal Government as it pertains to them, without regard to any court order that goes against the Constitution.

Sec. 4. Unenforceable Laws. Any laws, regulations, acts, or other legislation of the Federal Government that unconstitutionally provides for or regulates anything related to the areas served by the previously mentioned entities, and (if applicable) the functions of entities where particular functions have been ceased, will henceforward cease to be executed and will continue to cease to be executed unless and until the Constitution of the United States is amended to give Congress or the Federal Government the power to make laws regarding the areas served by the previously mentioned entities.

Sec. 5. Ending of Involvement. The United States is immediately and henceforward no longer involved with the United Nations and does not abide by any of its edicts.

Sec. 6. Reaffirmation of the Tenth Amendment of the Constitution. It is reaffirmed that, according to the Tenth Amendment of the Constitution of the United States, and implied by the Constitution before it was ever amended,

all powers of the previously mentioned entities are reserved to the States respectively, or to the People, and, therefore, none of the powers that these previously mentioned entities had will henceforward be exercised by the Federal Government, without there first being a ratified amendment to the Constitution that gives power over some area where these entities served to the Federal Government.

Sec. 7. Responsibilities of the People and their State Governments. Regarding the topic(s) of this Executive Order, the People and their respective State Governments, or the People alone, are urged to take care of anything previously attended to by the Federal Government. If any State desires to take action regarding a topic of this Executive Order, the Congress of the United States is urged to approve such State action so that the state may accomplish these or related things which were previously attended to by the Federal Government, if Congressional approval is Constitutionally required for the State to take such action.

Sec. 8. Pardons and Contracts. (a) A Full and Unconditional Pardon is hereby given to anyone who has been charged or convicted of any Federal crime or offense related to any of the unconstitutional laws that were deemed unenforceable according to this Executive Order.

(b) Regardless of any contracts or agreements that were signed or sworn to towards unconstitutional ends, anyone

who exposes the Federal Government for doing anything unconstitutional, including the items outlined in this Executive Order, will be given a Full and Unconditional Pardon for exposing such unconstitutional Federal actions. Also, regardless of any contracts or agreements that were signed or sworn to towards unconstitutional ends, anyone who has exposed the Federal Government for doing anything unconstitutional, including the items outlined in this Executive Order, is hereby given a Full and Unconditional Pardon for exposing such unconstitutional Federal actions.

Sec. 9. General Provisions. (a) This order is not intended to, and does not, create any right or benefit, substantive or procedural, enforceable at law or in equity by any party against the United States, its departments, agencies, or entities, its officers, employees, or agents, or any other person.

(b) This order is not intended to, and does not, go against the Constitution of the United States. Everything in this order has the intent of restoring the supreme law of the land, which is the Constitution of the United States of America; if any part of this order is deemed as going against the Constitution, any remedy must be at the discretion of each individual charged with that remedy, including judges, officials, secretaries, and people at any and every level of government. Those individuals are each urged to ask if the remedy is Constitutional according to the original intent and spirit of the Constitution when

written by our founding fathers in the seventeen hundreds. If any part of this order is ultimately deemed unconstitutional by any individual or institution, all other parts of this order will remain in full force and effect in perpetuity, or until the Constitution is amended or superseded.

[THE NAME AND SIGNATURE OF THE PRESIDENT OF THE UNITED STATES]

THE WHITE HOUSE,

[Date].

Office of Management and Budget

The president can create a budget.

Central Intelligence Agency (CIA)

This is a civilian (non-military) foreign intelligence gathering arm of the United States. It was created in 1947 after World War II with no Constitutional amendment. It is unconstitutional because it is non-military. The Army and Navy need to do the intelligence gathering under the Constitution. This agency needs to be dissolved immediately, and any necessary military intelligence operations from it should be immediately absorbed by the Army and Navy. The order:

Executive Order Immediately Dissolving the Central Intelligence Agency

EXECUTIVE ORDER

- - - - - - -

IMMEDIATELY DISSOLVING THE CENTRAL INTELLIGENCE AGENCY

By the authority vested in me as President by the Constitution and the laws of the United States of America, it is hereby affirmed, declared, and ordered as follows:

Section 1. Policy. It is the policy of the United States to not have a civilian Central Intelligence Agency.

Sec. 2. Constitutionality. The Constitution does not give Congress the power to create a civilian intelligence gathering entity.

Sec. 3. Presidential Duty and Immediacy. According to the President's duty to uphold the Constitution of the United States of America, as the President has sworn or affirmed to uphold such Constitution, all sections of this executive order will be immediately understood and carried out by all branches of the United States Federal

Government as it pertains to them, without regard to any court order that goes against the Constitution.

Sec. 4. Unenforceable Laws. Any laws, regulations, acts, or other legislation of the Federal Government that unconstitutionally provides for or regulates anything related to the areas served by the previously mentioned entities, and (if applicable) the functions of entities where particular functions have been ceased, will henceforward cease to be executed and will continue to cease to be executed unless and until the Constitution of the United States is amended to give Congress or the Federal Government the power to make laws regarding the areas served by the previously mentioned entities.

Sec. 5. Ending of the Agency. The Defense Department must immediately absorb any portions of the Central Intelligence Agency and their personnel that are performing Constitutional functions and are necessary for military intelligence, those absorbed portions and personnel are henceforward not a part of the Central Intelligence Agency. The United States must immediately and henceforward cease all operations of the Central Intelligence Agency.

Everyone working at the Central Intelligence Agency must permanently leave their respective entity offices or places of work immediately. Any State Government or other entity may reemploy any Federal worker who has lost a job in this way, to work in a similar or a different capacity.

All property of the Central Intelligence Agency will now be the property of the governments of the respective State, the District of Columbia, or the United States Territory where the property is situated. If the property is not contained in one of these locations, it will immediately come into the control of the first State government which has a representative at the property physically to claim the property. If two or more States lay claim to property at the same time, they may agree among themselves as to who will own the property, or they will share it among themselves. Any State, the District of Columbia, or any United States Territory that acquires property from the Federal Government in the above two ways may freely pay the Treasury of the United States for such property, if and in the amount that they desire to do so.

Sec. 6. Reaffirmation of the Tenth Amendment of the Constitution. It is reaffirmed that, according to the Tenth Amendment of the Constitution of the United States, and implied by the Constitution before it was ever amended, all powers of the previously mentioned entities are reserved to the States respectively, or to the People, and, therefore, none of the powers that these previously mentioned entities had will henceforward be exercised by the Federal Government, without there first being a ratified amendment to the Constitution that gives power over some area where these entities served to the Federal Government.

Sec. 7. Responsibilities of the People and their State Governments. Regarding the topic(s) of this Executive Order, the People and their respective State Governments, or the People alone, are urged to take care of anything previously attended to by the Federal Government. If any State desires to take action regarding a topic of this Executive Order, the Congress of the United States is urged to approve such State action so that the state may accomplish these or related things which were previously attended to by the Federal Government, if Congressional approval is Constitutionally required for the State to take such action.

Sec. 8. Pardons and Contracts. (a) A Full and Unconditional Pardon is hereby given to anyone who has been charged or convicted of any Federal crime or offense related to any of the unconstitutional laws that were deemed unenforceable according to this Executive Order.

(b) Regardless of any contracts or agreements that were signed or sworn to towards unconstitutional ends, anyone who exposes the Federal Government for doing anything unconstitutional, including the items outlined in this Executive Order, will be given a Full and Unconditional Pardon for exposing such unconstitutional Federal actions. Also, regardless of any contracts or agreements that were signed or sworn to towards unconstitutional ends, anyone who has exposed the Federal Government for doing anything unconstitutional, including the items outlined in this Executive Order, is hereby given a Full and Unconditional Pardon for exposing such unconstitutional Federal actions.

Sec. 9. General Provisions. (a) This order is not intended to, and does not, create any right or benefit, substantive or procedural, enforceable at law or in equity by any party against the United States, its departments, agencies, or entities, its officers, employees, or agents, or any other person.

(b) This order is not intended to, and does not, go against the Constitution of the United States. Everything in this order has the intent of restoring the supreme law of the land, which is the Constitution of the United States of America; if any part of this order is deemed as going against the Constitution, any remedy must be at the discretion of each individual charged with that remedy, including judges, officials, secretaries, and people at any and every level of government. Those individuals are each urged to ask if the remedy is Constitutional according to the original intent and spirit of the Constitution when written by our founding fathers in the seventeen hundreds. If any part of this order is ultimately deemed unconstitutional by any individual or institution, all other parts of this order will remain in full force and effect in perpetuity, or until the Constitution is amended or superseded.

[THE NAME AND SIGNATURE OF THE PRESIDENT OF THE UNITED STATES]

THE WHITE HOUSE,

[Date].

Environmental Protection Agency (EPA)

Created in 1970 with no constitutional amendment, this agency is utterly unconstitutional and needs to be dissolved immediately. Every single state has at least one entity related to the environment.[112] Let's bring back federalism and get rid of double government! The order:

Executive Order Immediately Dissolving the Environmental Protection Agency

EXECUTIVE ORDER

- - - - - - -

IMMEDIATELY DISSOLVING THE ENVIRONMENTAL PROTECTION AGENCY

By the authority vested in me as President by the Constitution and the laws of the United States of America, it is hereby affirmed, declared, and ordered as follows:

Section 1. Policy. It is the policy of the United States to operate no entity that seeks to protect the domestic environment.

Sec. 2. Constitutionality. The Constitution does not give Congress the power to create or operate an entity that protects the environment.

Sec. 3. Presidential Duty and Immediacy. According to the President's duty to uphold the Constitution of the United States of America, as the President has sworn or affirmed to uphold such Constitution, all sections of this executive order will be immediately understood and carried out by all branches of the United States Federal Government as it pertains to them, without regard to any court order that goes against the Constitution.

Sec. 4. Unenforceable Laws. Any laws, regulations, acts, or other legislation of the Federal Government that unconstitutionally provides for or regulates anything related to the areas served by the previously mentioned entities, and (if applicable) the functions of entities where particular functions have been ceased, will henceforward cease to be executed and will continue to cease to be executed unless and until the Constitution of the United States is amended to give Congress or the Federal Government the power to make laws regarding the areas served by the previously mentioned entities.

Sec. 5. Ending of the Agency. The United States must immediately and henceforward cease all operations of the Environmental Protection Agency.

Everyone working at the Environmental Protection Agency must permanently leave their respective entity offices or places of work immediately. Any State Government or other entity may reemploy any Federal worker who has lost a job in this way, to work in a similar or a different capacity.

All property of the Environmental Protection Agency will now be the property of the governments of the respective State, the District of Columbia, or the United States Territory where the property is situated. If the property is not contained in one of these locations, it will immediately come into the control of the first State government which has a representative at the property physically to claim the property. If two or more States lay claim to property at the same time, they may agree among themselves as to who will own the property, or they will share it among themselves. Any State, the District of Columbia, or any United States Territory that acquires property from the Federal Government in the above two ways may freely pay the Treasury of the United States for such property, if and in the amount that they desire to do so.

Sec. 6. Reaffirmation of the Tenth Amendment of the Constitution. It is reaffirmed that, according to the Tenth Amendment of the Constitution of the United States, and

implied by the Constitution before it was ever amended, all powers of the previously mentioned entities are reserved to the States respectively, or to the People, and, therefore, none of the powers that these previously mentioned entities had will henceforward be exercised by the Federal Government, without there first being a ratified amendment to the Constitution that gives power over some area where these entities served to the Federal Government.

Sec. 7. Responsibilities of the People and their State Governments. Regarding the topic(s) of this Executive Order, the People and their respective State Governments, or the People alone, are urged to take care of anything previously attended to by the Federal Government. If any State desires to take action regarding a topic of this Executive Order, the Congress of the United States is urged to approve such State action so that the state may accomplish these or related things which were previously attended to by the Federal Government, if Congressional approval is Constitutionally required for the State to take such action.

Sec. 8. Pardons and Contracts. (a) A Full and Unconditional Pardon is hereby given to anyone who has been charged or convicted of any Federal crime or offense related to any of the unconstitutional laws that were deemed unenforceable according to this Executive Order.

(b) Regardless of any contracts or agreements that were signed or sworn to towards unconstitutional ends, anyone who exposes the Federal Government for doing anything unconstitutional, including the items outlined in this Executive Order, will be given a Full and Unconditional Pardon for exposing such unconstitutional Federal actions. Also, regardless of any contracts or agreements that were signed or sworn to towards unconstitutional ends, anyone who has exposed the Federal Government for doing anything unconstitutional, including the items outlined in this Executive Order, is hereby given a Full and Unconditional Pardon for exposing such unconstitutional Federal actions.

Sec. 9. General Provisions. (a) This order is not intended to, and does not, create any right or benefit, substantive or procedural, enforceable at law or in equity by any party against the United States, its departments, agencies, or entities, its officers, employees, or agents, or any other person.

(b) This order is not intended to, and does not, go against the Constitution of the United States. Everything in this order has the intent of restoring the supreme law of the land, which is the Constitution of the United States of America; if any part of this order is deemed as going against the Constitution, any remedy must be at the discretion of each individual charged with that remedy, including judges, officials, secretaries, and people at any and every level of government. Those individuals are each

urged to ask if the remedy is Constitutional according to the original intent and spirit of the Constitution when written by our founding fathers in the seventeen hundreds. If any part of this order is ultimately deemed unconstitutional by any individual or institution, all other parts of this order will remain in full force and effect in perpetuity, or until the Constitution is amended or superseded.

[THE NAME AND SIGNATURE OF THE PRESIDENT OF THE UNITED STATES]

THE WHITE HOUSE,

[Date].

Small Business Administration (SBA)

Created in 1953 with no constitutional amendment, this entity is unconstitutional and needs to be dissolved. This needs to be and can be fully taken care of by the states and/or the people. Big business has so much pull in Washington, and yet it has conveniently opted out of having a Big Business Administration. They want their power to be secret. The order:

Executive Order Immediately Dissolving the Small Business Administration

EXECUTIVE ORDER

- - - - - - -

IMMEDIATELY DISSOLVING THE SMALL BUSINESS ADMINISTRATION

By the authority vested in me as President by the Constitution and the laws of the United States of America, it is hereby affirmed, declared, and ordered as follows:

Section 1. Policy. It is the policy of the United States to operate no entity that seeks to support small businesses.

Sec. 2. Constitutionality. The Constitution does not give Congress the power to create or operate an entity that specifically supports business, whether that business is small, medium, or large.

Sec. 3. Presidential Duty and Immediacy. According to the President's duty to uphold the Constitution of the United States of America, as the President has sworn or affirmed to uphold such Constitution, all sections of this executive order will be immediately understood and carried out by all branches of the United States Federal Government as it pertains to them, without regard to any court order that goes against the Constitution.

Sec. 4. Unenforceable Laws. Any laws, regulations, acts, or other legislation of the Federal Government that unconstitutionally provides for or regulates anything related to the areas served by the previously mentioned entities, and (if applicable) the functions of entities where particular functions have been ceased, will henceforward cease to be executed and will continue to cease to be executed unless and until the Constitution of the United States is amended to give Congress or the Federal Government the power to make laws regarding the areas served by the previously mentioned entities.

Sec. 5. Ending of the Agency. The United States must immediately and henceforward cease all operations of the Small Business Administration.

Everyone working at the Small Business Administration must permanently leave their respective entity offices or places of work immediately. Any State Government or other entity may reemploy any Federal worker who has lost a job in this way, to work in a similar or a different capacity.

All property of the Small Business Administration will now be the property of the governments of the respective State, the District of Columbia, or the United States Territory where the property is situated. If the property is not contained in one of these locations, it will immediately come into the control of the first State government which has a representative at the property physically to claim the property. If two or more States lay claim to property at the same time, they may agree among themselves as to who will own the property, or they will share it among themselves. Any State, the District of Columbia, or any United States Territory that acquires property from the Federal Government in the above two ways may freely pay the Treasury of the United States for such property, if and in the amount that they desire to do so.

Sec. 6. Reaffirmation of the Tenth Amendment of the Constitution. It is reaffirmed that, according to the Tenth Amendment of the Constitution of the United States, and implied by the Constitution before it was ever amended, all powers of the previously mentioned entities are reserved to the States respectively, or to the People, and, therefore, none of the powers that these previously mentioned entities had will henceforward be exercised by the Federal Government, without there first being a ratified amendment to the Constitution that gives power over some area where these entities served to the Federal Government.

Sec. 7. Responsibilities of the People and their State Governments. Regarding the topic(s) of this Executive Order, the People and their respective State Governments, or the People alone, are urged to take care of anything previously attended to by the Federal Government. If any State desires to take action regarding a topic of this Executive Order, the Congress of the United States is urged to approve such State action so that the state may accomplish these or related things which were previously attended to by the Federal Government,

if Congressional approval is Constitutionally required for the State to take such action.

Sec. 8. Pardons and Contracts. (a) A Full and Unconditional Pardon is hereby given to anyone who has been charged or convicted of any Federal crime or offense related to any of the unconstitutional laws that were deemed unenforceable according to this Executive Order.

(b) Regardless of any contracts or agreements that were signed or sworn to towards unconstitutional ends, anyone who exposes the Federal Government for doing anything unconstitutional, including the items outlined in this Executive Order, will be given a Full and Unconditional Pardon for exposing such unconstitutional Federal actions. Also, regardless of any contracts or agreements that were signed or sworn to towards unconstitutional ends, anyone who has exposed the Federal Government for doing anything unconstitutional, including the items outlined in this Executive Order, is hereby given a Full and Unconditional Pardon for exposing such unconstitutional Federal actions.

Sec. 9. General Provisions. (a) This order is not intended to, and does not, create any right or benefit, substantive or procedural, enforceable at law or in equity by any party against the United States, its departments, agencies, or entities, its officers, employees, or agents, or any other person.

(b) This order is not intended to, and does not, go against the Constitution of the United States. Everything in this order has the intent of restoring the supreme law of the land, which is the Constitution of the United States of America; if any part of this order is deemed as going against the Constitution, any remedy must be at the discretion of each individual charged with that remedy, including judges, officials, secretaries, and people at any and every level of government. Those individuals are each urged to ask if the remedy is Constitutional according to the original intent and spirit of the Constitution when written by our founding fathers in the seventeen hundreds. If any part of this order is ultimately deemed unconstitutional by any individual or institution, all other parts of this order will remain in full force and effect in perpetuity, or until the Constitution is amended or superseded.

[THE NAME AND SIGNATURE OF THE PRESIDENT OF THE UNITED STATES]

THE WHITE HOUSE,

[Date].

Other Entities in the Federal Government

That is the end of all the cabinet-level positions. There are 440 entities in the Federal Government that are not part of any cabinet-level Department or entity, according to the list of the Federal Register as of March 20th, 2017.[113] We've gone through dozens of them so far. Forty entities of those 440 will be listed just below because, as far as I can tell, they are already defunct, dissolved, inactive, or have been privatized. They will not be part of the rest of this section. Many of these entities would be illegal and unconstitutional if they functioned today.

The 40 Inactive or Privatized Entities:

International Development Cooperation Agency; Air Quality National Commission; Antitrust Modernization Commission; Assassination Records Review Board; Census Monitoring Board; Christopher Columbus Quincentenary Jubilee Commission; Commission on Immigration Reform; Commission on Protecting and Reducing Government Secrecy; Commission on Review of Overseas Military Facility Structure of the United States; Commission on Structural Alternatives for the Federal Courts of Appeals; Commission on the Advancement of Federal Law Enforcement; Commission on the Bicentennial of the United States Constitution; Competitiveness Policy Council; Defense Base Closure and Realignment Commission; Electronic Commerce Advisory Commission; Intergovernmental Relations Advisory Commission; Interstate Commerce Commission; National Bankruptcy Review Commission; National Commission on Intermodal Transportation; National Commission on Manufactured Housing; National Commission on Terrorist Attacks Upon the United States; National Commission on the Cost of Higher Education; National Education Goals Panel; National Gambling Impact Study Commission; National Partnership for Reinventing Government (I think this is defunct now); National Prison Rape Elimination Commission; Northeast Dairy Compact Commission; Ocean Policy Commission; Panama Canal Commission; President's Council on Sustainable Development; Presidential Advisory Committee on Gulf War Veterans' Illnesses; Presidential Commission on Assignment of Women in the Armed Forces; Prospective Payment Assessment Commission; Resolution Trust Corporation; Thrift Depositor Protection Oversight Board; Twenty-First Century Workforce Commission; U.S. Trade Deficit Review Commission; United States Enrichment Corporation (A company that does uranium enrichment. It's no longer Federally-owned because it has been privatized.); United States Information Agency; and Women's Progress Commemoration Commission.

In the rest of this section, I will first list all the remaining entities that are constitutional, along with a short idea related to some of them. Then, I will write the Executive Order to get rid of all the unconstitutional entities that includes a list of those entities within the Order. The list will sometimes include special instructions on how the entity must be dissolved. Finally, I will list entities that are partially unconstitutional within another Executive Order that describes what needs to be done with each of them. In all cases, I may provide context for what an entity is or does within parenthesis after the entity is listed. I have chosen this format to use fewer pages in the book than I would have used by listing them twice.

There are 48 entities that are constitutional:

Administrative Office of United States Courts (Helps administration of Federal courts); Architect of the Capitol; Armed Forces Retirement Home (Constitutional as pay for military); Committee for the Implementation of Textile Agreements (May only implement or recommend for treaties); Congressional Budget Office; Copyright Royalty Judges, Library of Congress; Council of the Inspectors General on Integrity and Efficiency (It OK for the executive branch to try to make sure government workers are efficient); Defense Nuclear Facilities Safety Board; Executive Council on Integrity and Efficiency (Stopping fraud is necessary and proper, and, given the size of our government, we might need a separate agency for it, rather than to let the President and his Cabinet do it more directly themselves); Executive Office of the President (Created in 1939, it helps the President to govern); Administration Office, Executive Office of the President (Created in 1977); Counsel to the President (Legal counsel started in 1943; hopefully the President's role will be so minimal because he's following the Constitution that we won't need this); Federal Accounting Standards Advisory Board; Federal Acquisition Regulation System; Federal Pay, Advisory Committee; Federal Register, Administrative Committee; Federal Retirement Thrift Investment Board (Allows additional savings to be invested by Federal employees; can be considered pay of employees, though I would recommend leaving this up to the private sector); Foreign Service Grievance Board (This is constitutional to the extent that it is serving diplomats and their underlings); General Services Administration (The nitty-gritty details of government, like Federal building maintenance); Geographic Names Board; Government Accountability Office; Government Ethics Office; Government Publishing Office; International Boundary and Water Commission, United States and Mexico (Deals with treaties between us); International Joint Commission-United States and Canada; International Trade Commission; Judicial Conference of the United States (They help run the courts); Library of Congress (Founded in 1800); Copyright Royalty Board; U.S. Copyright Office, Library of Congress; Federal Procurement Policy Office; Merit Systems Protection Board; Military Compensation and Retirement Modernization Commission; National Archives and Records Administration; Federal Register Office; Office of Government Information Services (Gives out Freedom of Information Act records); National Security Council; Office of Policy Development (Most of the policy areas that this office oversees are unconstitutional, but once all that unconstitutional policy is dissolved this Office will be fine); Personnel Management Office; Postal Rate Commission; Postal Regulatory Commission; Postal Service (The USPS is constitutional, but, personally, I would like to get this power pulled out of the Constitution through an amendment. I want the mail service to be totally privatized. However, it may be hard to find a private buyer for USPS, and it gives UPS and FedEx a run for their money in package shipping. At the very least, the Federal monopoly on mailing letters should be abolished, but that's for Congress to decide.); President's Council on Integrity and Efficiency (works against fraud and abuse within government; hopefully less needed as the government gets within constitutional bounds); Presidential Documents (I don't think this is an agency, but, perhaps ironically, it is listed as one in the Federal Register with absolutely no information.[114]); Regulatory Information Service Center (Will be very small once interstate commerce has no regulations from the Federal Government other than keeping the states from regulating it, which is what the Constitution demands); The White House Office; U.S. House of Representatives (Apparently the Federal Government, in its Registry, labels this as an agency, but it fails to list the U.S. Senate and the U.S. Supreme Court at all. These all are constitutional, although the people in these bodies could use some help on what the Constitution means.); U.S.-China Economic and Security Review Commission (It reports to Congress on the impact of trade and our economic relationship with China. Researching such things is constitutionally permissible, especially since this relates to international trade.); and United States Sentencing Commission (Created in 1984, we would hardly need this as a separate entity if we were only sentencing constitutional Federal crimes, of which there are very few).

On the Executive Order Dissolving 128 Federal Entities:

This is a monster executive order! Every one of these entities is unconstitutional. I'd like to comment on a few of these entities before I lay out the order.

National Counterintelligence Center – This is a counterterrorism entity. Islamic terrorism is a newer phenomenon and perhaps the Constitution should be amended to provide for it. But without an amendment this must be in the hands of the states and their people. **Court Services and Offender Supervision Agency for the District of Columbia** - This should be done by the local D.C. government; it was started in 1997. **Equal Employment Opportunity Commission** - The Federal Government has no authority to make laws against private discrimination; just because you think something is just or righteous doesn't mean the Constitution should be usurped; by usurping the Constitution you have effectively created a law that is illegal, null, and void, so it would be pointless anyway; an entity like this would require a constitutional amendment that I wouldn't support; this is best left to the people and their states. **Federal Communications Commission (FCC)** - Created in 1934 totally unconstitutionally; partly claiming that it's allowed to exist because of the interstate commerce clause; that was not the original intent of the clause and this "Commission" is illegal and these powers need to be left up to the states and the people). **Federal Maritime**

Commission - Congress must create laws, not a commission, otherwise this might be constitutional. **Indian Arts and Crafts Board** - This is one of the more rid-iculous and absurd entities that someone seems to have thought was constitutional. **James Madison Memorial Fellowship Foundation** - Started in 1986, it's all about getting the Constitution taught in schools. I like the Constitution, but this is unconstitutional. Unfortunately, the Federal Government of today has consistently shown to be one of the worst defenders of the Constitution. **Joint Board for Enrollment of Actuaries** - Congress does not have the power to declare someone an actuary. That's up to the people and the states. This is another absurd entity. **National Aeronautics and Space Admin-istration (NASA)** – This was once pivotal in our nation's history, but it was always unconstitutional. Although it may have been good to have a constitutional amendment to make NASA legitimate in the past, NASA is now obsolete, and the private sector is more than capable of producing in this arena. **National Nanotechnology Coordination Office** - Unbelievable. How can we even think that the founders could have enumerated this in the Constitution? And there's no amendment for it. "Nano" wasn't made a standard prefix until 1960. Only a constitutional amendment would allow for this. **President's Economic Policy Advisory Board** - It promotes economic growth. Why do we assume that growth is a good thing? It seems particularly American to think that bigger is better, but of course that isn't always true. If our assumption is that a higher growth rate is better, we need to challenge it. There are circumstances where shrinkage is better: this can easily be seen in certain industries, such as the early 1900's horse-drawn carriage industry during the disruption caused by cars. **Recovery Accountability and Transparency Board** – This is all about President Obama's Recovery Act from 2009, which was totally and utterly unconstitutional. By the way, the bubble that burst was largely caused by the Federal Government, which was messing with home loans and ensuring bank solvency. The Federal Government's causing of financial disasters is one of the many reasons we need the Federal Government out of all unconstitutional areas. I believe that the Federal Government is in large part creating the next great catastrophe. That's not including the catastrophe of the twenty trillion dollars of debt that they've already created. **Securities and Exchange Commission** - The SEC was created in 1934. This hideousness is authorized nowhere in the Constitution, and its functions must be left up to the states and their people. **Selective Service System** - This has personal significance for me. The last prosecution for failure to register with this System was in 1986. I felt that this failure to enforce the law was the government saying that it was no longer a law with which I needed to abide. Perhaps that's true. I did not register when I was 18. Then, when I was 25 and running for the Republican nomination for U.S. Congress, I decided to register in the hopes that people didn't view me as unpatriotic. I view myself as patriotic, simply because I have a very strong inner urge to do what's best for this country, and to change it for the better. I knowingly didn't register, essentially as a youthful defiance of the system. Then, at 25, I registered. It is through your 25th year that you are last required to register. There is no authority in the Constitution for Congress to force someone to serve in the military. Many people have honorably served in the United States military. If that's you, thank you so much for your service. But service needs to be voluntary, not forces. There's a great 1800s quote from Daniel Webster about the draft, "Where is it written in the Constitution, in what article or section is it contained, that you may take children from their parents, and parents from their children, and compel them to fight the battles of any war, in which the folly or the wickedness of Government may engage it?".[115] **Social Security Administration** - This will be gone and left up to the states and the people, but do not fear, everything you've paid into this will immediately be paid out to you plus interest according to the executive order) **Special Inspector General for Afghanistan Reconstruction** - "Needed" due to an undeclared, unconstitutional, illegal war. **Special Inspector General For Iraq Reconstruction** – Also "needed" due to an undeclared, unconstitutional, illegal war. **Utah Reclamation Mitigation and Conservation Commission** - Started in 1994-1995, it stores water. Why can't they just call it Utah Water Storage? They probably want to confuse the public and make it sound more important than it is, since it's unconstitutional.

Here's the Executive Order:

Executive Order Dissolving 128 Federal Entities

EXECUTIVE ORDER

- - - - - - -

DISSOLVING 128 FEDERAL ENTITIES

By the authority vested in me as President by the Constitution and the laws of the United States of America, it is hereby affirmed, declared, and ordered as follows:

Section 1. Policy. It is the policy of the United States to not be involved in anything not directly associated with the carrying out a power given to it by the Constitution of the United States.

Sec. 2. Constitutionality. One hundred twenty-eight entities in the United States Federal Government are unconstitutional. The entities listed in Section 5 of this Executive Order perform unconstitutional functions. No powers regarding the functions of these entities are ever given to the Federal Government or its Legislature in the Constitution.

Sec. 3. Presidential Duty and Immediacy. According to the President's duty to uphold the Constitution of the United States of America, as the President has sworn or affirmed to uphold such Constitution, all sections of this executive order will be immediately understood and carried out by all branches of the United States Federal Government as it pertains to them, without regard to any court order that goes against the Constitution.

Sec. 4. Unenforceable Laws. Any laws, regulations, acts, or other legislation of the Federal Government that unconstitutionally provides for or regulates anything related to the areas served by the previously mentioned entities, and (if applicable) the functions of entities where particular functions have been ceased, will henceforward cease to be executed and will continue to cease to be executed unless and until the Constitution of the United States is amended to give Congress or the Federal Government the power to make laws regarding the areas served by the previously mentioned entities.

Sec. 5. Ending 128 Entities of the Federal Government. The following entities within the United States Federal Government will immediately cease to function, except for the Social Security Administration which will cease to function according to the instructions listed with that entity, and any obligations owed by these entities to servants or from these entities to other entities will be taken over by the Federal Government in accordance with its historical commitment to pay debts, as Congress may prescribe:

ACTION (Organizes voluntary service from Americans); Administrative Conference of the United States (Uses non-volunteers to get experts to help with policy review); Advisory Council on Historic Preservation; African Development Foundation; Air Transportation Stabilization Board (Provides credit to airlines); American Battle Monuments Commission; Amtrak Reform Council; Appalachian Regional Commission; Appalachian States Low-Level Radioactive Waste Commission; Arctic Research Commission; Barry M. Goldwater Scholarship and Excellence in Education Foundation; Bipartisan Commission on Entitlement and Tax Reform (this started in 1994 to solve the high fiscal costs of government and came to no real conclusion[116]); Broadcasting Board of Governors (They broadcast information about the U.S. to places like the Middle East); Chemical Safety and Hazard Investigation Board (Investigates accidents); Commission of Fine Arts; Commission on the Future of the United States Aerospace Industry; Commission on the Social Security Notch Issue; Committee for Purchase From People Who Are Blind or Severely Disabled (Buys goods from organizations that use labor from people with disabilities); Commodity Futures Trading Commission; Consumer Financial Protection Bureau; Consumer Product Safety Commission; Corporation for National and Community Service; Court Services and Offender Supervision Agency for the District of Columbia; Crime and Security in U.S. Seaports, Interagency Commission; Delaware River Basin Commission (Started in 1961, it deals with water resources in the area); Denali Commission (Started in 1998, it provides services for Alaska); Election Assistance

Commission (Assists states in voting systems, started in 2002 in response to the year 2000 election issues[117]); Emergency Oil and Gas Guaranteed Loan Board; Emergency Steel Guarantee Loan Board; Equal Employment Opportunity Commission; Council on Environmental Quality; Export-Import Bank; Farm Credit Administration; Farm Credit System Insurance Corporation; Federal Communications Commission; Federal Deposit Insurance Corporation; Federal Election Commission (Has to do with monitoring election campaign funds, started in 1971); Federal Financial Institutions Examination Council; Federal Housing Finance Agency; Federal Housing Finance Board; Federal Labor Relations Authority (Started in 1979 from a Federal law that gives employees unionization rights); Federal Service Impasses Panel (Deals with Federal employee labor disputes); Federal Maritime Commission; Federal Mediation and Conciliation Service (Services related to collective bargaining through unions); Federal Mine Safety and Health Review Commission; Federal Trade Commission (Created in 1914, this is the anti-trust, anti-monopoly part of government); Financial Crisis Inquiry Commission (Created in 2009 to figure out the financial crisis); Financial Stability Oversight Council; Foreign Service Impasse Disputes Panel; Foreign Service Labor Relations Board; Gulf Coast Ecosystem Restoration Council; Harry S. Truman Scholarship Foundation; Indian Arts and Crafts Board; Institute of American Indian and Alaska Native Culture and Arts Development (An Indian college); Inter-American Foundation (Latin

America and Caribbean economic development); Interagency Floodplain Management Review Committee; International Broadcasting Board (Broadcasts United States' propaganda around the world); International Organizations Employees Loyalty Board; James Madison Memorial Fellowship Foundation; Japan-United States Friendship Commission (Makes grants); Joint Board for Enrollment of Actuaries; Judicial Review Commission on Foreign Asset Control (Deals with blocking someone's assets); Legal Services Corporation (Provides legal aid for poor people); Local Television Loan Guarantee Board; Marine Mammal Commission; Medicare Payment Advisory Commission; Millennium Challenge Corporation (Grants to poor countries who are "good"); Mississippi River Commission; Morris K. Udall and Stewart L. Udall Foundation (About environmental awareness); National Aeronautics and Space Administration (NASA); National Historical Publications and Records Commission (Makes grants to state and local archives); National Bipartisan Commission on Future of Medicare; National Commission on Libraries and Information Science; National Consumer Cooperative Bank (A bank for cooperatives); National Council on Disability; National Counterintelligence Center; National Credit Union Administration; National Crime Prevention and Privacy Compact Council; National Economic Council; National Foundation on the Arts and the Humanities; Institute of Museum and Library Services; National Endowment for the Arts; National Endowment for the Humanities; National Institute for

Literacy; National Labor Relations Board; National Mediation Board (Labor relations for railroads and airlines); National Nanotechnology Coordination Office; National Railroad Passenger Corporation (Amtrak); National Science Foundation; National Skill Standards Board; National Transportation Safety Board; National Women's Business Council; Navajo and Hopi Indian Relocation Office; Neighborhood Reinvestment Corporation; Northeast Interstate Low-Level Radioactive Waste Commission; Nuclear Regulatory Commission; Nuclear Waste Technical Review Board; Occupational Safety and Health Review Commission; Office of National Drug Control Policy; Oklahoma City National Memorial Trust (Oklahoma city bombing memorial); Ounce of Prevention Council (Crime prevention); Overseas Private Investment Corporation (Encourages private investment overseas, established in 1971); Pacific Northwest Electric Power and Conservation Planning Council; Peace Corps; Pension Benefit Guaranty Corporation (Payouts to private citizens for failed pension plans); Physician Payment Review Commission (Created in 1986 to look at how Medicare paid physicians); President's Critical Infrastructure Protection Board; President's Economic Policy Advisory Board (Promotes economic growth); Presidio Trust (A park in San Francisco); Reagan-Udall Foundation for the Food and Drug Administration (Provides more modernization and "accelerate[s] innovation"); Recovery Accountability and Transparency; Science and Technology Policy Office; Securities and Exchange Commission; Selective Service

System; Smithsonian Institution; Social Security Administration - Undisbursed inflows for each individual must be immediately paid out to living beneficiaries with fair interest, interest will be based on an act of Congress, if no act has passed interest will be based on the official Consumer Price Index as accrued for each inflow minus all outflows, the Social Security Administration must immediately stop accepting payments and must be dissolved as soon as all undisbursed inflows have been sent out, Congress may create a system of record for this Administration in case of disputes for debts owed, since the United States is Constitutionally allowed to pay its debts and historically has paid them; Special Counsel Office (Federal whistleblowers can blow at this office); Special Inspector General for Afghanistan Reconstruction; Special Inspector General For Iraq Reconstruction; State Justice Institute (Provides grants to bolster state courts); Surface Transportation Board; Susquehanna River Basin Commission; Tennessee Valley Authority; Trade and Development Agency (Started in 1980, it "advances economic development and U.S. commercial interest in developing and middle-income countries in […] regions of the world"); United States Institute of Peace; Utah Reclamation Mitigation and Conservation Commission (It stores water); Valles Caldera Trust (A New Mexico volcano park); and Women's Business Enterprise Interagency Committee.

Everyone working at the previously mentioned entities, except at the Social Security Administration which will dissolve as described in the above listing of it, must permanently leave their respective entity offices or places of work immediately. Any State Government or other entity may reemploy any Federal worker who has lost a job in this way, to work in a similar or a different capacity.

All property of the previously mentioned entities, except of the Social Security Administration which will dissolve as described in the above listing of it, will now be the property of the governments of the respective State, the District of Columbia, or the United States Territory where the property is situated. If the property is not contained in one of these locations, it will immediately come into the control of the first State government which has a representative at the property physically to claim the property. If two or more States lay claim to property at the same time, they may agree among themselves as to who will own the property, or they will share it among themselves. Any State, the District of Columbia, or any United States Territory that acquires property from the Federal Government in the above two ways may freely pay the Treasury of the United States for such property, if and in the amount that they desire to do so.

Sec. 6. Reaffirmation of the Tenth Amendment of the Constitution. It is reaffirmed that, according to the Tenth Amendment of the Constitution of the United States, and implied by the Constitution before it was ever amended, all powers of the previously mentioned entities are reserved to the States respectively, or to the People, and, therefore, none of the powers that these previously mentioned entities had will henceforward be exercised by the Federal Government, without there first being a ratified amendment to the Constitution that gives power over some area where these entities served to the Federal Government.

Sec. 7. Responsibilities of the People and their State Governments. Regarding the topic(s) of this Executive Order, the People and their respective State Governments, or the People alone, are urged to take care of anything previously attended to by the Federal Government. If any State desires to take action regarding a topic of this Executive Order, the Congress of the United States is urged to approve such State action so that the state may accomplish these or related things which were previously attended to by the Federal Government, if Congressional approval is Constitutionally required for the State to take such action.

Sec. 8. Pardons and Contracts. (a) A Full and Unconditional Pardon is hereby given to anyone who has been charged or convicted of any Federal crime or offense related to any of the unconstitutional laws that were deemed unenforceable according to this Executive Order.

(b) Regardless of any contracts or agreements that were signed or sworn to towards unconstitutional ends, anyone who exposes the Federal Government for doing anything unconstitutional, including the items outlined in this Executive Order, will be given a Full and Unconditional Pardon for exposing such unconstitutional Federal actions. Also, regardless of any contracts or agreements that were signed or sworn to towards unconstitutional ends, anyone who has exposed the Federal Government for doing anything unconstitutional, including the items outlined in this Executive Order, is hereby given a Full and Unconditional Pardon for exposing such unconstitutional Federal actions.

Sec. 9. General Provisions. (a) This order is not intended to, and does not, create any right or benefit, substantive or procedural, enforceable at law or in equity by any party against the United States, its departments, agencies, or entities, its officers, employees, or agents, or any other person.

(b) This order is not intended to, and does not, go against the Constitution of the United States. Everything in this order has the intent of restoring the supreme law of the land, which is the Constitution of the United States of America; if any part of this order is deemed as going against the Constitution, any remedy must be at the discretion of each individual charged with that remedy, including judges, officials, secretaries, and people at any and every level of government. Those individuals are each urged to ask if the remedy is Constitutional according to the original intent and spirit of the Constitution when written by our founding fathers in the seventeen hundreds. If any part of this order is ultimately deemed unconstitutional by any individual or institution, all other parts of this order will remain in full force and effect in perpetuity, or until the Constitution is amended or superseded.

[THE NAME AND SIGNATURE OF THE PRESIDENT OF THE UNITED STATES]

THE WHITE HOUSE,

[Date].

On the Executive Order Reducing the Functions of Eight Entities that are Partially Unconstitutional:

I'd like to point out two of these entities because they are interesting. The first is the Civil Rights Commission. This commission ensures "equal protection of the law." This is okay if it's limited to the original intent of that phrase, which is that being separate but equal is okay. Ironically, the Fourteenth Amendment ensures "equal protection" but cannot enforce equal protection of the law upon the federal government but only upon the states because the Constitution only provides for equal protection at the state level.

The second is the Coordinating Council on Juvenile Justice and Delinquency Prevention. This council is almost entirely unconstitutional except for dealing with children constitutionally detained for something such as a felony on the high seas, which I believe is exceedingly rare, so this needs to be moved to the Department of Justice.

Here's the Executive Order:

Executive Order Reducing the Functions of Eight Entities that are Partially Unconstitutional

EXECUTIVE ORDER

- - - - - - -

REDUCING THE FUNCTIONS OF EIGHT ENTITIES THAT ARE PARTIALLY UNCONSTITUTIONAL

By the authority vested in me as President by the Constitution and the laws of the United States of America, it is hereby affirmed, declared, and ordered as follows:

Section 1. Policy. It is the policy of the United States to have no involvement in matters not directly associated with the carrying out of a power given to it by the Constitution of the United States.

Sec. 2. Constitutionality. Portions of the United States Federal Government are partially unconstitutional. The partially unconstitutional entities are listed in Section 5.

No powers regarding the unconstitutional functions of these entities are ever given to the Federal Government or its Legislature in the Constitution.

Sec. 3. Presidential Duty and Immediacy. According to the President's duty to uphold the Constitution of the United States of America, as the President has sworn or affirmed to uphold such Constitution, all sections of this executive order will be immediately understood and carried out by all branches of the United States Federal Government as it pertains to them, without regard to any court order that goes against the Constitution.

Sec. 4. Unenforceable Laws. Any laws, regulations, acts, or other legislation of the Federal Government that unconstitutionally provides for or regulates anything related to the areas served by the previously mentioned entities, and (if applicable) the functions of entities where particular functions have been ceased, will henceforward cease to be executed and will continue to cease to be executed unless and until the Constitution of the United States is amended to give Congress or the Federal Government the power to make laws regarding the areas served by the previously mentioned entities.

Sec. 5. Ending some Functions of Several Federal Entities. The following entities within the United States Federal Government must immediately follow the instructions set forth here: Agency for International Development – All foreign aid must immediately and henceforward stop except that which is Constitutionally created by Congress through treaties directly written by Congress; Architectural and Transportation Barriers Compliance Board – Public access assurance for people with disabilities for Federal buildings may but creating and publishing access guidelines that the public can use are unconstitutional and must cease immediately and henceforward; Arms Control and Disarmament Agency – This Agency must immediately and henceforward cease all activities except for working on treaties and ensuring compliance with them; Civil Rights Commission – All functions of this Commission must immediately and henceforward cease except for those ensuring "equal protection of the law" when its meaning is simple that separate but equal is the most equality required by law; Coordinating Council on Juvenile Justice and Delinquency Prevention - Immediately cease all functions except for those regarding children Constitutionally detained for something such as a felony on the high seas, immediately move this Council to the Department of Justice; Information Security Oversight Office – This office must immediately and henceforward cease all functions regarding private industry, and it must cease all other functions except those where Federal Government information security is involved; National Capital Planning Commission – This Commission must immediately and henceforward cease all functions, including those dealing with D.C. parks; however, the previous portion notwithstanding, Federal buildings that carry out Constitutional functions may be dealt with;

Privacy and Civil Liberties Oversight Board – This Board must immediately and henceforward cease all functions, especially those regarding privacy or other rights not found in the Constitution, but it may continue ensuring Constitutional rights; and Railroad Retirement Board – The Federal Government owes a debt to Federal employees even though they were employed unconstitutionally, these debts will be paid according to legislation from Congress, henceforward no Federal retirement benefits will accrue for new work, and this entity must be dissolved as soon as all debts are paid.

Everyone working at the previously mentioned entities solely in ceased functions must permanently leave their respective entity offices or places of work immediately. Any State Government or other entity may reemploy any Federal worker who has lost a job in this way, to work in a similar or a different capacity.

All property of the previously mentioned entities ceased functions will now be the property of the governments of the respective State, the District of Columbia, or the United States Territory where the property is situated. If the property is not contained in one of these locations, it will immediately come into the control of the first State government which has a representative at the property physically to claim the property. If two or more States lay claim to property at the same time, they may agree among themselves as to who will own the property, or they will share it among themselves. Any State, the District of

Columbia, or any United States Territory that acquires property from the Federal Government in the above two ways may freely pay the Treasury of the United States for such property, if and in the amount that they desire to do so.

Sec. 6. Reaffirmation of the Tenth Amendment of the Constitution. It is reaffirmed that, according to the Tenth Amendment of the Constitution of the United States, and implied by the Constitution before it was ever amended, all powers of the previously mentioned entities are reserved to the States respectively, or to the People, and, therefore, none of the powers that these previously mentioned entities had will henceforward be exercised by the Federal Government, without there first being a ratified amendment to the Constitution that gives power over some area where these entities served to the Federal Government.

Sec. 7. Responsibilities of the People and their State Governments. Regarding the topic(s) of this Executive Order, the People and their respective State Governments, or the People alone, are urged to take care of anything previously attended to by the Federal Government. If any State desires to take action regarding a topic of this Executive Order, the Congress of the United States is urged to approve such State action so that the state may accomplish these or related things which were previously attended to by the Federal Government,

if Congressional approval is Constitutionally required for the State to take such action.

Sec. 8. Pardons and Contracts. (a) A Full and Unconditional Pardon is hereby given to anyone who has been charged or convicted of any Federal crime or offense related to any of the unconstitutional laws that were deemed unenforceable according to this Executive Order.

(b) Regardless of any contracts or agreements that were signed or sworn to towards unconstitutional ends, anyone who exposes the Federal Government for doing anything unconstitutional, including the items outlined in this Executive Order, will be given a Full and Unconditional Pardon for exposing such unconstitutional Federal actions. Also, regardless of any contracts or agreements that were signed or sworn to towards unconstitutional ends, anyone who has exposed the Federal Government for doing anything unconstitutional, including the items outlined in this Executive Order, is hereby given a Full and Unconditional Pardon for exposing such unconstitutional Federal actions.

Sec. 9. General Provisions. (a) This order is not intended to, and does not, create any right or benefit, substantive or procedural, enforceable at law or in equity by any party against the United States, its departments, agencies, or entities, its officers, employees, or agents, or any other person.

(b) This order is not intended to, and does not, go against the Constitution of the United States. Everything in this order has the intent of restoring the supreme law of the land, which is the Constitution of the United States of America; if any part of this order is deemed as going against the Constitution, any remedy must be at the discretion of each individual charged with that remedy, including judges, officials, secretaries, and people at any and every level of government. Those individuals are each urged to ask if the remedy is Constitutional according to the original intent and spirit of the Constitution when written by our founding fathers in the seventeen hundreds. If any part of this order is ultimately deemed unconstitutional by any individual or institution, all other parts of this order will remain in full force and effect in perpetuity, or until the Constitution is amended or superseded.

[THE NAME AND SIGNATURE OF THE PRESIDENT OF THE UNITED STATES]

THE WHITE HOUSE,

[Date].

CHAPTER 7

A CALL TO ARMS

After going through the 440 agencies that comprise the federal government (at least according to its Federal Register), I can confidently say that the federal government does nothing special. It is not special; it does nothing sacred or even important. All it does is take money from some people, waste a bunch of it, and then give a little bit of what's left to some other people. In the case of our government, it takes money from us and gives it not just to our own people, but to people and governments all over the world. Along the path of the take, waste, and spend cycle, the federal government also creates thousands upon thousands of restrictions on our people, which waste our time, energy, and money and lead to a horribly slow progress of business and innovation.

When we think of the government, we're tempted to give it some high and mighty status, but it's not high and mighty. When you look at its individual components, it is weak and mindless. It does almost nothing innovative, and when it does innovate, it costs the taxpayers billions of dollars. Private citizens or organizations can innovate for much less.

Never again do I want to be tempted to think that the Federal Government is in any way holding this nation together, or serving this nation. If anything, it is tearing us apart. Government is a necessary evil only because we make it that way. In ancient Israel, the people wanted government; they wanted a king. God said – No, a king is no good. I am your king. – but the people insisted, and eventually they got a king, and things have been worse for Israel ever since. We need government because we think we need it. I only accept government because some people can't accept our nation without government. In a perfect world there is no government other than the rule of God, but perhaps the best we'll ever get before God's rule is true, constitutionally limited government.

Perhaps never in the history of mankind has such an immense institution walked around headless and immoral and wasted so many people's lives, money, time, and resources. And much of that waste has been illegal because it is unconstitutional. We have sat back and relaxed while our government has "legally" stolen money from us in the form of taxes and then illegally spent much of the money on unconstitutional things.

We need to take a stand. We cannot back down. We must stand up to the military-industrial complex, the FDA drug industry cartel, the Medicare/Medicaid monstrosity, the Social Security money drain, and hundreds of other federal boondoggles, and we need to take back our Constitution and bring back our constitutional republic. We need to bring back our morals that will keep us following the Constitution, and we need to educate our kids, grandkids, and so on down the line into perpetuity to keep this government in check.

We the people have become we the impotent. We must rise up. Ron Paul called for a revolution, and I agree. We need a liberty revolution so that we start dismantling the government instead of building it up. We need federal, state, and local legislators who are not proud of the laws they passed but, rather, are proud of the laws they stopped. We need presidents and governors who laugh at what the federal government unconstitutionally tries to do, and then squash it, and we need judges who no longer create law but rather abolish laws because those laws go against the supreme law of the land, the Constitution of the United States of America.

We need to amend the Constitution to abolish the personal income tax because it was only when the Congress had the power to tax this way that it decided that 99% of what it did would be illegal and unconstitutional. We must take that power away from it.

This is God's nation, God's Earth, and we are God's creation. But God has made us stewards of those very things. I need to be a better steward of my mind, my body, my family, my home, and my relationships; and we need to be better stewards of this Earth and the Federal Government that has gotten so rotten.

I feel like I have no choice but to do what little I can to fix the federal government. Despite our government's incredible faults, we live in the greatest nation on Earth. And despite its faults, it is the best government I know of, and yet the government is so big and wastes so many lives through war, and wastes so many resources through unconstitutional programs that it may just be the biggest single man-made drag on humanity that the world has ever seen.

This call to arms is a call to minds and a call to justice. Let's use our hearts, minds, and voices to spread the knowledge of liberty to our friends, our family, and our neighbors and restore the Constitution in our nation once and for all! We must unite behind the Constitution: The Liberation Day Plan allows us to be on the same page while demanding liberty from our government.

CHAPTER 8

MORE EXECUTIVE ORDERS REGARDING ITEMS THAT ARE NOT FORMAL FEDERAL ENTITIES

On the Federal Reserve

We need to get back to constitutional government now because, otherwise, it won't be much longer until our $19.97 trillion of federal debt boils over into a default or hyperinflation. We're also looking at more frequent and more catastrophic bubbles bursting, and more government bailouts "required" due to crazy monetary manipulation by the bank-owned Federal Reserve.

You might think the Federal Reserve is owned by the government; even its website says it's "not 'owned' by anyone."[118] This is a lie. You can clearly see that it is owned by private banks at *Global Research*.[119]

I know that the Fed is privately owned from first-hand experience. My dad and I were walking in Chicago around 2009 or 2010, and there was the Federal Reserve Bank of Chicago. Out of curiosity, we went inside. As soon as we got in, they said something like, "Get Out!" and they were not friendly at all. I was confused why the door was unlocked. We talked a little more, but I can only tell you that I felt a strong sense of pressure to get out, and perhaps I also sensed something very dark.

My dad and I quickly got out of that building, and I don't want to go in a Federal Reserve building again unless we've fully gotten rid of the Federal Reserve System. This experience confirmed to me more than ever the darkness of the Federal Reserve and also suggested that it is not a public institution because a public institution would be answerable to taxpayers. The people in the building that day were angry that we were even there, let alone answer my questions.

The Federal Reserve is a private institution with no constitutional basis. Quite frankly, I don't even know if something like the Federal Reserve could exist under the Constitution because I don't think an organization with the power of government, but having private ownership, can coexist with the concept of the rule of law.

The rule of law implies that the government has certain powers that can't be given to private organizations such as the Federal Reserve. The Federal Reserve creates "money" out of nothing by adding digits to various banks' accounts. This is against any rule of law and should be reserved for the government, not a private institution, even if it were constitutional, which it's not.

I now call upon and urge every person working in the Federal Reserve System to immediately resign from this unconstitutional institution, which has the power of government and yet is privately owned and has virtually no oversight. I also call upon the Congress, the Supreme Court, and the President to put an immediate end to the institution that is the Federal Reserve.

Here's the Executive Order:

Executive Order Immediately Auditing and Dissolving the Federal Reserve

EXECUTIVE ORDER

- - - - - - -

IMMEDIATELY AUDITING AND DISSOLVING THE FEDERAL RESERVE

By the authority vested in me as President by the Constitution and the laws of the United States of America, it is hereby affirmed, declared, and ordered as follows:

Section 1. Policy. It is the policy of the United States to have no involvement with a central bank or any other banking services in matters not directly associated with the carrying out a power given to it by the Constitution of the United States.

Sec. 2. Constitutionality. The Federal Reserve is unconstitutional. It is a private entity given the power of Federal Government. As such, it has inadequate oversight and unfair freedom to use and abuse the public's purchasing power. Furthermore, no powers regarding the functions of the Federal Reserve are ever given to the Federal Government or its Legislature in the Constitution. While "Bankruptcies" are under the authority of the Federal Government according to the Constitution, the terms "Federal Reserve," "Central," "Bank," "Banks," and "Banking" never occur in the Constitution.

Sec. 3. Presidential Duty and Immediacy. According to the President's duty to uphold the Constitution of the United States of America, as the President has sworn or affirmed to uphold such Constitution, all sections of this executive order will be immediately understood and carried out by all branches of the United States Federal Government as it pertains to them, without regard to any court order that goes against the Constitution.

Sec. 4. Unenforceable Laws. Any laws, regulations, acts, or other legislation of the Federal Government that unconstitutionally provides for or regulates anything related to the areas served by the previously mentioned entities, and (if applicable) the functions of entities where particular functions have been ceased, will henceforward cease to be executed and will continue to cease to be executed unless and until the Constitution of the United States is amended to give Congress or the Federal Government the power to make laws regarding the areas served by the previously mentioned entities.

Sec. 5. Auditing and Ending the Entity. The Federal Reserve and all subentities must be immediately audited by an act of Congress in order to find any debts the Federal Government may owe because of actions of the Federal Reserve. If no such act has passed, it will be audited by a special task force of the President of the United States to find the same. The Federal Reserve and all subentities must immediately and henceforward cease to operate, and any Federal obligations owed by it to servants or from it to other entities will be taken over by the Federal Government in accordance with its historical commitment to pay debts, as Congress may prescribe. Any debts that the Federal Reserve owes that are not public debts, meaning debts not of the United States, must be paid for by the member banks of the Federal Reserve according to the law.

Everyone working at the Federal Reserve must permanently leave their respective offices or places of work immediately. Any State Government or other entity may reemploy any worker who has lost a job in this way, to work in a similar or a different capacity.

All property of the previously mentioned entities will now be private property or the property of the governments of the respective State, the District of Columbia, or the United States Territory where the property is situated, according to the law. If the property is not contained in one of these locations, it will immediately come into the control of the first State government which has a representative at the property physically to claim the property. If two or more States lay claim to property at the same time, they may agree among themselves as to who will own the property, or they will share it among themselves. Any State, the District of Columbia, or any United States Territory that acquires property from the Federal Government in the above two ways may freely pay the Treasury of the United States for such property, if and in the amount that they desire to do so.

Sec. 6. Reaffirmation of the Tenth Amendment of the Constitution. It is reaffirmed that, according to the Tenth Amendment of the Constitution of the United States, and implied by the Constitution before it was ever amended, all powers of the previously mentioned entities are reserved to the States respectively, or to the People, and, therefore, none of the powers that these previously mentioned entities had will henceforward be exercised by the Federal Government, without there first being a ratified amendment to the Constitution that gives power over some area where these entities served to the Federal Government.

Sec. 7. Responsibilities of the People and their State Governments. Regarding the topic(s) of this Executive Order, the People and their respective State Governments, or the People alone, are urged to take care of anything previously attended to by the Federal Government. If any State desires to take action regarding a topic of this Executive Order, the Congress of the United States is urged to approve such State action so that the state may accomplish these or related things which were previously attended to by the Federal Government, if Congressional approval is Constitutionally required for the State to take such action.

Sec. 8. Pardons and Contracts. (a) A Full and Unconditional Pardon is hereby given to anyone who has been charged or convicted of any Federal crime or offense related to any of the unconstitutional laws that were deemed unenforceable according to this Executive Order.

(b) Regardless of any contracts or agreements that were signed or sworn to towards unconstitutional ends, anyone who exposes the Federal Government for doing anything unconstitutional, including the items outlined in this Executive Order, will be given a Full and Unconditional Pardon for exposing such unconstitutional Federal actions. Also, regardless of any contracts or agreements that were signed or sworn to towards unconstitutional ends, anyone who has exposed the Federal Government for doing anything unconstitutional, including the items outlined in this Executive Order, is hereby given a Full

and Unconditional Pardon for exposing such unconstitutional Federal actions.

Sec. 9. General Provisions. (a) This order is not intended to, and does not, create any right or benefit, substantive or procedural, enforceable at law or in equity by any party against the United States, its departments, agencies, or entities, its officers, employees, or agents, or any other person.

(b) This order is not intended to, and does not, go against the Constitution of the United States. Everything in this order has the intent of restoring the supreme law of the land, which is the Constitution of the United States of America; if any part of this order is deemed as going against the Constitution, any remedy must be at the discretion of each individual charged with that remedy, including judges, officials, secretaries, and people at any and every level of government. Those individuals are each urged to ask if the remedy is Constitutional according to the original intent and spirit of the Constitution when written by our founding fathers in the seventeen hundreds. If any part of this order is ultimately deemed unconstitutional by any individual or institution, all other parts of this order will remain in full force and effect in perpetuity, or until the Constitution is amended or superseded.

[THE NAME AND SIGNATURE OF THE PRESIDENT OF THE UNITED STATES]

THE WHITE HOUSE,

[Date].

Abortion and Roe v. Wade:

Roe v. Wade **did not** legalize abortion! Abortion was already legal in some states. Roe v. Wade did the following: it made it illegal for the states to make abortion illegal.

It stripped the states of their constitutional right to regulate abortion under the Tenth Amendment. It is by far the worst decision that the Supreme Court has ever made. The word "privacy" does not exist in the Constitution, yet it is the constitutionally protected right of privacy that the Supreme Court cites as the reason that it ruled that abortion cannot be made illegal.

Not only does abortion kill a baby, but it is murder of varying degrees by both the practitioner(s) of the abortion and the consenting mother or father. Once a mother has had an abortion, she often experiences lifelong shame, guilt, and depression because of that murder. I searched on Google "I'm happy I aborted my baby" and "I'm happy that I aborted my baby," and neither search turned up even one result.[120] Could 30 trillion indexed pages have missed that any woman feels this way? I don't think so.

Many people want to declare that abortion is a right that must be protected, but my guess is that a very small proportion of women who have actually had abortions talk openly about them, let alone recommend them.

Adoption is desired in this country and other countries by many people. Even if we ignore the moral issue of murder, even children totally unwanted by the parent(s) should be allowed to live because others want to take care of those babies.

There have been well over 54 million murders as a result of abortion since the 1973 Roe v. Wade decision.[121] It's hard to fathom that many deaths or even to understand how we could let this happen. That's more death than if we killed every person living in South Korea, South Africa, Columbia, Kenya, or Spain.

If someone took the 94 least populated countries in the world and rounded up every single person living in them, and then shot and killed every single one of them, they still wouldn't have murdered as many people as have been murdered through abortion since the 1973 Roe v. Wade decision and only counting abortions in the United States.

That's as many dead babies as up to **10 times the number of Jewish people who were murdered in the Holocaust.**

I am surprised that more people aren't literally up in arms about this. I do not think more murder is the answer, but I'm still surprised. Killing someone who's not in the military is considered wrong; killing women and children is considered worse. Babies are considered one of the epitomes of innocence in our society. Murdering unborn babies can be argued to be the worst crime known to man. They had their whole life ahead of them.

Because of the disastrous Roe v. Wade decision and other poor decisions by the Supreme Court, we can no longer look to the Supreme Court to uphold the Constitution. They once did uphold it to some extent, but they likely never will again. The Roe v. Wade decision is the worst decision the Supreme Court has ever made: It has cost us 50 million or more American lives, perhaps.

We must not look to the Supreme Court for constitutional wisdom, but rather to the founders, the people, God, the states, and the Constitution itself for that wisdom.

We must not place our hope in the Supreme Court to bring us back to the Constitution, but rather, we must look to people, organizations, the states, and perhaps even the presidency and Congress. Roe v. Wade is a decision that is a radical disgrace to law, truth, justice, and our nation.

I now call upon and urge every person working for the federal government never again to enforce the outcome of the Roe v. Wade Supreme Court ruling. It is an unconstitutional decision, and it is illegal. I call upon every state to nullify the effects of Roe v. Wade as they see fit. I also call upon and urge Congress, the Supreme Court, and the president to immediately end any of the effects of the Roe v. Wade.

Here's the Executive Order:

Executive Order Immediately Ending All Effects of the Roe v. Wade Supreme Court Decision and Putting All Laws, Regulations, and Opinions Regarding the Murder of Human Embryos, Unborn Babies, and Born Babies in the Hands of the People and Their States

EXECUTIVE ORDER

- - - - - - -

IMMEDIATELY ENDING ALL EFFECTS OF THE ROE V. WADE SUPREME COURT DECISION AND PUTTING ALL LAWS, REGULATIONS, AND OPINIONS REGARDING THE MURDER OF HUMAN EMBRYOS, UNBORN BABIES, AND BORN BABIES IN THE HANDS OF THE PEOPLE AND THEIR STATES

By the authority vested in me as President by the Constitution and the laws of the United States of America, it is hereby affirmed, declared, and ordered as follows:

Section 1. Policy. It is the policy of the United States to have no involvement in issues of murder or abortion except on the high seas or by military personnel in times of war, whether the murder or abortion is of an adult, child, baby, unborn baby, or embryo.

Sec. 2. Constitutionality. The Roe v. Wade Supreme Court decision was falsely based on the Constitution. The words "privacy," "abortion," and "murder" do not occur in the Constitution. The Federal Government and its Legislature have no Constitutional grounds to do anything regarding these issues when they occur anywhere within the States under normal circumstances.

Sec. 3. Presidential Duty and Immediacy. According to the President's duty to uphold the Constitution of the United States of America, as the President has sworn or affirmed to uphold such Constitution, all sections of this executive order will be immediately understood and carried out by all branches of the United States Federal Government as it pertains to them, without regard to any court order that goes against the Constitution.

Sec. 4. Unenforceable Laws. Any Federal laws regarding abortion or murder within a State are null and void and unenforceable. All State and Federal courts, judges, and justices are must not uphold any judgements from any Federal Court, including the Roe v. Wade judgement, if it has anything to do with abortion or murder within the states, but they must uphold the concept that states may freely legalize or illegalize murder and abortion according to their state constitution and their laws.

Sec. 5. Reaffirmation of the Tenth Amendment of the Constitution. It is reaffirmed that, according to the Tenth Amendment of the Constitution of the United States, and

implied by the Constitution before it was ever amended, all powers of the previously mentioned entities are reserved to the States respectively, or to the People, and, therefore, none of the powers that these previously mentioned entities had will henceforward be exercised by the Federal Government, without there first being a ratified amendment to the Constitution that gives power over some area where these entities served to the Federal Government.

Sec. 6. Responsibilities of the People and their State Governments. Regarding the topic(s) of this Executive Order, the People and their respective State Governments, or the People alone, are urged to take care of anything previously attended to by the Federal Government. If any State desires to take action regarding a topic of this Executive Order, the Congress of the United States is urged to approve such State action so that the state may accomplish these or related things which were previously attended to by the Federal Government, if Congressional approval is Constitutionally required for the State to take such action.

Sec. 7. Pardons and Contracts. (a) A Full and Unconditional Pardon is hereby given to anyone who has been charged or convicted of any Federal crime or offense related to any of the unconstitutional laws that were deemed unenforceable according to this Executive Order.

(b) Regardless of any contracts or agreements that were signed or sworn to towards unconstitutional ends, anyone who exposes the Federal Government for doing anything unconstitutional, including the items outlined in this Executive Order, will be given a Full and Unconditional Pardon for exposing such unconstitutional Federal actions. Also, regardless of any contracts or agreements that were signed or sworn to towards unconstitutional ends, anyone who has exposed the Federal Government for doing anything unconstitutional, including the items outlined in this Executive Order, is hereby given a Full and Unconditional Pardon for exposing such unconstitutional Federal actions.

Sec. 8. General Provisions. (a) This order is not intended to, and does not, create any right or benefit, substantive or procedural, enforceable at law or in equity by any party against the United States, its departments, agencies, or entities, its officers, employees, or agents, or any other person.

(b) This order is not intended to, and does not, go against the Constitution of the United States. Everything in this order has the intent of restoring the supreme law of the land, which is the Constitution of the United States of America; if any part of this order is deemed as going against the Constitution, any remedy must be at the discretion of each individual charged with that remedy, including judges, officials, secretaries, and people at any and every level of government. Those individuals are each

urged to ask if the remedy is Constitutional according to the original intent and spirit of the Constitution when written by our founding fathers in the seventeen hundreds. If any part of this order is ultimately deemed unconstitutional by any individual or institution, all other parts of this order will remain in full force and effect in perpetuity, or until the Constitution is amended or superseded.

[THE NAME AND SIGNATURE OF THE PRESIDENT OF THE UNITED STATES]

THE WHITE HOUSE,

[Date].

Undeclared War, Overseas Military Bases, and Standing Armies:

The Constitution provides that Congress, and only Congress, may declare war. When Congress declares war, individuals in Congress put themselves on the chopping block if the war is not won or if the costs are high. That's probably why the United States has not won a "war" since World War II. None have been declared by Congress, so they are illegal and unconstitutional. And no one in Congress was blamed for our loss in those wars, because no one in Congress declared them. Korea, Vietnam, Iraq, and Afghanistan are all lost and undeclared "wars." We must declare war if we are to send our troops overseas.

A little side note: September 11th didn't happen in a vacuum. Osama bin Laden wanted our troops off a land that he felt was holy. That land was Saudi Arabia, home of the two holiest cities in Islam: Mecca and Medina.

Would you be angry if Saudi Arabia had an armed base with Saudi Arabian troops near St. Patrick's Cathedral in New York state? I bet you would. I bet we'd be calling to drive them out with guns blazing just like Osama bin Laden was calling against our troops in Saudi Arabia. This in no way justifies what Osama bin Laden did, but hopefully, it helps you see his line of thought. I hope you can see that getting our troops out of other countries will keep our nation safer because fewer people around the world will be angry at us, just like we would be less angry if foreign troops left our country.

The first overseas military base for the United States was on Guantánamo Bay in Cuba, established in 1898.[122] It was no accident that it took 110 years from the ratification of the Constitution for this first base to be established. Many of the people and legislators forgot the limits set forth in the Constitution. There is no authorization for Congress to have foreign military bases in the Constitution. In a war declared by Congress, there is a place for a temporary military base on foreign soil for the purpose of winning the war, but there can be no foreign military bases without a declaration of war.

We don't need all these bases either. We have more than any other country. It was just in July 2017 that China created its first formally established overseas military base.[123] Does China know something that we don't know? For the many decades without a base, was China less secure? I would argue that we are less safe because of our foreign bases because they cause resentment among the peoples of other nations.

Ron Paul's words from a 2007 Presidential debate strike a chord. He explained why an Islamic terrorist would attack us and said that what we do overseas is a "major contributing factor. Have you ever read the reasons they attacked us? They attacked us because we've been over there; we've been bombing Iraq for 10 years. We've been in the Middle East – I think Reagan was right. We don't understand the irrationality of Middle Eastern politics. So right now, we're building an embassy in Iraq that's bigger than the Vatican. We're building 14 permanent bases. What would we say here if China was doing this in our country or in the Gulf of Mexico? We would be objecting. We need to look at what we do from the perspective of what would happen if somebody else did it to us."[124]

Our military bases on foreign soil seed hatred among the peoples of that soil. In 1951 "the U.S. established a permanent U.S. Military Training Mission" in Saudi Arabia.[125] After this time, the United States built multiple military bases in that country. Osama bin Laden, the leader of the September 11th, 2001 attacks on the United States, is from Saudi Arabia.

What extremist Islamic leader wouldn't be angry that an armed people virtually entirely of a different religion and race is occupying what he considers his religion's Holy Land? A hatred of that kind is reasonable, considering his background. I do not agree with the way he fought against what he considered a horrible problem for his home country, but I can understand his hatred.

Here are the results from an interesting survey: "Opinion polls conducted by Gallup from 2006–2008, found that many in Muslim majority countries strongly objected to U.S. military bases in Saudi Arabia. 52% of Saudis agreed that removing military bases from Saudi Arabia would very significantly improve their opinion of the United States. Also, 60% of Egyptians, 39% of Jordanians, 40% of Syrians and Palestinians, 55% of Tunisians, 13% of Iranians, 29% of Turks, 40% of Lebanese, and 30% of Algerians gave that opinion, too."[126] Permanent foreign military bases are unconstitutional, and they are typically not in our best interest.

Regarding standing armies, please read this information from Wikipedia: "After the war the Continental Army was quickly disbanded as part of the American distrust of standing armies, and irregular state militias became the new nation's sole ground army, with the exception of a regiment to guard the Western Frontier and one battery of artillery guarding West Point's arsenal. However, because of continuing conflict with Native Americans, it was soon realized that it was necessary to field a trained standing army. The first of these, the Legion of the United States, was established in 1791."[127] The Constitution tells us that Congress has the pow-er to "To raise and support Armies, but no Appropriation of Money to that Use shall be for a longer Term than two Years." Armies are allowed, but there are limits on the funds used for them. People were fearful of standing armies then, and while not a constitutional issue in particular, I personally believe that we should greatly downsize the size and number of our standing armies when not in a declared war.

At the time of writing, the United States is in no constitutional wars. Here's the Executive Order that a President must sign to get us in line with the Constitution in this area:

Executive Order Immediately Ending All Undeclared War and Immediately Dissolving All Foreign Military Bases

EXECUTIVE ORDER

- - - - - - -

IMMEDIATELY ENDING ALL UNDECLARED WAR AND IMMEDIATELY DISSOLVING ALL FOREIGN MILITARY BASES

By the authority vested in me as President by the Constitution and the laws of the United States of America, it is hereby affirmed, declared, and ordered as follows:

Section 1. Policy. It is the policy of the United States to be involved in no war unless the war is Constitutionally declared by Congress.

Sec. 2. Constitutionality. War by the United States that is undeclared by Congress is unconstitutional and thereby illegal.

Sec. 3. Presidential Duty and Immediacy. According to the President's duty to uphold the Constitution of the United States of America, as the President has sworn or affirmed to uphold such Constitution, all sections of this executive order will be immediately understood and carried out by all branches of the United States Federal Government as it pertains to them, without regard to any court order that goes against the Constitution.

Sec. 4. Military Orders. Unless towards the ends of a congressionally declared, Constitutional war [there are none as of this December 22nd, 2017 writing], I order that all troops and equipment on foreign soil begin their journey home as soon as possible while still maintaining their safety. All Federally employed contractors on foreign soil, not part of an embassy or consulate, may cease to serve the United States as all of their contracts are hereby ended. All foreign bases will be sold back to their parent countries, or leases immediately terminated, and any equipment that can be returned to the United States must be returned by the foreign countries.

Going forward, no troops or military contractors will touch foreign soil without a formal, congressional, Constitutional declaration of war.

All acts of aggression such as drone strikes, bombings, and covert operations will immediately cease and continue to cease unless there is a formal, congressional, Constitutional declaration of war, or an immediate, credible threat to our nation's soil, skies, waters, or the people on and in them.

Sec. 5. Reaffirmation of the Tenth Amendment of the Constitution. It is reaffirmed that, according to the Tenth Amendment of the Constitution of the United States, and implied by the Constitution before it was ever amended, all powers of the previously mentioned entities are reserved to the States respectively, or to the People, and, therefore, none of the powers that these previously mentioned entities had will henceforward be exercised by the Federal Government, without there first being a ratified amendment to the Constitution that gives power over some area where these entities served to the Federal Government.

Sec. 6. Responsibilities of the People and their State Governments. Regarding the topic(s) of this Executive Order, the People and their respective State Governments, or the People alone, are urged to take care of anything previously attended to by the Federal Government. If any State desires to take action regarding a topic of this Executive Order, the Congress of the United States is urged to approve such State action so that the state may accomplish these or related things which were previously attended to by the Federal Government,

if Congressional approval is Constitutionally required for the State to take such action.

Sec. 7. Pardons and Contracts. (a) A Full and Unconditional Pardon is hereby given to anyone who has been charged or convicted of any Federal crime or offense related to any of the unconstitutional laws that were deemed unenforceable according to this Executive Order.

(b) Regardless of any contracts or agreements that were signed or sworn to towards unconstitutional ends, anyone who exposes the Federal Government for doing anything unconstitutional, including the items outlined in this Executive Order, will be given a Full and Unconditional Pardon for exposing such unconstitutional Federal actions. Also, regardless of any contracts or agreements that were signed or sworn to towards unconstitutional ends, anyone who has exposed the Federal Government for doing anything unconstitutional, including the items outlined in this Executive Order, is hereby given a Full and Unconditional Pardon for exposing such unconstitutional Federal actions.

Sec. 8. General Provisions. (a) This order is not intended to, and does not, create any right or benefit, substantive or procedural, enforceable at law or in equity by any party against the United States, its departments, agencies, or entities, its officers, employees, or agents, or any other person.

(b) This order is not intended to, and does not, go against the Constitution of the United States. Everything in this order has the intent of restoring the supreme law of the land, which is the Constitution of the United States of America; if any part of this order is deemed as going against the Constitution, any remedy must be at the discretion of each individual charged with that remedy, including judges, officials, secretaries, and people at any and every level of government. Those individuals are each urged to ask if the remedy is Constitutional according to the original intent and spirit of the Constitution when written by our founding fathers in the seventeen hundreds. If any part of this order is ultimately deemed unconstitutional by any individual or institution, all other parts of this order will remain in full force and effect in perpetuity, or until the Constitution is amended or superseded.

[THE NAME AND SIGNATURE OF THE PRESIDENT OF THE UNITED STATES]

THE WHITE HOUSE,

[Date].

CHAPTER 9

CONCLUSION

As of February 2017, we're at 19.97 trillion dollars of Federal debt. If we continue for the next 15 years as we have for the past 15 years (from 2000 to 2015), we'll be at 64 trillion dollars of debt by 2032. I want to write that out to help visualize how much money that is: $64,000,000,000,000.00.

The tallest building in the world is the Burj Khalifa. It weighs one billion pounds when empty.[128] Even if the entire building were made of pure gold, it would take over three and a half Burj Khalifas to pay back that debt.[129]

By regular, earthly powers, I do not think we can bear a burden that large. I believe we face two options: either we have drastic cuts to the federal government where hundreds of thousands of federal employees lose their jobs and the federal redistribution of wealth and income is drastically cut or constitutionally ends, with the states and the people taking care of these things, or the cuts we need to make will be forced upon us when our financial system crumbles because we default on our debt virtually, through inflation, or we actually default.

If we choose default, we will be like Greece over the past several years, only there will be nobody to bail us out. Perhaps even more federal employees will lose their jobs than if we had done the cuts before the collapse.

Beyond this, trillions of dollars of wealth will be wiped out because people's dollars will be much less valuable or will be worthless; dollar-denominated savings will be much less valuable or will be worthless; or if we don't have hyperinflation, we will have defaulted on our debt, and many people's retirement and other savings will largely be wiped out since people relied on the ability of the United States to pay its debt. Whether we have hyperinflation or an actual default, federal bonds will lose much or all of their value.

We can't keep kicking the can to the next generation. This is it. This generation either will save this nation from collapse, or it won't. I want us to save the nation from collapse, and I want us to do it in perhaps the simplest way possible—a return to the rule of law in our country: a return to our constitution.

APPENDIX

ON THE U.S. CONSTITUTION

"The death of democracy is not likely to be an assassination from ambush. It will be a slow extinction from apathy, indifference, and undernourishment." —Robert M. Hutchins[130]

At this point, for your reference, I'm adding a copy of the Constitution. With this Constitution, I'm going to add some underlining. I will underline the powers given to the United States Federal Government by the Constitution. I'm going to double underline the items that the Constitution forbids the states from doing. There may be some spelling mistakes or minor errors, as I have tried to use the original text of the Constitution.

After the text, I'm going to list the Federal powers and the things forbidden to the states so that we can focus on them. As you'll recall, the things listed in the Constitution that the Federal Government can do are exclusive, which means that there's nothing beyond those things that the Federal Government can do.

This means that any limits to the Federal Government listed in the Constitution are not needed, but may help to clarify the original intent of the Constitution.

The Tenth Amendment does not change the intent of the Constitution in any way, but it makes clear to us, over 200 years later, what the exact intent of the Constitution is, "The powers not delegated to the United States by the Constitution, nor prohibited by it to the States, are reserved to the States respectively, or to the people."

One of the things I'm not always underlining is powers of the Federal Government that are the operations of government business such as electing the president and electing Congress. I may have skipped anything mechanical having to do with the government even though it is a power of government. These are the powers of government that allow the people to control it, and they also allow the government to control itself.

I think we are following this mechanical part of the Constitution pretty well, so we don't need to worry too much about it. I'm going to focus on powers that the Federal Government has external to itself.

Feel free to skip the Constitution or the original intent explanations if you feel you already have a good knowledge of those topics you can move on to the Executive Order section, or anywhere else in the book.

A few notes before we get to the text:

The Bill of Rights is almost totally implied by the Constitution and doesn't change the rights of the states at all, contrary to some rulings of the Supreme Court. Amendments 11-27 are as found on yale.edu and may include corrections of minor errors in the original.

Some double underlines are also single underlines; in other words, some limits on state power are also powers of the Federal Government, and I have tried to explicitly call this out after the entire Constitution. This happens quite a bit in amendments where Congress is granted the power to enforce the rest of an article upon the states.

The Constitution can be a little tricky to understand for a few reasons. It has some misspellings or typos because this is largely in its original form. It's also tricky because some of the English is less than modern as it was written over two hundred years ago. The final tricky part is the way it has been updated. Since it is updated through amendments, there are some amendments which invalidate certain older parts of the Constitution. You can usually tell when the Constitution is making a previous portion invalid because it will be in the form of an amendment that typically directly references text from the Constitution.

If you're already familiar with the Constitution, feel free to skip it and move on to the Original Intent of the Constitution portion. If you're already familiar with the original intent of the Constitution, feel free to skip that part as well.

The Constitution of the United States of America

The Preamble

We the People of the United States, in Order to form a more perfect Union, establish Justice, insure domestic Tranquility, provide for the common defence, promote the general Welfare, and secure the Blessings of Liberty to ourselves and our Posterity, do ordain and establish this Constitution for the United States of America.

Article. I.

Section. 1.

All legislative Powers herein granted shall be vested in a Congress of the United States, which shall consist of a Senate and House of Representatives.

Section. 2.

The House of Representatives shall be composed of Members chosen every second Year by the People of the several States, and the Electors in each State shall have the Qualifications requisite for Electors of the most numerous Branch of the State Legislature.

No Person shall be a Representative who shall not have attained to the Age of twenty five Years, and been seven Years a Citizen of the United States, and who shall not, when elected, be an Inhabitant of that State in which he shall be chosen.

Representatives and direct Taxes shall be apportioned among the several States which may be included within this Union, according to their respective Numbers, which shall be determined by adding to the whole Number of free Persons, including those bound to Service for a Term of Years, and excluding Indians not taxed, three fifths of all other Persons. <u>The actual Enumeration shall be made within three Years after the first Meeting of the Congress of the United States, and within every subsequent Term of ten Years, in such Manner as they shall by Law direct.</u> The Number of Representatives shall not exceed one for every thirty Thousand, but each State shall have at Least one Representative; and until such enumeration shall be made, the State of New Hampshire shall be entitled to chuse three, Massachusetts eight, Rhode-Island and Providence Plantations one, Connecticut five, New-York six, New Jersey four, Pennsylvania eight, Delaware one, Maryland six, Virginia ten, North Carolina five, South Carolina five, and Georgia three.

When vacancies happen in the Representation from any State, the Executive Authority thereof shall issue Writs of Election to fill such Vacancies.

<u>The House of Representatives shall chuse their Speaker and other Officers; and shall have the sole Power of Impeachment.</u>

Section. 3.

The Senate of the United States shall be composed of two Senators from each State, chosen by the Legislature thereof, for six Years; and each Senator shall have one Vote.

Immediately after they shall be assembled in Consequence of the first Election, they shall be divided as equally as may be into three Classes. The Seats of the Senators of the first Class shall be vacated at the Expiration of the second Year, of the second Class at the Expiration of the fourth Year, and of the third Class at the Expiration of the sixth Year, so that one third may be chosen every second Year; and if Vacancies happen by Resignation, or otherwise, during the Recess of the Legislature of any State, the Executive thereof may make temporary Appointments until the next Meeting of the Legislature, which shall then fill such Vacancies.

No Person shall be a Senator who shall not have attained to the Age of thirty Years, and been nine Years a Citizen of the United States, and who shall not, when elected, be an Inhabitant of that State for which he shall be chosen.

The Vice President of the United States shall be President of the Senate, but shall have no Vote, unless they be equally divided.

The Senate shall chuse their other Officers, and also a President pro tempore, in the Absence of the Vice President, or when he shall exercise the Office of President of the United States.

The Senate shall have the sole Power to try all Impeachments. When sitting for that Purpose, they shall be on Oath or Affirmation. When the President of the United States is tried, the Chief Justice shall preside: And no Person shall be convicted without the Concurrence of two thirds of the Members present.

Judgment in Cases of Impeachment shall not extend further than to removal from Office, and disqualification to hold and enjoy any Office of honor, Trust or Profit under the United States: but the Party convicted shall nevertheless be liable and subject to Indictment, Trial, Judgment and Punishment, according to Law.

Section. 4.

The Times, Places and Manner of holding Elections for Senators and Representatives, shall be prescribed in each State by the Legislature thereof; but the Congress may at any time by Law make or alter such Regulations, except as to the Places of chusing Senators.

The Congress shall assemble at least once in every Year, and such Meeting shall be on the first Monday in December, unless they shall by Law appoint a different Day.

Section. 5.

Each House shall be the Judge of the Elections, Returns and Qualifications of its own Members, and a Majority of each shall constitute a Quorum to do Business; but a smaller Number may adjourn from day to day, and may be authorized to compel the Attendance of absent

Members, in such Manner, and under such Penalties as each House may provide.

Each House may determine the Rules of its Proceedings, punish its Members for disorderly Behaviour, and, with the Concurrence of two thirds, expel a Member.

Each House shall keep a Journal of its Proceedings, and from time to time publish the same, excepting such Parts as may in their Judgment require Secrecy; and the Yeas and Nays of the Members of either House on any question shall, at the Desire of one fifth of those Present, be entered on the Journal.

Neither House, during the Session of Congress, shall, without the Consent of the other, adjourn for more than three days, nor to any other Place than that in which the two Houses shall be sitting.

Section. 6.

The Senators and Representatives shall receive a Compensation for their Services, to be ascertained by Law, and paid out of the Treasury of the United States. They shall in all Cases, except Treason, Felony and Breach of the Peace, be privileged from Arrest during their Attendance at the Session of their respective Houses, and in going to and returning from the same; and for any Speech or Debate in either House, they shall not be questioned in any other Place.

No Senator or Representative shall, during the Time for which he was elected, be appointed to any civil Office under the Authority of the United States, which have been created, or the Emoluments whereof shall have been encreased during such time; and no Person holding any Office under the United States, shall be a Member of either House during his Continuance in Office.

Section. 7.

All Bills for raising Revenue shall originate in the House of Representatives; but the Senate may propose or concur with Amendments as on other Bills.

Every Bill which shall have passed the House of Representatives and the Senate, shall, before it become a Law, be presented to the President of the United States; If he approve he shall sign it, but if not he shall return it, with his Objections to that House in which it shall have originated, who shall enter the Objections at large on their Journal, and proceed to reconsider it. If after such Reconsideration two thirds of that House shall agree to pass the Bill, it shall be sent, together with the Objections, to the other House, by which it shall likewise be reconsidered, and if approved by two thirds of that House, it shall become a Law. But in all such Cases the Votes of both Houses shall be determined by yeas and Nays, and the Names of the Persons voting for and against the Bill shall be entered on the Journal of each House respectively. If any Bill shall not be returned by the President within ten Days (Sundays excepted) after it shall have been presented to him, the Same shall be a Law, in like Manner as if he had signed it, unless the Congress by their Adjournment prevent its Return, in which Case it shall not be a Law.

Every Order, Resolution, or Vote to which the Concurrence of the Senate and House of Representatives may be necessary (except on a question of Adjournment) shall be presented to the President of the United States; and before the Same shall take Effect, shall be approved by him, or being disapproved by him, shall be repassed by two thirds of the Senate and House of Representatives, according to the Rules and Limitations prescribed in the Case of a Bill.

Section. 8.

The Congress shall have Power To lay and collect Taxes, Duties, Imposts and Excises, to pay the Debts and provide for the common Defence and general Welfare of the United States; but all Duties, Imposts and Excises shall be uniform throughout the United States;

To borrow Money on the credit of the United States;

To regulate Commerce with foreign Nations, and among the several States, and with the Indian Tribes;

To establish an uniform Rule of Naturalization, and uniform Laws on the subject of Bankruptcies throughout the United States;

To coin Money, regulate the Value thereof, and of foreign Coin, and fix the Standard of Weights and Measures;

To provide for the Punishment of counterfeiting the Securities and current Coin of the United States;

To establish Post Offices and post Roads;

To promote the Progress of Science and useful Arts, by securing for limited Times to Authors and Inventors the exclusive Right to their respective Writings and Discoveries;

To constitute Tribunals inferior to the supreme Court;

To define and punish Piracies and Felonies committed on the high Seas, and Offences against the Law of Nations;

To declare War, grant Letters of Marque and Reprisal, and make Rules concerning Captures on Land and Water;

To raise and support Armies, but no Appropriation of Money to that Use shall be for a longer Term than two Years;

To provide and maintain a Navy;

To make Rules for the Government and Regulation of the land and naval Forces;

To provide for calling forth the Militia to execute the Laws of the Union, suppress Insurrections and repel Invasions;

To provide for organizing, arming, and disciplining, the Militia, and for governing such Part of them as may be employed in the Service of the United States, reserving to the States respectively, the Appointment of the Officers, and the Authority of training the Militia according to the discipline prescribed by Congress;

To exercise exclusive Legislation in all Cases whatsoever, over such District (not exceeding ten Miles square) as may, by Cession of particular States, and the Acceptance of Congress, become the Seat of the Government of the United States, and to exercise like Authority over all Places purchased by the Consent of the Legislature of the State in which the Same shall be, for the Erection of

Forts, Magazines, Arsenals, dock-Yards, and other needful Buildings;—And

To make all Laws which shall be necessary and proper for carrying into Execution the foregoing Powers, and all other Powers vested by this Constitution in the Government of the United States, or in any Department or Officer thereof.

Section. 9.

The Migration or Importation of such Persons as any of the States now existing shall think proper to admit, shall not be prohibited by the Congress prior to the Year one thousand eight hundred and eight, but a Tax or duty may be imposed on such Importation, not exceeding ten dollars for each Person.

The Privilege of the Writ of Habeas Corpus shall not be suspended, unless when in Cases of Rebellion or Invasion the public Safety may require it.

No Bill of Attainder or ex post facto Law shall be passed.

No Capitation, or other direct, Tax shall be laid, unless in Proportion to the Census or enumeration herein before directed to be taken.

No Tax or Duty shall be laid on Articles exported from any State.

No Preference shall be given by any Regulation of Commerce or Revenue to the Ports of one State over those of another: nor shall Vessels bound to, or from, one State, be obliged to enter, clear, or pay Duties in another.

No Money shall be drawn from the Treasury, but in Consequence of Appropriations made by Law; and <u>a regular Statement and Account of the Receipts and Expenditures of all public Money shall be published from time to time.</u>

No Title of Nobility shall be granted by the United States: <u>And no Person holding any Office of Profit or Trust under them, shall, without the Consent of the Congress, accept of any present, Emolument, Office, or Title, of any kind whatever, from any King, Prince, or foreign State.</u>

Section. 10.

<u>No State shall enter into any Treaty, Alliance, or Confederation; grant Letters of Marque and Reprisal; coin Money; emit Bills of Credit; make any Thing but gold and silver Coin a Tender in Payment of Debts; pass any Bill of Attainder, ex post facto Law, or Law impairing the Obligation of Contracts, or grant any Title of Nobility.</u>

<u>No State shall, without the Consent of the Congress, lay any Imposts or Duties on Imports or Exports, except what may be absolutely necessary for executing its inspection Laws: and the net Produce of all Duties and Imposts, laid by any State on Imports or Exports, shall be for the Use of the Treasury of the United States; and all such Laws shall be subject to the Revision and Controul of the Congress.</u>

<u>No State shall, without the Consent of Congress, lay any Duty of Tonnage, keep Troops, or Ships of War in</u>

time of Peace, enter into any Agreement or Compact with another State, or with a foreign Power, or engage in War, unless actually invaded, or in such imminent Danger as will not admit of delay.

Article. II.

Section. 1.

The executive Power shall be vested in a President of the United States of America. He shall hold his Office during the Term of four Years, and, together with the Vice President, chosen for the same Term, be elected, as follows

Each State shall appoint, in such Manner as the Legislature thereof may direct, a Number of Electors, equal to the whole Number of Senators and Representatives to which the State may be entitled in the Congress: but no Senator or Representative, or Person holding an Office of Trust or Profit under the United States, shall be appointed an Elector.

The Electors shall meet in their respective States, and vote by Ballot for two Persons, of whom one at least shall not be an Inhabitant of the same State with themselves. And they shall make a List of all the Persons voted for, and of the Number of Votes for each; which List they shall sign and certify, and transmit sealed to the Seat of the Government of the United States, directed to the President of the Senate. The President of the Senate shall, in the Presence of the Senate and House of Representatives, open all the Certificates, and the Votes shall then be counted. The Person having the greatest Number of Votes shall be the President, if such Number be a Majority of the whole Number of Electors appointed; and if there be more than one who have such Majority, and have an equal Number of Votes, then the House of Representatives shall immediately chuse by Ballot one of them for President; and if no Person have a Majority, then from the five highest on the List the said House shall in like Manner chuse the President. But in chusing the President, the Votes shall be taken by States, the Representation from each State having one Vote; A quorum for this Purpose shall consist of a Member or Members from two thirds of the States, and a Majority of all the States shall be necessary to a Choice. In every Case, after the Choice of the President, the Person having the greatest Number of Votes of the Electors shall be the Vice President. But if there should remain two or more who have equal Votes, the Senate shall chuse from them by Ballot the Vice President.

The Congress may determine the Time of chusing the Electors, and the Day on which they shall give their Votes; which Day shall be the same throughout the United States.

No Person except a natural born Citizen, or a Citizen of the United States, at the time of the Adoption of this Constitution, shall be eligible to the Office of President; neither shall any Person be eligible to that Office who shall not have attained to the Age of thirty five Years, and been fourteen Years a Resident within the United States.

In Case of the Removal of the President from Office, or of his Death, Resignation, or Inability to discharge the Powers and Duties of the said Office, the Same shall devolve on the Vice President, and <u>the Congress may by Law provide for the Case of Removal, Death, Resignation or Inability, both of the President and Vice President, declaring what Officer shall then act as President, and such Officer shall act accordingly, until the Disability be removed, or a President shall be elected.</u>

The President shall, at stated Times, receive for his Services, a Compensation, which shall neither be encreased nor diminished during the Period for which he shall have been elected, and he shall not receive within that Period any other Emolument from the United States, or any of them.

Before he enter on the Execution of his Office, he shall take the following Oath or Affirmation:—"I do solemnly swear (or affirm) that I will faithfully execute the Office of President of the United States, and will to the best of my Ability, preserve, protect and defend the Constitution of the United States."

Section. 2.

The President shall be Commander in Chief of the Army and Navy of the United States, and of the Militia of the several States, when called into the actual Service of the United States; he may require the Opinion, in writing, of the principal Officer in each of the executive Departments, upon any Subject relating to the Duties of their respective Offices, and he shall have Power to grant

Reprieves and Pardons for Offences against the United States, except in Cases of Impeachment.

He shall have Power, by and with the Advice and Consent of the Senate, to make Treaties, provided two thirds of the Senators present concur; and he shall nominate, and by and with the Advice and Consent of the Senate, shall appoint Ambassadors, other public Ministers and Consuls, Judges of the supreme Court, and all other Officers of the United States, whose Appointments are not herein otherwise provided for, and which shall be established by Law: but the Congress may by Law vest the Appointment of such inferior Officers, as they think proper, in the President alone, in the Courts of Law, or in the Heads of Departments.

The President shall have Power to fill up all Vacancies that may happen during the Recess of the Senate, by granting Commissions which shall expire at the End of their next Session.

Section. 3.

He shall from time to time give to the Congress Information of the State of the Union, and recommend to their Consideration such Measures as he shall judge necessary and expedient; he may, on extraordinary Occasions, convene both Houses, or either of them, and in Case of Disagreement between them, with Respect to the Time of Adjournment, he may adjourn them to such Time as he shall think proper; he shall receive Ambassadors and other public Ministers; he shall take

Care that the Laws be faithfully executed, and shall Commission all the Officers of the United States.

Section. 4.

The President, Vice President and all civil Officers of the United States, shall be removed from Office on Impeachment for, and Conviction of, Treason, Bribery, or other high Crimes and Misdemeanors.

Article III.

Section. 1.

<u>The judicial Power of the United States, shall be vested in one supreme Court, and in such inferior Courts as the Congress may from time to time ordain and establish.</u> The Judges, both of the supreme and inferior Courts, shall hold their Offices during good Behaviour, and shall, at stated Times, receive for their Services, a Compensation, which shall not be diminished during their Continuance in Office.

Section. 2.

The judicial Power shall extend to all Cases, in Law and Equity, arising under this Constitution, the Laws of the United States, and Treaties made, or which shall be made, under their Authority;—to all Cases affecting Ambassadors, other public Ministers and Consuls;—to all Cases of admiralty and maritime Jurisdiction;—to Controversies to which the United States shall be a Party;—to Controversies between two or more States;—

between a State and Citizens of another State,—between Citizens of different States,—between Citizens of the same State claiming Lands under Grants of different States, and between a State, or the Citizens thereof, and foreign States, Citizens or Subjects.

In all Cases affecting Ambassadors, other public Ministers and Consuls, and those in which a State shall be Party, the supreme Court shall have original Jurisdiction. In all the other Cases before mentioned, the supreme Court shall have appellate Jurisdiction, both as to Law and Fact, with such Exceptions, and under such Regulations as the Congress shall make.

The Trial of all Crimes, except in Cases of Impeachment, shall be by Jury; and such Trial shall be held in the State where the said Crimes shall have been committed; but when not committed within any State, the Trial shall be at such Place or Places as the Congress may by Law have directed.

Section. 3.

Treason against the United States, shall consist only in levying War against them, or in adhering to their Enemies, giving them Aid and Comfort. No Person shall be convicted of Treason unless on the Testimony of two Witnesses to the same overt Act, or on Confession in open Court.

The Congress shall have Power to declare the Punishment of Treason, but no Attainder of Treason shall work Corruption of Blood, or Forfeiture except during the Life of the Person attainted.

Article. IV.

Section. 1.

Full Faith and Credit shall be given in each State to the public Acts, Records, and judicial Proceedings of every other State. And the Congress may by general Laws prescribe the Manner in which such Acts, Records and Proceedings shall be proved, and the Effect thereof.

Section. 2.

The Citizens of each State shall be entitled to all Privileges and Immunities of Citizens in the several States.

A Person charged in any State with Treason, Felony, or other Crime, who shall flee from Justice, and be found in another State, shall on Demand of the executive Authority of the State from which he fled, be delivered up, to be removed to the State having Jurisdiction of the Crime.

No Person held to Service or Labour in one State, under the Laws thereof, escaping into another, shall, in Consequence of any Law or Regulation therein, be discharged from such Service or Labour, but shall be delivered up on Claim of the Party to whom such Service or Labour may be due.

Section. 3.

New States may be admitted by the Congress into this Union; but no new State shall be formed or erected within the Jurisdiction of any other State; nor any State be formed by the Junction of two or more States, or Parts of States, without the Consent of the Legislatures of the States concerned as well as of the Congress.

The Congress shall have Power to dispose of and make all needful Rules and Regulations respecting the Territory or other Property belonging to the United States; and nothing in this Constitution shall be so construed as to Prejudice any Claims of the United States, or of any particular State.

Section. 4.

The United States shall guarantee to every State in this Union a Republican Form of Government, and shall protect each of them against Invasion; and on Application of the Legislature, or of the Executive (when the Legislature cannot be convened), against domestic Violence.

Article. V.

The Congress, whenever two thirds of both Houses shall deem it necessary, shall propose Amendments to this Constitution, or, on the Application of the Legislatures of two thirds of the several States, shall call a Convention for proposing Amendments, which, in either Case, shall be valid to all Intents and Purposes, as Part of this Constitution, when ratified by the Legislatures of three fourths of the several States, or by Conventions in three fourths thereof, as the one or the other Mode of Ratification may be proposed by the Congress; Provided that no Amendment which may be made prior to the Year

One thousand eight hundred and eight shall in any Manner affect the first and fourth Clauses in the Ninth Section of the first Article; and that no State, without its Consent, shall be deprived of its equal Suffrage in the Senate.

Article. VI.

All Debts contracted and Engagements entered into, before the Adoption of this Constitution, shall be as valid against the United States under this Constitution, as under the Confederation.

This Constitution, and the Laws of the United States which shall be made in Pursuance thereof; and all Treaties made, or which shall be made, under the Authority of the United States, shall be the supreme Law of the Land; and the Judges in every State shall be bound thereby, any Thing in the Constitution or Laws of any State to the Contrary notwithstanding.

The Senators and Representatives before mentioned, and the Members of the several State Legislatures, and all executive and judicial Officers, both of the United States and of the several States, shall be bound by Oath or Affirmation, to support this Constitution; but no religious Test shall ever be required as a Qualification to any Office or public Trust under the United States.

Article. VII.

The Ratification of the Conventions of nine States, shall be sufficient for the Establishment of this Constitution between the States so ratifying the Same.

The Word, "the," being interlined between the seventh and eighth Lines of the first Page, The Word "Thirty" being partly written on an Erazure in the fifteenth Line of the first Page, The Words "is tried" being interlined between the thirty second and thirty third Lines of the first Page and the Word "the" being interlined between the forty third and forty fourth Lines of the second Page.

Attest William Jackson Secretary

done in Convention by the Unanimous Consent of the States present the Seventeenth Day of September in the Year of our Lord one thousand seven hundred and Eighty seven and of the Independance of the United States of America the Twelfth In witness whereof We have hereunto subscribed our Names,

G°. Washington, Presidt and deputy from Virginia

Delaware - Geo: Read, Gunning Bedford jun, John Dickinson, Richard Bassett, Jaco: Broom

Maryland - James McHenry, Dan of St Thos. Jenifer, Danl. Carroll

Virginia - John Blair, James Madison Jr.

North Carolina - Wm. Blount, Richd. Dobbs Spaight, Hu Williamson

South Carolina - J. Rutledge, Charles Cotesworth Pinckney, Charles Pinckney, Pierce Butler

Georgia - William Few, Abr Baldwin

New Hampshire - John Langdon, Nicholas Gilman

Massachusetts - Nathaniel Gorham, Rufus King

Connecticut - Wm. Saml. Johnson, Roger Sherman

New York - Alexander Hamilton

New Jersey - Wil: Livingston, David Brearley, Wm. Paterson, Jona: Dayton

Pennsylvania - B Franklin, Thomas Mifflin, Robt. Morris, Geo. Clymer, Thos. FitzSimons, Jared Ingersoll, James Wilson, Gouv Morris

[The first ten amendments to the original Constitution are next - they are also known as the Bill of Rights and were ratified just over three years after the original Constitution was ratified]

Amendment I

Congress shall make no law respecting an establishment of religion, or prohibiting the free exercise thereof; or abridging the freedom of speech, or of the press; or the right of the people peaceably to assemble, and to petition the Government for a redress of grievances.

Amendment II

A well regulated Militia, being necessary to the security of a free State, the right of the people to keep and bear Arms, shall not be infringed.

Amendment III

No Soldier shall, in time of peace be quartered in any house, without the consent of the Owner, nor in time of war, but in a manner to be prescribed by law.

Amendment IV

The right of the people to be secure in their persons, houses, papers, and effects, against unreasonable searches and seizures, shall not be violated, and no Warrants shall issue, but upon probable cause, supported by Oath or affirmation, and particularly describing the place to be searched, and the persons or things to be seized.

Amendment V

No person shall be held to answer for a capital, or otherwise infamous crime, unless on a presentment or indictment of a Grand Jury, except in cases arising in the land or naval forces, or in the Militia, when in actual service in time of War or public danger; nor shall any person be subject for the same offence to be twice put in jeopardy of life or limb; nor shall be compelled in any criminal case to be a witness against himself, nor be deprived of life, liberty, or property, without due process of law; nor shall private property be taken for public use, without just compensation.

Amendment VI

In all criminal prosecutions, the accused shall enjoy the right to a speedy and public trial, by an impartial jury of the State and district wherein the crime shall have been committed, which district shall have been previously ascertained by law, and to be informed of the nature and cause of the accusation; to be confronted with the witnesses against him; to have compulsory process for obtaining witnesses in his favor, and to have the Assistance of Counsel for his defence.

Amendment VII

In Suits at common law, where the value in controversy shall exceed twenty dollars, the right of trial by jury shall be preserved, and no fact tried by a jury, shall be otherwise re-examined in any Court of the United States, than according to the rules of the common law.

Amendment VIII

Excessive bail shall not be required, nor excessive fines imposed, nor cruel and unusual punishments inflicted.

Amendment IX

The enumeration in the Constitution, of certain rights, shall not be construed to deny or disparage others retained by the people.

Amendment X

The powers not delegated to the United States by the Constitution, nor prohibited by it to the States, are reserved to the States respectively, or to the people.

Amendment XI

The judicial power of the United States shall not be construed to extend to any suit in law or equity, commenced or prosecuted against one of the United States by citizens of another State, or by citizens or subjects of any foreign state.

Amendment XII

The electors shall meet in their respective states and vote by ballot for President and Vice-President, one of whom, at least, shall not be an inhabitant of the same state with themselves; they shall name in their ballots the person voted for as President, and in distinct ballots the person voted for as Vice-President, and they shall make distinct lists of all persons voted for as President, and of all persons voted for as Vice-President, and of the number of votes for each, which lists they shall sign and certify, and transmit sealed to the seat of the government of the United States, directed to the President of the Senate;--

The President of the Senate shall, in the presence of the Senate and House of Representatives, open all the certificates and the votes shall then be counted;--the person having the greatest number of votes for President, shall be the President, if such number be a majority of the whole number of electors appointed; and if no person have such majority, then from the persons having the highest numbers not exceeding three on the list of those voted for as President, the House of Representatives shall choose immediately, by ballot, the President. But in choosing the President, the votes shall be taken by states, the representation from each state having one vote; a quorum for this purpose shall consist of a member or members from two-thirds of the states, and a majority of all the states shall be necessary to a choice. And if the House of Representatives shall not choose a President whenever the right of choice shall devolve upon them, before the fourth day of March next following, then the Vice-President shall act as President, as in the case of the death or other constitutional disability of the President. The person having the greatest number of votes as Vice-President, shall be the Vice-President, if such number be a majority of the whole number of electors appointed, and if no person have a majority, then from the two highest numbers on the list, the Senate shall choose the Vice-President; a quorum for the purpose shall consist of two-thirds of the whole number of Senators, and a majority of the whole number shall be necessary to a choice. But no person constitutionally ineligible to the office of President shall be eligible to that of Vice-President of the United States.

Amendment XIII

1. <u>Neither slavery nor involuntary servitude, except as a punishment for crime whereof the party shall have been duly convicted, shall exist within the United States, or any place subject to their jurisdiction.</u>

2. <u>Congress shall have power to enforce this article by appropriate legislation.</u>

Amendment XIV

1. All persons born or naturalized in the United States, and subject to the jurisdiction thereof, are citizens of the United States and of the State wherein they reside. <u>No State shall make or enforce any law which shall abridge the privileges or immunities of citizens of the United States; nor shall any State deprive any person of life, liberty, or property, without due process of law; nor to deny to any person within its jurisdiction the equal protection of the laws.</u>

2. Representatives shall be apportioned among the several States according to their respective numbers, counting the whole number of persons in each State, excluding Indians not taxed. <u>But when the right to vote at</u>

<u>any election for the choice of Electors for President and Vice-President of the United States, Representatives in Congress, the executive and judicial officers of a State, or the members of the legislature thereof, is denied to any of the male inhabitants of such State, being twenty-one years of age, and citizens of the United States, or in any way abridged, except for participation in rebellion, or other crime, the basis of representation therein shall be reduced in the proportion which the number of such male citizens shall bear to the whole number of male citizens twenty-one years of age in such State.</u>

3. No person shall be a Senator or Representative in Congress, or Elector of President and Vice-President, or hold any office, civil or military, under the United States, or under any State, who, having previously taken an oath, as a member of Congress, or as an officer of the United States, or as a member of any State Legislature, or as an executive or judicial officer of any State, to support the Constitution of the United States, shall have engaged in insurrection or rebellion against the same, or given aid or comfort to the enemies thereof. But Congress may by a vote of two-thirds of each House, remove such disability.

4. The validity of the public debt of the United States, authorized by law, including debts incurred for payment of pensions and bounties for services in suppressing insurrection or rebellion, shall not be questioned. <u>But neither the United States nor any State shall assume or</u>

pay any debt or obligation incurred in aid of insurrection or rebellion against the United States, or any claim for the loss or emancipation of any slave; but all such debts, obligations and claims shall be held illegal and void.

5. The Congress shall have the power to enforce, by appropriate legislation, the provisions of this article.

Amendment XV

1. The right of citizens of the United States to vote shall not be denied or abridged by the United States or by any State on account of race, color, or previous condition of servitude.

2. The Congress shall have the power to enforce this article by appropriate legislation.

Amendment XVI

The Congress shall have power to lay and collect taxes on incomes, from whatever sources derived, without apportionment among the several States, and without regard to any census or enumeration.

Amendment XVII

1. The Senate of the United States shall be composed of two Senators from each State, elected by the people thereof, for six years; and each Senator shall have one

vote. The electors in each State shall have the qualifications requisite for electors of the most numerous branch of the State Legislatures.

2. When vacancies happen in the representation of any State in the Senate, the executive authority of such State shall issue writs of election to fill such vacancies: Provided, That the Legislature of any State may empower the Executive thereof to make temporary appointments until the people fill the vacancies by election as the Legislature may direct.

3. This amendment shall not be so construed as to affect the election or term of any Senator chosen before it becomes valid as part of the Constitution.

Amendment XVIII

1. After one year from the ratification of this article the manufacture, sale, or transportation of intoxicating liquors within, the importation thereof into, or the exportation thereof from the United States and all territory subject to the jurisdiction thereof for beverage purposes is hereby prohibited.

2. The Congress and the several States shall have concurrent power to enforce this article by appropriate legislation.

3. This article shall be inoperative unless it shall have been ratified as an amendment to the Constitution by the Legislatures of the several States, as provided in the Constitution, within seven years from the date of the submission hereof to the States by the Congress.

Amendment XIX

1. <u>The right of citizens of the United States to vote shall not be denied or abridged by the United States or by any State on account of sex.</u>

2. Congress shall have power to enforce this article by appropriate legislation.

Amendment XX

1. The terms of the President and the Vice-President shall end at noon on the 20th day of January, and the terms of Senators and Representatives at noon on the 3rd day of January, of the years in which such terms would have ended if this article had not been ratified; and the terms of their successors shall then begin.

2. The Congress shall assemble at least once in every year, and such meeting shall begin at noon on the 3rd day of January, unless they shall by law appoint a different day.

3. If, at the time fixed for the beginning of the term of the President, the President elect shall have died, the Vice-President elect shall become President. If a President shall not have been chosen before the time fixed for the beginning of his term, or if the President elect shall have failed to qualify, then the Vice-President elect shall act as President until a President shall have qualified; and <u>the Congress may by law provide for the case wherein neither a President elect nor a Vice-President shall have qualified, declaring who shall then act as President, or the manner in which one who is to act shall be selected, and such person shall act accordingly until a President or Vice-President shall have qualified.</u>

4. <u>The Congress may by law provide for the case of the death of any of the persons from whom the House of representatives may choose a President whenever the right of choice shall have devolved upon them, and for the case of the death of any of the persons from whom the Senate may choose a Vice-President whenever the right of choice shall have devolved upon them.</u>

5. Sections 1 and 2 shall take effect on the 15th day of October following the ratification of this article.

6. This article shall be inoperative unless it shall have been ratified as an amendment to the Constitution by the

Legislatures of three-fourths of the several States within seven years from the date of its submission.

Amendment XXI

1. The Eighteenth article of amendment to the Constitution of the United States is hereby repealed.

2. The transportation or importation into any State, Territory, or Possession of the United States for delivery or use therein of intoxicating liquors, in violation of the laws thereof, is hereby prohibited.

3. This article shall be inoperative unless it shall have been ratified as an amendment to the Constitution by conventions in the several States, as provided in the Constitution, within seven years from the date of the submission hereof to the States by the Congress.

Amendment XXII

1. No person shall be elected to the office of the President more than twice, and no person who has held the office of President, or acted as President, for more than two years of a term to which some other person was elected President shall be elected to the office of the President more than once. But this article shall not apply to any person holding the office of President when this article was proposed by the Congress, and shall not

prevent any person who may be holding the office of President, or acting as President, during the term within which this article becomes operative from holding the office of President or acting as President during the remainder of such term.

2. This article shall be inoperative unless it shall have been ratified as an amendment to the Constitution by the legislatures of three-fourths of the several states within seven years from the date of its submission to the states by the Congress.

Amendment XXIII

1. The District constituting the seat of Government of the United States shall appoint in such manner as Congress may direct:

A number of electors of President and Vice President equal to the whole number of Senators and Representatives in Congress to which the District would be entitled if it were a State, but in no event more than the least populous State; they shall be in addition to those appointed by the States, but they shall be considered, for the purposes of the election of President and Vice President, to be electors appointed by a State; and they shall meet in the District and perform such duties as provided by the twelfth article of amendment.

2. The Congress shall have power to enforce this article by appropriate legislation.

Amendment XXIV

1. <u>The right of citizens of the United States to vote in any primary or other election for President or Vice President, for electors for President or Vice President, or for Senator or Representative in Congress, shall not be denied or abridged by the United States or any State by reason of failure to pay poll tax or any other tax.</u>

2. Congress shall have power to enforce this article by appropriate legislation.

Amendment XXV

1. In case of the removal of the President from office or of his death or resignation, the Vice President shall become President.

2. Whenever there is a vacancy in the office of the Vice President, the President shall nominate a Vice President who shall take the office upon confirmation by a majority vote of both houses of Congress

3. Whenever the President transmits to the President Pro tempore of the Senate and the Speaker of the House of Representatives his written declaration that he is unable

to discharge the powers and duties of his office, and until he transmits to them a written declaration to the contrary, such powers and duties shall be discharged by the Vice President as Acting President.

4. Whenever the Vice President and a majority of either the principal officers of the executive departments or of such other body as Congress may by law provide, transmits to the President Pro tempore of the Senate and the Speaker of the House of Representatives their written declaration that the President is unable to discharge the powers and duties of his office, the Vice President shall immediately assume the powers and duties of the office as Acting President.

5. Thereafter, when the President transmits to the President Pro tempore of the Senate and the Speaker of the House of Representatives his written declaration that no inability exists, he shall resume the powers and duties of his office unless the Vice President and a majority of either the principal officers of the executive departments or of such other body as Congress may by law provide, transmits within four days to the President Pro tempore of the Senate and the Speaker of the House of Representatives their written declaration that the President is unable to discharge the powers and duties of his office. Thereupon Congress shall decide the issue, assembling within forty-eight hours for that purpose if not in session. If the Congress, within twenty-one days

after receipt of the latter written declaration, or, if Congress is not in session within twenty-one days after Congress is required to assemble, determines by two-thirds vote of both houses that the President is unable to discharge the powers and duties of his office, the Vice President shall continue to discharge the same as Acting President; otherwise, the President shall resume the powers and duties of his office.

Amendment XXVI

<u>The right of citizens of the United States, who are 18 years of age or older, to vote shall not be denied or abridged by the United States or any state on account of age.</u>

The Congress shall have power to enforce this article by appropriate legislation.

Amendment XXVII

No law, varying the compensation for services of the Senators and Representatives, shall take effect, until an election of Representatives shall have intervened.

The End of the Constitution

Some comments on the Constitution before we revisit the items that have been underlined. The Preamble to the

Constitution is the first paragraph of the Constitution. It doesn't have any legally binding text. That's why I italicized it. Please don't think that when the preamble says, "promote the general Welfare" it means that the Constitution is providing a legal way for the Federal Government to have welfare of any form. It is not. But even if the Preamble is binding it is simply giving the reasons that the Constitution is being established, not giving any particular power to government.

Article 1 Section 1 is pretty interesting because it says, "All legislative Powers herein granted shall be vested in a Congress of the United States [...]" That word "All" is extremely important. It means that the Federal Government of the United States cannot have anyone else writing laws. It is only the Congress that can write laws, no one else, not the President, not the Supreme Court, not an agency or department, can write laws. The idea that no one else can write laws is very key.

The other extremely important part of the Constitution I'll print again here. It's the 10th Amendment:

The powers not delegated to the United States by the Constitution, nor prohibited by it to the States, are reserved to the States respectively, or to the people.

This book is based on the Tenth Amendment. Perhaps one of the reasons that people don't grasp the Tenth Amendment is that we are told that this amendment was implied by the original Constitution. This is true, but don't make the mistake of glossing over it. Just because it was implied doesn't mean that it's not extremely important. To reiterate, **there is not one thing that the Federal Government <u>can do</u> beyond what is written in the Constitution**. And under the Constitution, **there is not one thing that the states or people <u>cannot do</u> except for the restrictions for the states that are written in the Constitution**. In other words, the states, being republican forms of government, have virtually unlimited power, and the United States, the Federal Government, has extremely limited power.

The Original Intent of the Constitution

Here I will list all portions from above that I previously underlined in the entire Constitution. First I am listing the things that are powers of the Federal Government. These were single-underlined, and in some cases, they were double-underlined if they were also a limit on the states. I've added explanations on the text's meaning, original intent, and current ramifications in some cases.

From Article 1, Section 2:

<u>The actual Enumeration shall be made within three Years after the first Meeting of the Congress of the United States, and within every subsequent Term of ten Years, in such Manner as they shall by Law direct.</u> - This is the power and duty of Congress: do a Census every 10 years.

The House of Representatives shall chuse their Speaker and other Officers; and shall have the sole Power of Impeachment.

From Article 1, Section 3:

The Senate shall have the sole Power to try all Impeachments. When sitting for that Purpose, they shall be on Oath or Affirmation. When the President of the United States is tried, the Chief Justice shall preside: And no Person shall be convicted without the Concurrence of two thirds of the Members present.

From Article 1, Section 4: The Times, Places and Manner of holding Elections for Senators and Representatives, shall be prescribed in each State by the Legislature thereof; but the Congress may at any time by Law make or alter such Regulations, except as to the Places of chusing Senators. - Congress has the power to change the time, place, and manner of elections for Representatives in the House.

From Article 1, Section 5: Each House shall keep a Journal of its Proceedings, and from time to time publish the same, excepting such Parts as may in their Judgment require Secrecy; and the Yeas and Nays of the Members of either House on any question shall, at the Desire of one fifth of those Present, be entered on the Journal.

From Article 1, Section 5: and paid out of the Treasury of the United States - This is confirmation that Congress can establish and run a Treasury.

Article 1, Section 8: [The following 18 powers are the Enumerated Powers and form the core of what the Federal Government can do.]

The Congress shall have Power To lay and collect Taxes, Duties, Imposts and Excises, to pay the Debts and provide for the common Defence and general Welfare of the United States; but all Duties, Imposts and Excises shall be uniform throughout the United States;

To borrow Money on the credit of the United States; - I hope enacting this book's executive orders will help us do less of this borrowing, but it's not a constitutional requirement.

To regulate Commerce with foreign Nations, and among the several States, and with the Indian Tribes; - This "Commerce Clause" has been the reason behind a lot of misguided Federal regulation. I explained this topic in detail in the chapter title "The Commerce Clause", but to reiterate: all that the Commerce Clause allows is for the Federal Government to regulate international commerce. The only thing the Federal Government can do to regulate interstate commerce is to ensure that no regulations for or taxes on interstate commerce are created by the states. This interpretation is based on the original intent of the Founders. You can read about the Founders' original intent for the Commerce Clause in more detail in the Commerce chapter.

We know that the Founders wanted us to interpret the Constitution based on their line of thought. Here's one of the most important keys to understanding how the Constitution is meant to be understood: Here's Thomas

Jefferson in 1823, "**On every question of construction carry ourselves back to the time when the Constitution was adopted, recollect the spirit manifested in the debates and instead of trying what meaning may be squeezed out of the text or invented against it, conform to the probable one in which it was passed.**" The publication *What Would The Founders Think?* has this quote and more on how the Founders wanted the Constitution to be interpreted.[131]

To establish an uniform Rule of Naturalization, and uniform Laws on the subject of Bankruptcies throughout the United States; - Notice here that Congress is given power over naturalization, or granting citizenship. It is not given power over immigration: that is a state's right. I could understand if the American people wanted the Constitution amended to Federalize immigration, but until that amendment is ratified the Federal Government needs to stop involving itself with immigration.

To coin Money, regulate the Value thereof, and of foreign Coin, and fix the Standard of Weights and Measures; - At first glance, we might think that coining money and printing money are the same thing, but they are not. The founders did not want paper money from the government. They wanted money that was coins made out of metal. So, we cannot have printed money from government.

A related note: someone might think that the Constitution allows for Congress to have a bank, but it does not. Congress does not have the power to create a bank.

To provide for the Punishment of counterfeiting the Securities and current Coin of the United States;

To establish Post Offices and post Roads; - Arguments have been made either way as to whether Congress can build roads or designate roads as "post" roads, so it may currently be Constitutional to build post roads, but much of the current road building by the Federal Government has nothing to do with the Post or the Postal Service, so it is unconstitutional.

While presently the post office is Constitutional, I personally would support an amendment that stripped the Federal Government of these Postal powers, and the Post Office could be auctioned off to any domestic entity and deregulated. Powers of Congress like this one are optional. We wouldn't need an amendment to force the end of the post office, just Congressional action, but an amendment would make its removal more permanent.

In an age of the internet, email, and messaging apps, the government should not be required to secure cheap communication for all.

Affordable, nationwide communication was the goal of this power that has been delegated to the Federal Government, and since we now easily meet this goal without this Federal power, I would like to see the nation do away with it. Wouldn't the Founders be proud to see us stripping away even more powers from the Federal Government, than their original intent?

To promote the Progress of Science and useful Arts, by securing for limited Times to Authors and Inventors the exclusive Right to their respective Writings and

Discoveries; - Here's a power where I think the length of time of the exclusive right could be more limited, but it seems to be up to Congress to limit them as they see fit. Notice that there's nothing about Trademarks in this clause.

To constitute Tribunals inferior to the supreme Court;

To define and punish Piracies and Felonies committed on the high Seas, and Offences against the Law of Nations; - This is where the Federal Government is given the power to punish people for crimes, but notice that the power to punish people for crimes is on the high seas or against the Law of Nations.

This section is about punishing people for actions while on the oceans and for those disobeying the international laws of the times. Law of Nations in particular refers to things such as providing for the protection of diplomats and prisoners of war.[132]

The key is that Congress has been given no power to punish people for crimes within any of the states' physical borders (except in the case of infractions of international law), and as far as I know Congress doesn't try to do that. It's a beautiful thing - this is one of the few places where the Federal Government realizes there are states' rights and they abide by them.

I have to mention Roe v. Wade here, which is a related example where a Supreme Court decision made it illegal to make certain abortions illegal. This is not Constitutional.

When people do acts of terrorism within a state's borders or when people commit crimes in multiple states, the FBI likes to get involved. This is unconstitutional. The one exception to this would if there was something like a war or insurrection within a state, in which case the Congress may declare war and the Federal Government could get involved. Typically, crime can be taken care of by local police, or at worst the state's militia.

To declare War, grant Letters of Marque and Reprisal, and make Rules concerning Captures on Land and Water;

Congress has the power to declare war, but Congress has since given the powers of war over to the President through the Tonkin Gulf Resolution,[133] and this was unconstitutional. Presidents are still unilaterally going to war with no declaration of war from Congress. That's probably why we've lost virtually every "war" that we've been in since World War II, which was the last war which was declared by Congress. It would be Constitutional for Congress to give this power to the President only through a Constitutional amendment.

Congressional declaration of war is so important because it puts Representatives and Senators on the chopping block of the American people if anything goes wrong with a war. This makes us much less likely to go to war because a bad "yes" vote for a bad war could ruin a Congressperson's career.

To raise and support Armies, but no Appropriation of Money to that Use shall be for a longer Term than two Years;

The appropriation, or designation, of money for raising or supporting an Army can last only two years. Pretty clear stuff. The next power is about the Navy. Notice there's nothing about air forces, planes, or forces in space. This would require an amendment to the Constitution. I would recommend this amendment but also recommend that any new President agree to sign the executive order to remove our Air Force if the Constitution is not amended prior to him taking office. I think the threat of this executive order would quickly convince the nation to amend the Constitution to allow for Air and Space Forces.

To provide and maintain a Navy;

To make Rules for the Government and Regulation of the land and naval Forces;

The above power would also need to be amended to add air and space forces, to make those rules Constitutional.

To provide for calling forth the Militia to execute the Laws of the Union, suppress Insurrections and repel Invasions;

This power and the next one have to do with a military force from the people. It can be argued that the National Guard is not the Militia as stated above and below because the Federal Government, and no longer the states, hold the power to appoint officers, unlike the state power prescribed below.[134] So if it's not a militia, what is it? It seems to be part of the Army. If the National Guard is a militia according to the above power, then it would never be deployed overseas, as its duties are for domestic protection. But it has been deployed overseas. The National Guard needs to be incorporated into the Army, and states need to know that they can have their own Militia if they would like to.

To provide for organizing, arming, and disciplining, the Militia, and for governing such Part of them as may be employed in the Service of the United States, reserving to the States respectively, the Appointment of the Officers, and the Authority of training the Militia according to the discipline prescribed by Congress;

To exercise exclusive Legislation in all Cases whatsoever, over such District (not exceeding ten Miles square) as may, by Cession of particular States, and the Acceptance of Congress, become the Seat of the Government of the United States, and to exercise like Authority over all Places purchased by the Consent of the Legislature of the State in which the Same shall be, for the Erection of Forts, Magazines, Arsenals, dock-Yards, and other needful Buildings;—And

The power above is essentially a two-part power. The first power is what became Washington D.C., where the Federal Government primarily does its business. The key here is that Congress must in all cases create the laws for Washington D.C. The second power here is similar in that the Federal Government has to exercise exclusive legislation and the legislature of the state has to agree that land may be purchased from them.

The land must be for magazines, arsenals, dockyards, and other needful buildings. The key here is that Congress has "like Authority" as their powers over Washington D.C.[135] The authority Congress has is to do anything which the enumerated powers of the Constitution allow it to do, and nothing more.

<u>To make all Laws which shall be necessary and proper for carrying into Execution the foregoing Powers, and all other Powers vested by this Constitution in the Government of the United States, or in any Department or Officer thereof.</u>

This "necessary and proper" clause does not give the Congress any additional powers, it just clarifies that Congress can make laws which enable the other powers to happen. For instance, Congress may legislate that it is necessary and proper to hire someone to set up a plant to coin money since Congress has the power to coin money. Necessary and Proper means that Congress can legislate to achieve the powers given to them by the enumerated powers, nothing more.

The previous 18 underlined powers are known as the Enumerated Powers. These are the ones we really need to pay attention to because these powers form the baseline for our government. They show us that the focus of the Federal Government is meant to be on international trade and war, and on collecting taxes primarily for those purposes.

Notice it says the Congress "shall have Power To." These are optional powers. Please always remember that the Congress does not have to exercise any of these powers if it chooses not to.

Here are more powers granted to Congress, further down in the Constitution:

The following powers are from Article 1, Section 9:

<u>The Migration or Importation of such Persons as any of the States now existing shall think proper to admit, shall</u>

not be prohibited by the Congress prior to the Year one
thousand eight hundred and eight, but a Tax or duty may
be imposed on such Importation, not exceeding ten
dollars for each Person.

This is a power related to limiting the slave trade. A law
related to it came into effect on January 1st, 1808, the
first day it could be. The law made importing slaves from
other nations into the United States illegal. It was signed
into law by President Thomas Jefferson.[136]

The Privilege of the Writ of Habeas Corpus shall not be
suspended, unless when in Cases of Rebellion or Invasion
the public Safety may require it.

It's arguable whether this is a power granted to
Congress. I would say that the Writ of Habeas Corpus
was implied by establishing a Supreme Court. The Writ
of Habeas Corpus is the right of a person in prison to ask
courts for relief from wrongful imprisonment - the court
does not have to grant any relief. But the power granted is
that the Writ can be suspended in times of Rebellion or
Invasion, by Congress. Some Founders did not want this
suspension allowed.[137]

a regular Statement and Account of the Receipts and
Expenditures of all public Money shall be published from
time to time. - This regular publication of money coming
into and out of government is a power and duty of
Congress.

And no Person holding any Office of Profit or Trust
under them, shall, without the Consent of the Congress,
accept of any present, Emolument, Office, or Title, of any
kind whatever, from any King, Prince, or foreign State. -

This is the power of Congress to approve the acceptance of gift, pay, or official title from another nation, for anyone who serves the United States. Anything not approved by Congress must be rejected by the servant.

From Article 1, Section 10: <u>No State shall, without the Consent of the Congress, lay any Imposts or Duties on Imports or Exports, except what may be absolutely necessary for executing its inspection Laws: and the net Produce of all Duties and Imposts, laid by any State on Imports or Exports, shall be for the Use of the Treasury of the United States; and all such Laws shall be subject to the Revision and Controul of the Congress.</u> - This gives Congress the power to approve import and export duties or tariffs from the states, and all of the money collected must go to the Federal Treasury. It limits the ability for states to have tariffs on foreign trade and tariffs on trade among the states.[138]

From Article 1, Section 10: <u>No State shall, without the Consent of Congress, lay any Duty of Tonnage, keep Troops, or Ships of War in time of Peace, enter into any Agreement or Compact with another State, or with a foreign Power, or engage in War, unless actually invaded, or in such imminent Danger as will not admit of delay.</u> - Congress may approve state powers regarding tariffs, troops, ships, interstate and international agreements, and war.

From Article II:

<u>The President of the Senate shall, in the Presence of the Senate and House of Representatives, open all the Certificates, and the Votes shall then be counted. The</u>

Person having the greatest Number of Votes shall be the President, if such Number be a Majority of the whole Number of Electors appointed; and if there be more than one who have such Majority, and have an equal Number of Votes, then the House of Representatives shall immediately chuse by Ballot one of them for President; and if no Person have a Majority, then from the five highest on the List the said House shall in like Manner chuse the President. But in chusing the President, the Votes shall be taken by States, the Representation from each State having one Vote; A quorum for this Purpose shall consist of a Member or Members from two thirds of the States, and a Majority of all the States shall be necessary to a Choice. In every Case, after the Choice of the President, the Person having the greatest Number of Votes of the Electors shall be the Vice President. But if there should remain two or more who have equal Votes, the Senate shall chuse from them by Ballot the Vice President. - In the rare case that there is not a majority of electors for the election of President, or if there's a tie for President or Vice President, the House and Senate may get involved through voting. Some of the above section has been modified by amendment.

The Congress may determine the Time of chusing the Electors, and the Day on which they shall give their Votes; which Day shall be the same throughout the United States.

the Congress may by Law provide for the Case of Removal, Death, Resignation or Inability, both of the President and Vice President, declaring what Officer shall then act as President, and such Officer shall act accordingly, until the Disability be removed, or a President shall be elected. - Some of these Congressional powers over presidential succession are modified by amendment.

He shall have Power, by and with the Advice and Consent of the Senate, to make Treaties, provided two thirds of the Senators present concur; and he shall nominate, and by and with the Advice and Consent of the Senate, shall appoint Ambassadors, other public Ministers and Consuls, Judges of the supreme Court, and all other Officers of the United States, whose Appointments are not herein otherwise provided for, and which shall be established by Law: but the Congress may by Law vest the Appointment of such inferior Officers, as they think proper, in the President alone, in the Courts of Law, or in the Heads of Departments. - The Senate has the power to approve the following from the President: Treaties, appointments of Ambassadors, Judges of the Supreme Court, and other officers. Congress may, by law, let lower appointments be made without the Senate's consent.

From Article III:

The judicial Power of the United States, shall be vested in one supreme Court, and in such inferior Courts as the Congress may from time to time ordain and establish. - The last part of this sentence is the power of Congress to create inferior Courts.

In all the other Cases before mentioned, the supreme Court shall have appellate Jurisdiction, both as to Law and Fact, with such Exceptions, and under such Regulations as the Congress shall make.

but when not committed within any State, the Trial shall be at such Place or Places as the Congress may by Law have directed.

The Congress shall have Power to declare the Punishment of Treason, but no Attainder of Treason shall work Corruption of Blood, or Forfeiture except during the Life of the Person attainted.

From Article IV:

[For context, the following text is preceded by "Full Faith and Credit shall be given in each State to the public Acts, Records, and judicial Proceedings of every other State."] And the Congress may by general Laws prescribe the Manner in which such Acts, Records and Proceedings shall be proved, and the Effect thereof.

New States may be admitted by the Congress into this Union; but no new State shall be formed or erected within the Jurisdiction of any other State; nor any State be formed by the Junction of two or more States, or Parts of States, without the Consent of the Legislatures of the States concerned as well as of the Congress.

The Congress shall have Power to dispose of and make all needful Rules and Regulations respecting the Territory or other Property belonging to the United States;

From Article V:

The Congress, whenever two thirds of both Houses shall deem it necessary, shall propose Amendments to this Constitution, or, on the Application of the Legislatures of

two thirds of the several States, shall call a Convention for
proposing Amendments,

This concludes the powers given to Congress in the
original Constitution. Next, I will go over powers
provided through the amendments, but first I want to
comment on the Bill of Rights, which includes the first
ten amendments to the Constitution.

The first nine Amendments have nothing to do with
state governments. These amendments are rights for citizens that state governments can abridge. These amendments are limits on the Federal Government so that the
Federal Government can't make any laws infringing these
various rights. The state governments can make any law
abridging or granting these rights, at least according to
the Constitution. The state constitutions already protect
many rights, but that's for the states to decide.

When the founders wrote the first nine amendments
to the Bill of Rights, they intended for them to have
nothing to do with limiting state governments.[139]

Not only that but before the Bill of Rights was
ratified, some didn't want the Bill of Rights at all. They
feared that people would say the Constitution is a list of
things that the Federal Government can't do. But that's
not at all what the Constitution is; rather, the Constitution is a very short list of the only things that the Federal Government can do.[140]

Before the Bill of Rights, things like the freedom of
religion, freedom of the press, and the right to bear arms
were already protected at the Federal level because there

was nothing in the Constitution giving the Federal Government power over these things.

So that there is no question that the Bill of Rights was not intended to limit state governments, check out what Chief Justice John Marshall wrote about the Bill of Rights in 1833: "Had the framers of these amendments intended them to be limitations on the powers of the state governments, they would have imitated the framers of the original constitution, and have expressed that intention. Had Congress engaged in the extraordinary occupation of improving the constitutions of the several states, by affording the people additional protection from the exercise of power by their own governments, in matters which concerned themselves alone, they would have declared this purpose in plain and intelligible language."[141]

Some claim that the 14th Amendment allows some or all of Amendments 1 to 10 to be forced as rights upon the states. This concept is called incorporation. Here's the main part of the 14th Amendment that has been argued to create a need for incorporation: "No State shall make or enforce any law that shall abridge the privileges or immunities of citizens of the United States; nor shall any State deprive any person of life, liberty, or property, without due process of law; nor deny to any person within its jurisdiction the equal protection of the laws." The idea that the states need to incorporate any of the Federal Bill of Rights simply isn't true.

The 14th Amendment was passed after slaves were freed and after the Civil Rights Act of 1866. When the Civil Rights Act of 1866 was passed, it was unconstitutional, and so Congress then amended the Constitution with the 14th Amendment, essentially to make the act legal.[142]

However, I do not think this act created any new rights for the states to comply with. Incorporation was not implied. The purpose of the act was to give blacks in our country the same rights, privileges, and immunities as whites. In simple terms, this act, and the amendment obliged states to treat people of different races equally.

We know that the act did not confer new rights because it declared that American blacks "**shall have the same right**, in every State and Territory in the United States, to make and enforce contracts, to sue, be parties, and give evidence, to inherit, purchase, lease, sell, hold, and convey real and personal property, and to full and equal benefit of all laws and proceedings for the security of person and property, as is enjoyed by white citizens, and shall be subject to like punishment, pains, and penalties, and to none other, any law, statute, ordinance, regulation, or custom, to the contrary notwithstand-ing".[143] There's nothing about new rights.

The quote above is key to understanding the act and the amendment. No new rights are granted; the act merely gives to black citizens, and all other races, except "Indians not taxed," the same rights and protections that whites already had and will have going forward.

The 11th Amendment:
The judicial power of the United States shall not be construed to extend to any suit in law or equity,

commenced or prosecuted against one of the United States by citizens of another State, or by citizens or subjects of any foreign state. - This doesn't give the Federal Government any new power, but I wanted to include it because it clarifies the Judicial Power and confirms that the Federal Judiciary has less power.

The 13th Amendment:

1. Neither slavery nor involuntary servitude, except as a punishment for crime whereof the party shall have been duly convicted, shall exist within the United States, or any place subject to their jurisdiction.

2. Congress shall have power to enforce this article by appropriate legislation.

Seeing just the first section you could assume that perhaps the states or the people somehow had to enforce this prohibition of slavery, but the second section makes it clear that the Federal Government has the power to enforce the first section.

The 14th Amendment:

No State shall make or enforce any law which shall abridge the privileges or immunities of citizens of the United States; nor shall any State deprive any person of

<u>life, liberty, or property, without due process of law; nor to deny to any person within its jurisdiction the equal protection of the laws.</u> - This Amendment was ratified in 1868, essentially making the Civil Rights Act of 1866 Constitutional.

The Act makes virtually all who were previously American slaves into citizens of the United States, and it gives to them and all citizens equal protections under state law. In other words, blacks and whites were to have the same protections as each other, and it was to be equal for other races as well. To reiterate, this act and this Amendment do not create any new rights or protections.

Isn't it funny that this is a limit on states according to the 14th Amendment's text, to be enforced by the Federal Government, but the Federal Government does not say in this amendment that they themselves must ensure "equal protection of the laws" among citizens at a Federal level? Perhaps this was just missed by the writers of the amendment, or perhaps it was on purpose to force states to conform to equal protection but to leave the Federal Government to not give equal protection if they don't feel like it.

<u>The Congress shall have the power to enforce, by appropriate legislation, the provisions of this article.</u> Congress, and thereby the Federal Government, get to enforce this "equal protection of the laws" upon the States. State governments must provide "equal protection of the laws."

The 15th Amendment:

1. <u>The right of citizens of the United States to vote shall not be denied or abridged by the United States or by any State on account of race, color, or previous condition of servitude.</u> - Some states have used tricky ways to get around the intent of this clause (the intent was to give blacks and former slaves the right to vote), such as requiring literacy tests but giving exemptions to everyone who was "grandfathered," perhaps because they had voted before the tests.[144] The original intent, I believe, is to allow the states to make any requirement to vote as long as it isn't specifically to disenfranchise blacks, slaves, or other races. So, the "grandfather" exemption law should be prohibited because it is meant to circumvent this intent. I like to err on the side of giving states their rights, even if those rights might be morally wrong, rather than giving the Federal Government more power.

2. <u>The Congress shall have the power to enforce this article by appropriate legislation.</u> - The Federal Government can enforce the first section above.

The 16th Amendment:

<u>The Congress shall have power to lay and collect taxes on incomes, from whatever sources derived, without apportionment among the several States, and without regard to</u>

any census or enumeration. - Unfortunately, the income tax does seem to be Constitutional, for now. I would support, in a heartbeat, an amendment to repeal the income tax, but a proposed amendment that does this would have to be ratified by three-fourths of state legislatures or by three-fourths of conventions in each of the states. A president has virtually no say in the constitutional amendment process.

Arguments against the legitimacy of the 16th amendment have been made. Perhaps the best argument against the income tax is that with it, we are asked to submit income tax returns. These returns are, in a way, forcing us to testify against ourselves, which can be argued to go against the fifth amendment, which reads, in part, that no person shall "be compelled in any criminal case to be a witness against himself."[145] Not paying income taxes is criminal, but since 1913, when the income tax amendment was ratified, Congress has required returns to be filed.[146]

You can argue that forcing the filing of returns is necessary and proper to carry out the income tax and that it was part of the original intent of the amendment: the very year it was ratified, in 1913, is the year that Congress made tax return filing part of the law, and it was just a few years earlier that Congress had formally proposed the amendment, in 1909.

While I'd like to make the argument that the income tax is unconstitutional because of the Fifth Amendment, I can't do that in good conscience, in light of my belief that we need to follow the Constitution based on its original intent. We need to be consistent: our founders wanted us to interpret the Constitution based on the meaning of the words when they were written, and that is what I intend to do. Anything less than interpreting the Constitution based on original intent makes the Constitutional malleable, inconcrete, unenforceable, and therefore no law at all.

As far as I know, since 1913, the requirement to file has never been successfully overturned, so it seems to me that the intent of the 16th Amendment was to require the filing of returns for the income tax regardless of the Fifth Amendment. For consistency, because of the Fifth Amendment, the writers of the amendment should have specified that requiring a tax return could be enforced without regard to the 5th Amendment.

Just a little history on the income tax: an income tax law was first passed, unconstitutionally, in 1861 during the Civil War.[147] For U.S. Residents the income tax for 1861 was to be 3 percent on all income over $800 per year, except U.S. Treasuries which were taxed at 1.5%. And income over $10,000 was taxed at 5%. But National, State, and Local property taxes were first deducted when calculating income.

How long was the law? Just under 4 pages.[148] There's no reason we can't abolish the income tax, because as Ron Paul said in 2008:

> I want to abolish the income tax, but I don't want to replace it with anything. About 45 percent of all federal revenue comes from the personal income tax.

That means that about 55 percent — over half of all revenue — comes from other sources, like excise taxes, fees, and corporate taxes.

We could eliminate the income tax, replace it with nothing, and still fund the same level of big government we had in the late 1990s.[149]

If we do have an income tax, there's no reason the law can't be four pages. The reason it's so long is that the special interests and super-rich have a stranglehold on Congress. Because of this stranglehold, the super-rich can get out of paying almost all income taxes because they weave complicated deductions and exclusions into the law that only they have the money and resources to take advantage of.

You could make $800 in 1861 and pay no taxes. In 2016, the typical amount that you could make without having to pay any taxes was $10,350. Not bad, right? Oh wait, there's inflation. Taking into account inflation, this untaxed amount from 1861 would be around $160,220.84 in 2016 dollars. If we must have an income tax, let's go back to that level of no taxation, and let's make it a three-percent tax at most, please. And the five-percent tax, the higher rate, would kick in at over $2,000,000 in 2016 dollars. Sounds almost fair to me.[150]

The 1861 income tax was also illegal because it was unconstitutional. It was unconstitutional not only because it was not authorized in the Constitution, but also be-cause it forced people to testify against themselves:

"And the several collectors and assistants" [...] if they can't find property to sell to pay for the income tax, "shall have the power" [...] "to examine under oath the person assessed under this act or any other person" [...] and then they can sell stock, etc. owned by the person to satisfy the income tax, "**and in case he refuses to testify**, the said several collectors and assistants shall have the power to arrest such person and commit him to prison, to be held in custody until the same shall be paid, with interest thereon, at the rate of six per centum per annum, from the time when the same was payable as aforesaid, and all fees and charges of such commitment and custody."[151]

Part of the 18th Amendment:

1. After one year from the ratification of this article the manufacture, sale, or transportation of intoxicating liquors within, the importation thereof into, or the exportation thereof from the United States and all territory subject to the jurisdiction thereof for beverage purposes is hereby prohibited.

2. The Congress and the several States shall have concurrent power to enforce this article by appropriate legislation. - This is the "prohibition" of alcohol, ratified in 1919. We fully repealed it by 1933 with the 21st Amendment.

Notice how the Federal Government has since made Marijuana, Cocaine, and a lot of other drugs illegal at a national level, without even worrying about amending the Constitution to do so. An amendment would be needed to make any substance illegal when created within a state's borders.

It seems as though almost everyone in 1919 and 1933 knew that amendment was needed for a national prohibition because they modified the Constitution to regulate and then deregulate alcohol. But for some reason, we had a bit of belief that narcotics could be regulated at a Federal level before 1919 without any Constitutional Amendment, even though it makes no logical sense.

In 1914 some drugs were limited in the "Harrison Narcotics Tax Act."[152] Some of that law was overturned by a judge in 1925.[153] Perhaps the biggest Constitutional blow came in 1970 in the Controlled Substances Act, where even "simple possession" of controlled substances could be penalized.[154] This is unquestionably unconstitutional according to the original intent of the Constitution.

The Tenth Amendment clearly shows us that anything such as drugs, alcohol, guns, healthcare, or any other power not specifically delegated to the United States is to be left up to the people or the states. I do not personally agree with the use of Marijuana for recreational purposes, but the Federal Government needs to stay out of it. Any of the Federal Government's penalties related to any "controlled" substance, as long as the activity is domestic to a state and as long as we're not talking about excise taxes, are unconstitutional.

The first thing any Representative or Senator or President should ask when presented with any law is, "Where is this authorized in the Constitution?". If, and only if, a law passes this litmus test should it be considered further, for any possible merits, to become law.

Part of the 20th Amendment:

the Congress may by law provide for the case wherein neither a President elect nor a Vice-President shall have qualified [to be President or Vice-President], declaring who shall then act as President, or the manner in which one who is to act shall be selected, and such person shall act accordingly until a President or Vice-President shall have qualified.

4. The Congress may by law provide for the case of the death of any of the persons from whom the House of representatives may choose a President whenever the right of choice shall have devolved upon them, and for the case of the death of any of the persons from whom the Senate may choose a Vice-President whenever the right of choice shall have devolved upon them.

This concludes the list of the powers of Congress. I have not included a few of the powers of Congress related to the inner workings of government, such as some powers related to Presidential Succession. However, I have tried to include in this list all powers of Congress external to government itself, meaning those powers which can apply to foreign affairs, taxation, war, the military, the people, their property, U.S. territories, and the States.

Specific Limits on State Governments:

This list of limits on state governments is extremely important because infractions upon these limits, in conjunction with interference in constitutionally granted federal powers, are the only legitimate places where the Federal Supreme Court can strike down as unconstitutional a state law, regulation, or action.

Above this, we list all external constitutional federal powers, and below, we have all limits on state governments. These are the only ends that the Federal Government can strive for, and these are the only places where states can be limited. This is made perfectly clear in the 10th Amendment of the Constitution, which is also the 10th Article of the Bill of Rights.

The 10th Amendment says, "The powers not delegated to the United States by the Constitution, nor prohibited by it to the States, are reserved to the States respectively, or to the people." From this, we see that the only actions, inactions, laws, or Supreme Court decisions that can be used to impose any authority whatsoever on the states from the Federal Government is in areas where the Constitution prohibits the states from doing things, or where a conflict between constitutionally granted federal power and state power exists.

In recent years the United States Supreme Court has struck down many state laws as unconstitutional, often because the Court says that the state law somehow violates the Federal Constitution's Bill of Rights. This is a totally inaccurate and a very confused interpretation of the Bill of Rights. The Bill of Rights in no way imposes any upholding of rights upon the states.

All that the Bill of Rights is doing is imposing limits upon the Federal Government, and many of those limits were already 100% implied by the Constitution before the Bill of Rights was ratified.

The Supreme Court has said over the years that states need to "incorporate" certain rights guaranteed by the U.S. Constitution. This was not the intent of the Founders or any of the amendment writers, other than the rights that the Constitution explicitly imposes upon the states through Amendments beyond the first ten amendments. The amendments beyond the first ten abridge the rights of the states in very clear language, generally by using the phrase "any State, and they only do it a few times.

What follows is my attempt to list every single prohibition on state governments from the Constitution.

I hope this list will be a nice reference if the Supreme Court strikes down another state law: unless the Court properly references something on this list, using the original intent of the words when written as their basis, the decision is almost definitely null, void, and should not be obeyed by anyone, be it the states, the people, the President, the Congress, or any state or Federal courts. The Supreme Court has overturned its own decisions from time to time, so we must concede that they make mistakes.[155] As there are 3 branches of the Federal Government, we need to be open to the Executive,

Legislative, and even lower parts of the Judicial branch not carrying out the Supreme Court's mistakes.

In fact, according to the Constitution, every member of Congress, every President, and every judicial officer must have sworn or affirmed that they will uphold the Constitution, and that means that whenever the Supreme Court makes a Constitutional mistake, Congress, the President, and the lower Federal courts shouldn't just be open to defying the Supreme Court, they are bound by oath or affirmation to defy the Supreme Court. Here's the text from the Constitution: "The Senators and Representatives before mentioned, and the Members of the several State Legislatures, and all executive and judicial Officers, both of the United States and of the several States, shall be bound by Oath or Affirmation, to support this Constitution."

Roe v. Wade is a perfect example of an unconstitutional Supreme Court decision that should be undermined by everyone in the Federal Government, and by everyone in state governments. It is the right of the people or the states to illegalize, legalize, or regulate abortion. This is stated in the Tenth Amendment and is just as true as the right of the people or the states (but not the Federal Government) to illegalize or legalize murder within a state's borders.

The following are the limits on state governments according to the Constitution of the United States

All of Article 1, Section 10 are some of the limits on the state governments:

No State shall enter into any Treaty, Alliance, or Confederation; grant Letters of Marque and Reprisal; coin Money; emit Bills of Credit; make any Thing but gold and silver Coin a Tender in Payment of Debts; pass any Bill of Attainder, ex post facto Law, or Law impairing the Obligation of Contracts, or grant any Title of Nobility.

No State shall, without the Consent of the Congress, lay any Imposts or Duties on Imports or Exports, except what may be absolutely necessary for executing its inspection Laws: and the net Produce of all Duties and Imposts, laid by any State on Imports or Exports, shall be for the Use of the Treasury of the United States; and all such Laws shall be subject to the Revision and Controul of the Congress.

No State shall, without the Consent of Congress, lay any Duty of Tonnage, keep Troops, or Ships of War in time of Peace, enter into any Agreement or Compact with another State, or with a foreign Power, or engage in War, unless actually invaded, or in such imminent Danger as will not admit of delay.

Article IV:

Part of Section 1: <u>Full Faith and Credit shall be given in each State to the public Acts, Records, and judicial Proceedings of every other State.</u> - This limits states so that they can't invalidate another state's laws.[156]

Section 4: <u>The United States shall guarantee to every State in this Union a Republican Form of Government,</u>- State governments must be governmental systems by the people. They can't be run by dictators. It's essentially a limit on how states can operate, and includes a requirement for the "rule of law." It is guaranteed by the United States.[157]

From the 14 Amendment:

<u>No State shall make or enforce any law which shall abridge the privileges or immunities of citizens of the United States; nor shall any State deprive any person of life, liberty, or property, without due process of law; nor to deny to any person within its jurisdiction the equal protection of the laws.</u>

<u>But when the right to vote at any election for the choice of Electors for President and Vice-President of the United States, Representatives in Congress, the executive and judicial officers of a State, or the members of the legislature thereof, is denied to any of the male</u>

inhabitants of such State, being twenty-one years of age, and citizens of the United States, or in any way abridged, except for participation in rebellion, or other crime, the basis of representation therein shall be reduced in the proportion which the number of such male citizens shall bear to the whole number of male citizens twenty-one years of age in such State. - This is not really a limit on state governments, but rather a penalty to the states, giving the state less representation in the Federal House of Representatives if the state doesn't give suffrage to all male citizens 21 years or older. The suffrage must be for Federal and State positions.

But neither the United States nor any State shall assume or pay any debt or obligation incurred in aid of insurrection or rebellion against the United States, or any claim for the loss or emancipation of any slave; but all such debts, obligations and claims shall be held illegal and void. - States can't pay money owed from lending to the Confederacy or as payments for freed slaves. Going forward states can't pay debts for similar situations.

From the 15th Amendment:

1. The right of citizens of the United States to vote shall not be denied or abridged by the United States or by any State on account of race, color, or previous condition of servitude.

From the 19th Amendment:

1. <u>The right of citizens of the United States to vote shall not be denied or abridged by the United States or by any State on account of sex.</u>

From the 24th Amendment:

<u>The right of citizens of the United States to vote in any primary or other election for President or Vice President, for electors for President or Vice President, or for Senator or Representative in Congress, shall not be denied or abridged by the United States or any State by reason of failure to pay poll tax or any other tax.</u> - It's interesting that the amendment did not limit poll taxes for state elections, perhaps it would not have passed otherwise.

From the 26th Amendment:

<u>The right of citizens of the United States, who are 18 years of age or older, to vote shall not be denied or abridged by the United States or any state on account of age.</u>

This concludes the list of all the limits on state governments by the Constitution of the United States. I have tried to include them all; barring an omission, these are the only federal limits on the states or the people, other than areas where the Federal Government has constitutional power, which supplants state power. Those supplantable areas would at most include any items on the federal power list, which was listed before this state limit list. Any additional limits on state governments would need to be imposed by the people themselves, or the states, not the Federal Government. The only way the Federal Government can impose additional limits on the states is through constitutional amendments.

Eric Martin

ENDNOTES

[1] "Are You a Three Percenter?" Kellene Bishop. May 14, 2009.
https://freedomintelligence.wordpress.com/2009/05/14/are-you-a-three-percenter/

[2] *The Washington Times.* "1M kids stop school lunch due to Michelle Obama's standards." March 6, 2014.
https://www.washingtontimes.com/news/2014/mar/6/1m-kids-stop-school-lunch-due-michelle-obamas-stan/

[3] Data as of February 2017, from
http://www.usdebtclock.org/

[4] http://www.foxnews.com/politics/2011/08/04/us-debt-reaches-100-percent-countrys-gdp.html

[5]
https://www.treasurydirect.gov/govt/reports/pd/histdebt/histdebt_histo5.htm

[6] See http://www.tradingeconomics.com/country-list/government-debt-to-gdp

[7] http://www.tradingeconomics.com/united-states/gdp-growth

[8] Retrieved 2/10/2017 from http://www.usdebtclock.org/

[9]
https://www.census.gov/newsroom/releases/archives/income_wealth/cb12-172.html from 2/10/2017

[10] http://blogs.census.gov/2013/03/21/household-wealth-and-debt-in-the-u-s-2000-to-2011/

[11]
https://www.brainyquote.com/quotes/quotes/t/thomaspai

n100996.html

[12] Source: OMB, National Priorities Project. Licensed under Creative Commons. Used under fair use.

[13]13 See https://www.chesterton.org/wrong-with-world/

[14] http://www.forumfed.org/countries/

[15] Chapter 75. English interpretation by S. Mitchell. Originally written around the 6th century BC. http://acc6.its.brooklyn.cuny.edu/~phalsall/texts/taote-v3.html

[16]

http://www.beliefnet.com/resourcelib/docs/115/message_from_john_adams_to_the_officers_of_the_first_brigade_1.html

[17] http://www.rma.usda.gov/other/stateag.html

[18] https://www.thebalance.com/history-of-bankruptcy-in-the-united-states-316225

[19] http://www.bartleby.com/73/1593.html

[20]

https://www.brainyquote.com/quotes/quotes/t/thomasjeff135368.html?src=t_liberty

[21] This is based on the 1969 chart by David Nolan. See https://en.wikipedia.org/wiki/Nolan_Chart

[22] Sheldon Richman. "The Commerce Clause: Route to Omnipotent Government", 1995. http://www.fff.org/explore-freedom/article/commerce-clause-route-omnipotent-government/

[23]

http://www.federalistblog.us/2011/06/how_commerce_was_regulated/

[24] https://constitutionmythbuster.com/2013/04/15/do-federal-regulations-violate-the-constitution/

[25] http://www.fff.org/explore-freedom/article/commerce-clause-route-omnipotent-government/

[26] Emphasis added. Source: http://press-pubs.uchicago.edu/founders/documents/a1_8_3_commerces19.html

[27] http://www.shmoop.com/constitution/article-1-section-9.html

[28] http://www.federalistblog.us/2011/06/how_commerce_was_regulated/

[29] Emphasis added. Source: http://www.presidency.ucsb.edu/ws/?pid=67965

[30] https://en.wikipedia.org/wiki/James_Monroe#Governor_of_Virginia_and_diplomat

[31] https://founders.archives.gov/documents/Hamilton/01-08-02-0045

[32] https://en.wikipedia.org/wiki/Interstate_Commerce_Act_of_1887

[33] https://en.wikipedia.org/wiki/Economy_of_the_United_States

[34] Retrieved 2/10/2017 from http://www.usdebtclock.org/

[35] https://www.census.gov/newsroom/releases/archives/inco

me_wealth/cb12-172.html from 2/10/2017

[36] http://blogs.census.gov/2013/03/21/household-wealth-and-debt-in-the-u-s-2000-to-2011/

[37]

https://www.forbes.com/sites/realspin/2014/01/17/you-think-the-deficit-is-bad-federal-unfunded-liabilities-exceed-127-trillion/#fddacde9bf8a

[38] see http://www.tradingeconomics.com/united-states/gdp-growth

[39]

https://www.treasurydirect.gov/govt/reports/pd/histdebt/histdebt_histo5.htm

[40] http://money.cnn.com/2016/05/10/news/economy/us-debt-ownership/

[41] https://www.federalregister.gov/agencies/child-support-enforcement-office

[42] This list is almost entirely from Wikipedia, accessed on 2/18/2017:

https://en.wikipedia.org/wiki/United_States_federal_executive_departments

[43] https://en.wikipedia.org/wiki/Marine_Hospital_Service

[44] Expenditure and revenue figures are from http://www.usdebtclock.org, accessed 2/18/2017

[45] https://cei.org/blog/nobody-knows-how-many-federal-agencies-exist, https://www.federalregister.gov/agencies

[46]

https://en.wikipedia.org/wiki/List_of_federal_agencies_in_the_United_States

[47] https://en.wikipedia.org/wiki/Category:Quasi-public_entities_in_the_United_States

[48] https://en.wikipedia.org/wiki/Cabinet_of_the_United_States, retrieved on 2/6/2017

[49] https://www.federalregister.gov/agencies, this federal government site was quite slow at times, which I should have expected

[50] See https://en.wikipedia.org/wiki/Community_Development_Financial_Institutions_Fund

[51] https://ratical.org/many_worlds/cc/NMfHC/chp6.html

[52] https://en.wikipedia.org/wiki/Numismatic_history_of_the_United_States

[53] https://en.wikipedia.org/wiki/United_States_Department_of_Justice

[54] https://en.wikipedia.org/wiki/Walgreens

[55] http://jacksonandwilson.com/which-is-more-dangerous-a-gun-or-a-swimming-pool/

[56] http://www.americanbar.org/publications/insights_on_law_andsociety/14/spring-2014/who-is-responsible-for-u-s--immigration-policy-.html

[57] https://en.wikipedia.org/wiki/History_of_laws_concerning_immigration_and_naturalization_in_the_United_States

58

https://en.wikipedia.org/wiki/United_States_Fish_and_
Wildlife_Service

59 https://www.fws.gov/offices/statelinks.html

60

https://en.wikipedia.org/wiki/United_States_Geological_
Survey

61

https://en.wikipedia.org/wiki/Bureau_of_Indian_Affairs

62

https://en.wikipedia.org/wiki/Bureau_of_Land_Managem
ent

63

https://en.wikipedia.org/wiki/National_Indian_Gaming_
Commission

64 https://en.wikipedia.org/wiki/National_Park_Service

65

https://en.wikipedia.org/wiki/Bureau_of_Ocean_Energy_
Management

66

https://en.wikipedia.org/wiki/United_States_Bureau_of_
Reclamation

67

https://en.wikipedia.org/wiki/Bureau_of_Safety_and_Env
ironmental_Enforcement

68 https://www.scientificamerican.com/article/how-
microbes-helped-clean-bp-s-oil-spill/

69

https://en.wikipedia.org/wiki/Office_of_Surface_Mining

[70] http://www.rma.usda.gov/other/stateag.html

[71]

https://en.wikipedia.org/wiki/United_States_Department_of_Agriculture

[72]

https://en.wikipedia.org/wiki/Agricultural_Marketing_Service

[73]

https://en.wikipedia.org/wiki/Agricultural_Research_Service

[74]

https://en.wikipedia.org/wiki/Animal_and_Plant_Health_Inspection_Service

[75] https://en.wikipedia.org/wiki/Farm_Service_Agency

[76]

https://en.wikipedia.org/wiki/Food_and_Nutrition_Service

[77]

https://en.wikipedia.org/wiki/Food_Safety_and_Inspection_Service

[78]

https://en.wikipedia.org/wiki/United_States_Forest_Service

[79]

https://en.wikipedia.org/wiki/Grain_Inspection,_Packers_and_Stockyards_Administration

[80]

https://en.wikipedia.org/wiki/United_States_Department_of_Commerce

81

https://en.wikipedia.org/wiki/Economic_Development_Administration

[82] https://en.wikipedia.org/wiki/Foreign-trade_zones_of_the_United_States

83

https://en.wikipedia.org/wiki/Bureau_of_Industry_and_Security

84

https://en.wikipedia.org/wiki/International_Trade_Administration

85

https://en.wikipedia.org/wiki/National_Oceanic_and_Atmospheric_Administration

86

https://en.wikipedia.org/wiki/National_Telecommunications_and_Information_Administration

87

https://en.wikipedia.org/wiki/United_States_trademark_law#History_of_US_trademark_law

88

https://en.wikipedia.org/wiki/United_States_Maritime_Administration

89

https://en.wikipedia.org/wiki/United_States_Department_of_Labor

[90] https://www.dol.gov/whd/contacts/state_of.htm

91

http://web.archive.org/web/20110629183749/http://ww

w.house.gov/jec/cost-gov/regs/minimum/50years.htm
92

https://en.wikipedia.org/wiki/Employee_Benefits_Securit
y_Administration
93

https://en.wikipedia.org/wiki/United_States_Department
_of_Health_and_Human_Services
94 https://www.fsis.usda.gov/wps/wcm/connect/fsis-
content/internet/main/topics/recalls-and-public-health-
alerts/additional-recall-links/state-departments-of-public-
health/ct_index
95 See it here:
http://housedocs.house.gov/energycommerce/ppacacon.p
df, accessed on 2/21/2017.
96

https://en.wikipedia.org/wiki/Medicare_(United_States)#
Program_history
97 "An Indexed Comparison of Health Care Inflation and
Consumer Price Index in US from 1935 to 2009"
(Source: US Census 2013) Credit to the Mises Institute
for this chart. CC BY-NC-ND 4.0
https://creativecommons.org/licenses/by-nc-nd/4.0/
(From https://mises.org/blog/how-government-
regulations-made-healthcare-so-expensive)
98

https://en.wikipedia.org/wiki/United_States_Department
_of_Housing_and_Urban_Development
99 See: https://drrobertowens.com/2015/01/29/
100 See here for proof:

https://ntl.bts.gov/tools/statedot.html

[101] See

https://www.fhwa.dot.gov/interstate/faq.cfm#question7

[102]

https://en.wikipedia.org/wiki/Office_of_Energy_Efficiency_and_Renewable_Energy

[103] https://en.wikipedia.org/wiki/State_education_agency

[104]

https://en.wikipedia.org/wiki/No_Child_Left_Behind_Act

[105]

https://en.wikipedia.org/wiki/Every_Student_Succeeds_Act

[106] From: http://www.capenet.org/benefits4.html

[107] http://www.moneycrashers.com/private-vs-public-school-cost-comparison/

[108] See http://www.governing.com/gov-data/education-data/state-education-spending-per-pupil-data.html

[109]

https://en.wikipedia.org/wiki/Federal_Emergency_Management_Agency

[110] https://www.federalregister.gov/agencies/secret-service

[111]

https://en.wikipedia.org/wiki/White_House_Chief_of_Staff

[112]

https://en.wikipedia.org/wiki/List_of_environmental_agencies_in_the_United_States

[113] https://www.federalregister.gov/agencies

[114] https://www.federalregister.gov/agencies/presidential-documents

[115] https://www.rutherford.org/publications_resources/john_whiteheads_commentary/the_draft_unwise_immoral_and_unconstitutional

[116] https://www.federalregister.gov/agencies/bipartisan-commission-on-entitlement-and-tax-reform

[117] See https://www.federalregister.gov/agencies/election-assistance-commission

[118] https://www.federalreserve.gov/faqs/about_14986.htm

[119] http://www.globalresearch.ca/who-owns-the-federal-reserve/10489

[120] Searched on 2/21/2017

[121] http://www.politifact.com/new-jersey/statements/2012/mar/18/chris-smith/chris-smith-says-more-54-million-abortions-have-be/

[122] See http://apjjf.org/2013/11/32/Paul-A.-Kramer/3983/article.html

[123] http://www.cnn.com/2017/07/12/asia/china-djibouti-military-base/index.html

[124] See https://mises.org/library/ron-paul-blowback

[125] See https://en.wikipedia.org/wiki/Saudi_Arabia%E2%80%93United_States_relations

[126] From https://en.wikipedia.org/wiki/United_States_withdrawal_from_Saudi_Arabia, retrieved December 26th, 2017

[127] From

https://en.wikipedia.org/wiki/History_of_the_United_Sta
tes_Army, section titled, "Early national period (1783-
1812)", retrieved on 12/19/2017

128

http://blogs.discovermagazine.com/80beats/2010/01/04/
10-things-you-didnt-know-about-the-burj-khalifa-the-
new-tallest-building-in-the-world/#.WKzYWTvyu00

[129] The price of gold at the time of writing was about
$1,235 per ounce.

[130] Robert M. Hutchins. (Great Books of the Western
World, Volume 1: The Great Conversation. 1952. p. 80.)

[131] http://www.whatwouldthefoundersthink.com/the-
founders-on-a-living-constitution

[132] See

http://www.constitution.org/cmt/law_of_nations.htm

[133] http://www.e-ir.info/2014/11/19/presidential-war-
powers-in-vietnam/

134

http://www.heritage.org/constitution/#!/articles/1/essays/
56/organizing-the-militia

[135] See

http://tenthamendmentcenter.com/2016/02/05/federally-
administered-lands-the-original-intent/

[136] See

https://en.wikipedia.org/wiki/Act_Prohibiting_Importati
on_of_Slaves

137

http://www.heritage.org/constitution/#!/articles/1/essays/
61/habeas-corpus

[138] See
http://www.heritage.org/constitution/#!/articles/1/essays/74/import-export-clause

[139] See
http://tenthamendmentcenter.com/2014/10/13/was-the-bill-of-rights-meant-to-apply-to-the-states/

[140] http://www.cnsnews.com/commentary/ed-feulner/we-almost-didnt-have-bill-rights

[141] See
http://tenthamendmentcenter.com/2012/03/12/the-14th-amendment-and-the-bill-of-rights/

[142] http://tenthamendmentcenter.com/2012/03/12/the-14th-amendment-and-the-bill-of-rights/

[143] See
http://www.supremelaw.org/ref/1866cra/1866.cra.htm. I added the emphasis.

[144]
http://www.heritage.org/constitution#!/amendments/15/essays/176/suffrage-race

[145] https://www.irs.gov/businesses/small-businesses-self-employed/anti-tax-law-evasion-schemes-law-and-arguments-section-iv

[146] http://legisworks.org/sal/38/stats/STATUTE-38-Pg114.pdf

[147]
https://en.wikipedia.org/wiki/Legal_history_of_income_tax_in_the_United_States#Second_income_tax_law

[148] http://memory.loc.gov/cgi-bin/ampage?collId=llsl&fileName=012/llsl012.db&recNu

m=340, and
https://en.wikipedia.org/wiki/Revenue_Act_of_1861
[149] http://www.ronpaul.com/taxes/
[150] This is based on the Consumer Price Index from
1861-1969, and based on ShadowStats from 1969-2016,
see http://www.halfhill.com/inflation_js.html
[151] Author's bolding added, text from Thirty-Seventh
Congress, Sess. I., Ch. 45, 1861, Sec. 51. P.310, see
http://memory.loc.gov/cgi-
bin/ampage?collId=llsl&fileName=012/llsl012.db&recNu
m=341
[152] https://en.wikipedia.org/wiki/War_on_Drugs#History
[153]
https://en.wikipedia.org/wiki/Harrison_Narcotics_Tax_A
ct
[154] https://www.gpo.gov/fdsys/pkg/STATUTE-
84/pdf/STATUTE-84-Pg1236.pdf
[155]
https://en.wikipedia.org/wiki/List_of_overruled_United_
States_Supreme_Court_decisions
[156]
http://www.heritage.org/constitution/#!/articles/4/essays/
121/full-faith-and-credit-clause
[157] See
http://www.heritage.org/constitution/#!/articles/4/essays/
128/guarantee-clause

EXECUTIVE ORDER INDEX

Eric Martin

It does not take a majority to prevail … but rather an irate, tireless minority, keen on setting brushfires of freedom in the minds of men.

—SAMUEL ADAMS

Eric Martin

ACKNOWLEDGMENTS

This book was made possible by my wife. Thank you so much, Melody! She spent countless hours caring for our three young daughters, for me, for our house, and for herself, while I was often absent physically or mentally while working on this book. She also reviewed much of the book and encouraged me throughout.

Thank you to my daughters for being who God created you to be, and for being amazing even when I'm absent.

Thank you to my parents and Melody's parents for supporting me on this journey and for collectively reviewing early versions.

Thank you to my sister, Claudia, for the author photo she took, and to my brother, Elliot, for giving constructive criticism.

Thank you to Josh Rae for getting me started on the libertarian path, to Dr. Ron Paul for inspiring me, and to God for grounding me in his Word and, I hope, his wisdom.

Eric Martin

JOIN THE MOVEMENT

The hope of the Liberation Day Movement is to see freedom restored in the United States of America.

www.liberationday.com

Made in the USA
Middletown, DE
27 January 2020